Re-Visioning Education in Africa

Emefa J. Takyi-Amoako
N'Dri Thérèse Assié-Lumumba
Editors

Re-Visioning Education in Africa

Ubuntu-Inspired Education for Humanity

Editors
Emefa J. Takyi-Amoako
Oxford ATP
Oxford, UK

N'Dri Thérèse Assié-Lumumba
Africana Studies and Research Center
Cornell University
Ithaca, NY, USA

ISBN 978-3-319-70042-7   ISBN 978-3-319-70043-4   (eBook)
https://doi.org/10.1007/978-3-319-70043-4

Library of Congress Control Number: 2017960955

This Palgrave Macmillan imprint is published by Springer Nature
The registered company is Springer International Publishing AG
The registered company address is: Gewerbestrasse 11, 6330 Cham, Switzerland

CONTENTS

v

NOTES ON CONTRIBUTORS

Ali A. Abdi is Professor of Social Development Education in the Department of Educational Studies at the University of British Columbia. Previously, he was Professor of Education and Co-founding Director of the Centre for Global Citizenship Education and Research (CGCER) at the University of Alberta. His research interests include global citizenship and human rights education, social development education, multi-centric philosophies and methodologies of education, and anti-colonial studies in education. His edited/co-edited volumes include *The Education of African Canadian children* (Montreal: McGill-Queen's University Press, 2016), *Indigenous Discourses on Development in Africa* (New York: Routledge, 2014), *Decolonizing Philosophies of Education* (Rotterdam: Sense Publishers, 2012), and *Education and the Politics of Difference: Select Canadian Perspectives* (Toronto: Canadian Scholar's Press, 2004).

N'Dri Thérèse Assié-Lumumba is a Professor of African, African Diaspora, and Comparative/International Education at Cornell University in the Africana Studies and Research Center. She is currently serving as President of Comparative and International Education Society (CIES). She is a Fellow of the World Academy of Art and Science, Chercheur Associé at Université Félix Houphouët-Boigny in Abidjan and Research Affiliate at the Institute for Higher Education Law and Governance of the University of Houston, Houston (Texas). She is co-founder/Associate Director of CEPARRED (Centre PanAfricain d'Etudes et de Recherches en Relations Internationales et en Education pour le Développement). She has been a visiting Professor at Hiroshima University in Japan and the

American University in Cairo (Egypt). She has served as Director of the graduate field of Africana Studies and Director of the former Cornell program on Gender and Global Change (GGC). Dr. Assié-Lumumba is a leading scholar and policy analyst with several published books, numerous articles in refereed journals and book chapters, and major reports especially on higher education, gender, equity, and ICT. She has served as a senior advisor for numerous national and international development projects.

Hamidou Boukary is an educationist by training. His primary interests are in the role of education and training in fostering social and economic transformation in Africa. He has contributed to educational development in Africa during his long service at the Association for the Development of Education in Africa (ADEA). He specializes in comparative education and has expertise in education policy analysis, education systems design, education program implementation design, evaluation, and monitoring of education programs and projects. As a practitioner, he has worked on issues related to the full spectrum of the education and training system: from ECD and TVSD, to higher education as well as non-formal education. He is currently an independent consultant working for governments, different multilateral, and regional development agencies.

José Cossa is a Mozambican scholar, writer/author, researcher, poet, blogger, "twitterer," podcaster, entrepreneur, and a Senior Lecturer at Peabody College, Vanderbilt University. Prior to Vanderbilt, Cossa was a Visiting Associate Professor at the American University in Cairo. Cossa holds a Ph.D. in Cultural and Educational Policy Studies with a depth area in Comparative and International Education from Loyola University Chicago. He is the author of *Power, Politics, and Higher Education: International Regimes, Local Governments, and Educational Autonomy* (New York: Cambria Press, 2008) and the recipient of the 2012 Joyce Cain Award for Distinguished Research on People of African Descent, awarded by the Comparative and International Education Society (CIES). Cossa's research focus is on power dynamics in negotiation over educational policy, higher education policy and administration, system transfer, international development, and global and social justice.

Mohamed Chérif Diarra is an education specialist who has authored several publications on various education topics in Africa such as educational systems, higher education, teacher education, financing and planning as well as human capital development.

Eric Kemeh born in Accra, Ghana, is an e-learning implementation specialist. He is currently the Principal ICT Assistant at University of Ghana, responsible for administration and implementation of E-learning at the institution. He is also a part-time lecturer at the Computer Science Department of the university where he teaches Advance Database Management Systems and Information Communication Technology (ICT) in the global economy. His research interest is in the following areas: innovative curriculum in e-learning, instructional design for e-learning, intelligent e-learning technology, interactive e-learning systems, knowledge management in e-learning, learning and content management systems, multimedia-based e-learning systems, organizational e-learning strategies, educational technology for e-learning, information design for e-learning, learning experience design for e-learning, and attitudinal behavior to adoption of e-learning.

Tukumbi Lumumba-Kasongo is a Professor of Political Science and Education.

His specific interests in political science are varied and timely, and relate to comparative politics, international relations, political economy, education, philosophy, and classical studies are all intertwined in the classes he teaches. He has published numerous works including those on education.

Pai Obanya is an international education strategist, known as the Grand Sage of Education in Africa, named Outstanding Mentor of Educational Researchers in Africa (2012) by ADEA, designer of Nigeria's Universal Basic Education (UBE) program, Chairman of Presidential Task Team on Education in Nigeria (2011), immediate past Chairman of the West African Examinations Council (WAEC), retired ADG/Director of UNESCO Regional Office for Education in Africa (BREDA) and a widely-sought-after keynote speaker on Education, who attained the rank of full Professor in October 1979, and is currently Emeritus Professor in the Institute of Education, University of Ibadan-Nigeria.

Benjamin A. Ogwo is an associate professor and coordinator, occupational competency assessment program, Department of Vocational Teacher Preparation, State University of New York (SUNY) Oswego, United States of America. He holds a doctoral degree in industrial technical education and has broad experiences in intervention program design and implementation in technical vocational education and training (TVET) in sub-Saharan Africa. His research interests are in program design, change management, policy issues in TVET, and informal sector workforce development in sub-Saharan Africa. Dr. Ogwo has participated in different trainings as well as development initiatives sponsored by the following agencies, the World Bank, UNESCO, UNICEF, AfDB, USAID, ILO, and African Technology Policy Studies Network (ATPS). He has also published more than 80 books, book chapters, and articles in various peer-reviewed learned journals and technical papers and presented several international workshop papers in Botswana, Democratic Republic of Congo (DRC), France, Germany, India, Italy, Jamaica, Kenya, Mozambique, Nigeria, South Africa, Uganda, United Kingdom, and the United States of America.

Emefa J. Takyi-Amoako is Executive Director of Oxford ATP International Education and Education, Gender and Research Consultant, who holds a doctorate in Comparative and International Education from Oxford University, UK. Prior to this, she obtained her Bachelor's and two Master's Degrees from University of Cape Coast, Ghana, and Oxford University, Wadham College, and St Anne's Colleges, respectively. Her research interests are in the areas of education policy, globalization, foreign aid partnerships, power, gender, postcolonial and feminist theories, education and technology, as well as pre-tertiary and higher education. She has published works and authored a number of reports on education. They include *Education in West Africa* (2015) by Bloomsbury Publishing and "Education and Gender in the Global South: Inadequate Policy Environment at the Confluence in Sub-Saharan Africa", in P. Amakasu Raposo, D. Arase, S. Cornelissen, *Routledge Handbook of Africa–Asia Relations* (2017). Dr. Takyi-Amoako has taught at undergraduate and graduate levels and is also a Senior Quality Assurance Expert on higher education.

Yusef Waghid is a distinguished professor of Philosophy of Education in the Department of Education Policy Studies at Stellenbosch University in South Africa. He is the author of the following books: *African Philosophy of Education Reconsidered: On Being Human* (London & New York: Routledge, 2014); (with Nuraan Davids) *Education, Assessment and the Desire for Dissonance* (New York: Peter Lang, 2017); and *Tolerance and Dissent Within Education: Towards Debate and Understanding* (London: Palgrave Macmillan, 2017).

LIST OF FIGURES

List of Tables

LIST OF BOXES

Introduction: Re-visioning Education in Africa—Ubuntu-Inspired Education for Humanity

Emefa J. Takyi-Amoako
and N'Dri Thérèse Assié-Lumumba

BACKGROUND

It is an established historical fact that certain peoples in the world value every piece of their history, identity, and culture, both the highly significant and what may seem inconsequential, and are ready to purchase them at exorbitant prices![1] Can the same be said of the African peoples? Perhaps, Africans too have in the past valued their history and culture which are manifest in varying forms, as they were emboldened by their culture in their fight against Europeans, for instance, against colonial rule. However, what is the current state of Africans' knowledge of their history and their mind-set in general toward the value of their history and culture? Thus the

E. J. Takyi-Amoako (✉)
Oxford ATP, Oxford, UK

N. T. Assié-Lumumba
Africana Studies and Research Center, Cornell University,
Ithaca, NY, USA

© The Author(s) 2018
E. J. Takyi-Amoako, N. T. Assié-Lumumba (eds.),
Re-Visioning Education in Africa,
https://doi.org/10.1007/978-3-319-70043-4_1

1

likes of the long list of African freedom fighters before and after the Berlin Conference and its aftermath until the process of independence: Donna Beatrice (Kimpa Vita by her African name) of the Kongo Empire from the end of the seventeenth to the beginning of the eighteenth centuries who lived a short life as she was put to death by the Portuguese forces during the period of informal colonization; Queen Nzinga/Jinga, the reformist who assigned women to important government positions in present-day Angola and organized and led a powerful guerrilla army; Nehanda Charwe Nyakasikana of Zimbabwe who led resistance against colonial occupation and was put to death by the British forces; Yaa Asantewaa who became Queen of the Ashanti Kingdom (now part of modern-day Ghana) and who led her people to fight the onslaught of colonialism after the Ashanti Court was sent into exile and was also ultimately sent to and died in exile; the women who in Côte d'Ivoire took over the Grand-Bassam prison where the French colonial administration had imprisoned anti-colonial leaders; the range of the African leaders who fought in the transition between colonial rules and independence among whom, Félix Houphouët-Boigny who fought for the eradication of forced labor in African countries colonized by France and became the first President of Côte d'Ivoire; Kwame Nkrumah, a vanguard in the colonial struggle, strong advocate of Pan-Africanism, and first President of the Republic of Ghana; Leopold Sedar Senghor, first President of Senegal and a founding member of the La Négritude Movement; Nelson Mandela, the first black President of South Africa and a countless others who fought apartheid; the Aba Women from six ethnic groups (Igbo, Ibibio, Andoni, Orgoni, Bonny, and Opobo) in Nigeria known for reclaiming their political power; Chinua Achebe of Nigeria, known as the Father of the African novel; Ngugi wa Thiong'o of Kenya with his theory of de-colonizing the mind and appeal to Africans to employ their own indigenous languages in their writings and as media of instruction in schools; West African in general such as Ghana's Makola Women and Togo's Nana Benz, market women famous for their economic clout and ingenuity; Aliko Dangote, Africa's top billionaire who confidently believes that "we will be able to transform Africa by ourselves. Not alone, but we will lead and others will follow" (African Business Magazine, October Issue 2015, Emphasis in the original); as well as other countless past and present renowned (pan) Africans, both male and female have demonstrated unequivocally across Africa that Africans too have always treasured and utilized their identity, history, and culture and above all their natural potential and achieved capabilities and boldness to lead their societies over the generations toward improved lives.

However, the main question in this analysis is, to what extent are contemporary Africans willing to acknowledge, value, and integrate these manifestations of human distinctiveness, chronicle, assertiveness, intellectual philosophy, values, achievements, and leadership regarded collectively, into their educational systems, be it formal from pre-school to the tertiary level or non-formal so as to shape the contemporary education that genuinely represents and simultaneously equips the African to take on the challenges of her/his world? Dangote's assertive words in terms of Africa's ability in the world to assume the leadership position in shaping its own present and future destinies remain poignant: "we will be able to transform Africa by ourselves. Not alone, but we will lead and others will follow". These words echo when Nsamenang and Tchombe (2011, p. xxvii) rightly point out that:

> We have learned that no people entirely dislodged from their ancestral roots have ever made collective progress with development and that the era of outsiders deciding and "supplying" what Africans need has not yielded hoped-for outcomes...Their powers should not be used to 'show the way', but to support Africa's efforts to hear its own education theories and see its education practices, among others, and to seek its own way forward.

This book represents one symbolic instance of Africa's leadership efforts to "show the way", "hear its own education theories and see its education practices...and...seek its own way forward" (Nsamenang and Tchombe 2011, p. xxvii). This is what it sets out to do.

This book is one of several publication projects that have been inspired by the 59th Comparative and International Education Society (CIES) Conference, held in Washington, DC, from 8 to 13 March 2015. The conference was framed in the spirit of the main theme: "Ubuntu! Imagining a Humanist Education Globally". At the conference, the African Special Interest Group highlighted paper session entitled "Re-visioning Education in Africa and Beyond: Ubuntu, Humanism and Social Change" featured paper presentations that argued clearly that education in Africa, particularly, can no longer be "business as usual", and that a re-visioning process for education in Africa was urgently needed. These paper presentations shape a number of the chapters in this book.

RATIONALE AND OBJECTIVES

Re-visioning Education in Africa: Ubuntu-Inspired Education for Humanity argues that Africa needs a revolution or at least some profound transformation as far as its educational systems with poor outcomes are concerned—a conceptual and pragmatic revolution. Its purpose is to seek fresh paths for education in Africa by theoretically and practically interrogating and re-visioning education within the African cultural and philosophical concept of Ubuntu. Within this setting, it aims to: unpack the concept of an Ubuntu-inspired education for Africa and humanity; explore ways in and extent to which the continent can harness the potential of its very youthful populations rather than be confronted with the risk that untapped talents and capabilities of the youth pose; examine types of policy questions that national/regional/continental governments ought to be asking themselves with regard to educational systems and the global partnership for development processes in Africa; problematize the type and level of education quality offered to these growing young populations in the various countries; probe the issue of how educational systems in the different countries in Africa are enabling their graduates or beneficiaries with the above considerations in mind; investigate the choices that governments and decision makers are making to ensure these conditions are fulfilled; take a critical look into ways and extent to which governments can convert or are converting the fast technological and economic advancement in the international sphere into tangible transformation and enhanced opportunities for Africa's youth; interrogate the gender dimension; and finally, explore the relationship and impact of re-visioned education on socio-economic and political development of Africa and provide a critique of the current situation from an Ubuntu perspective, and how the Ubuntu philosophy will inspire a new type of education. For instance, what values and mind-set will the concept of Ubuntu bring into content and practice of education? Overall, the book proposes to instigate a rekindling of the debate on seeking new paths for education in Africa and encourage fresh thinking and ways of seeing and practicing education in Africa in order to increase its relevance to society and national/regional/continental development.

FOCUS

While briefly taking stock of educational recommendation of the global community with a special reference to the Education for All (EFA) goals and Millennium Development Goals (MDGs) as it related to education and partnership in Africa, particularly, this book examines the Sustainable Development Goals (SDGs) of the Post-2015 Agenda, with specific focus on SDG 4, which aims to guarantee inclusive and equitable quality education and promote lifelong learning prospects, and SDG 17, which aspires to consolidate the means of implementation and revive the global partnership for sustainable development within the context of Africa. While focus is on the education and partnership SDGs, the book also refers to the Education for All Global Monitoring Reports (EFA/GMRs) published the year prior to and on the cusp of the launch of the Post-2015 Agenda, the Global Education Monitoring (GEM) Report 2016, Africa's own education strategies such as the African Union Commission (AUC) Agenda 2063's ten-year Continental Education Strategy for Africa 2016–2025 (CESA 16–25), and the Common Africa Position (CAP) on the Post-2015 Development Agenda (AUC 2014, 2015, n.d.). Reference is also made to the education strategies of regional economic communities (RECs) of Africa and other documents where relevant.

Poor Education Outcomes: The Problem

First, why the argument that Africa needs to seek fresh paths in regard to its educational systems? Africa is lagging behind all the other regions of the world as far as formal education is concerned, and it is high time the education of the subcontinent was re-visioned (UNESCO 2014; Takyi-Amoako 2015a, b). When it comes to issues regarding its public educational systems from the basic level right through to the tertiary level, the subcontinent is found wanting (ibid.). Global engagements with stated goals of addressing Africa's educational shortcomings repeatedly miss their targets in great part because the problems are inadequately analyzed and the solutions are ill-conceived (Andrews et al. 2015, Assié-Lumumba 2015). The expansion and mass provision of basic education albeit of low quality has exerted pressure on the higher levels. Moreover, policy decisions over the years spearheaded internationally and by international agents, bodies, and financial institutions ensured that secondary and tertiary education were deprived of the necessary resources that would enable both levels to expand concomitantly in readiness for the high demand leading to crowding sometimes mistakenly referred to as "massification" of basic education. Therefore, not surprising are statements such as,

Mass higher education…, spread to Europe and East Asia in the 20th [century] and is **now happening pretty much everywhere except sub-Saharan Africa**. (The Economist 28 March 2015; our emphasis)

Thus, in spite of the substantial national and international financial and technical support of the education systems in Africa, the continent can only lay claim to negligible educational returns when compared to other regions worldwide. Africa trails the rest of the world as far as educational progress is concerned. Generally, its educational outcomes are disappointing and the future of education in the region seems bleak (UNESCO 2014, 2015, 2016; Takyi-Amoako 2015a, b). By the close of 2015, the date set as the deadline for the attainment of the Millennium Development Goals (MDGs) and Education for All (EFA), studies indicated that 30 million of the 59 million children out of school globally lived in Africa? Half of these out-of-school children would never set foot in the classroom. Despite improvement in access, high dropout rate persists. In 32 countries, less than 20 percent of children enrolled are expected to complete primary school. Additionally, the region currently remains home to a third of the 65 million adolescents out of school—a proportion larger than that recorded in the year 2000 (ibid.).

Attempts from the year 2000 to promote education globally were nearly akin to guaranteeing school access to every child. Since this EFA and MDG target of universal access to primary schooling was more focused on poorer nations, it was seemingly irrelevant to the wealthier ones. Temporarily, the exclusive concentration on universal primary enrollment implied a repudiation of equally critical sectors like education quality, early childhood care and education (ECCE), adult literacy, secondary, technical/vocational, and higher education. Generally, there was failure in attaining even this goal of universal primary education, a less ambitious goal of all the EFA goals. Thus, the most deprived in society continue to lose out (UNESCO 2015). It is fair to admit that the EFA agenda achieved only limited gains, and partners, perhaps, failed to keep their promises. Also, interesting was the assertion that while a decade and half of EFA agenda certified the significance of technical solutions, acquiring political authority and grip was even more important in regard to the extent of reform and action needed to attain EFA nationally (UNESCO 2016).

Global and Continental Responses to the Problem

Consequently, in May 2015, the World Education Forum assembled 1600 delegates from 160 nations in Incheon, the Republic of Korea with the sole objective of how to ensure inclusive and equitable quality education and lifelong learning for all by 2030. This Incheon Declaration for Education 2030 has been crucial in shaping the SDG on education— "Ensure inclusive and equitable quality education and promote lifelong learning opportunities for all" when in September 2015, during the 70th Session of the United Nations General Assembly, member states adopted a fresh global development strategy: "Transforming our world: the 2030 Agenda for Sustainable Development". This new agenda blends both global development and environmental objectives in a single framework. UNESCO has been assigned the management and monitoring of the Education 2030 Agenda, and the Global Education Monitoring (GEM) team has been tasked to provide independent monitoring and reporting of the SDG 4, and on education in the other SDGs, for the subsequent decade and half (UNESCO 2016).

Additionally, the AUC emphasizes that CESA 16–25 of Agenda 2063 represents an attempt to not only own the 2030 Agenda for sustainable development but also appropriate it to suit Africa's own vision for education and development. It represents a strategy that emerged from the Conference of Education Ministers held in Kigali and the World Education Forum in Incheon, Korea (AUC/CESA 2016). It is acknowledged that the goals of CESA 16–25 are bold as they pursue superior outcomes to earlier continental or global education strategic plans.

Effectiveness of Global and Continental Responses: Re-visioning (Education) Is Key

The book argues that for the above newly minted global and continental development agendas to attain their goals for Africa, and forestall the depressing educational outcomes, an urgent re-visioned or alternative education paradigm(s) is needed. In other words, this book represents a quest for innovative ways that will guarantee more relevant and effectively appropriated type of formal education, imbued with an indigenous and cultural comprehensiveness that tackles the challenges with more sophistication. Remarkably, most of the national populations in the region—that is, 60–70 percent—are under the age of 30 years or lower. These youthful populations represent a tremendous resource that ought to be tapped, by means of quality and relevant education and training (AUC/CESA 2016; AfDB-OECD-UNDP 2016, 2017). Indeed, education in Africa portrays a depressing picture, but there is a silver lining to the dark cloud, a glimmer of hope, which is represented by Africa's burgeoning youth, if developed can forestall the continent's weak socio-economic standing.

Africa's Population, Human Development, and Socio-economic Profile

Population in Africa is very young. In 2017, children under the age of 15 constitute 41 percent of the population, and the youth between the ages of 15 and 24 years make up an extra 19 percent (United Nations 2017). Most countries on this vast continent boast of between 60 and 70 percent of their population as youthful—under the age of 30 years and lower (UNESCO 2014, 2015, 2016; Takyi-Amoako 2015a, b).

In terms of regional disparity, North Africa records the maximum share of medium and high human development nations. Southern Africa and Central Africa also comprise a blend of low and medium human development countries. Conversely, in East and West Africa, most of the countries belong to the low human development group. Hence development initiatives ought to catalyze and uphold growth, especially, for low human development nations in Africa.

Young people in Africa face the problem of stagnant or sluggish human development. The tremendous gap in regard to skills and opportunities has ramifications for them. Whereas one in every five persons worldwide is a citizen of nations with weak bases for human progress, in Africa, there are three out of every four Africans. The deficit undermines inclusive growth and progress in Africa in both short and long terms. Countries in Africa demonstrate the highest inequity in human progress globally. These forecasts show that the bold targets of the Agenda 2030 and Agenda 2063 will not be achieved especially if the present speed of human development persists as poverty eradication goals will remain unattained.

Productive capacities, competencies, and entrepreneurship are the factors to maximize the potential of Africa's youth as human progress is about generating capacities and prospects for innovation (AfDB-OECD-UNDP 2016, 2017). Catering to the health, education, and employment needs of this demographic will be pivotal to the effective execution of the

2030 Agenda for sustainable development in Africa and African Union Commission Agenda 2063. States with comparatively more work force than dependent population hold the prospect of profiting from a "demographic dividend", if adequate openings are available to the huge labor force to participate productively in the labor market (ibid.). To accomplish this, ample investment in the human capital of the young populations by means of universal access to education at all levels and health care is obligatory.

In Africa, the share of the population aged 25–59 is expected to rise from 35 percent in 2017 to 45 percent in 2090 (United Nations 2017). This is and will continue to be an incredible resource now and for a long time to come. However, this extraordinary human resource could become the curse of Africa's present and future if not managed and exploited effectively for the progress of the continent. Besides, over half of the anticipated growth in population from now till 2050 is expected to transpire in Africa. Of the 2.2 billion people that may heighten global population, 1.3 billion will be incorporated in Africa. The continent will be the chief contributor to world population growth after 2050 (ibid.).

As a result, the book reiterates its argument that in order to efficiently develop this substantial human resource potential for Africa's progress and avert a looming disaster, current education in Africa ought to undergo an urgent fundamental transformation—a process that will set on course a re-visioning of its systems, subjected to the scrutiny it urgently requires, and must undergo methodical and rational processes as well as coherent thinking and analysis while trading ideas through debate. Indeed, this philosophical process when done diligently has the power to enable African governments with their stakeholders and partners to put on the right track, steer and regulate what we know as education on the continent. This exercise is needed as it contemplates and reassesses the entire state of education for the benefit of its people (Venter 2004; Mkabela and Luthuli 1997: 3). We argue that this re-visioning requires the notion of *Ubuntu* at its core.

Ubuntu-Inspired Education for Humanity

In the cultural and philosophical fundament of Africa, the individual forms an essential component of the community or society and, for that matter, can only exist corporately, that is, inextricably from the community (Venter 2004; Teffo 1996: 103; Schiele 1994). This worldview, which pervades Africa, is embodied by the South African word "*Ubuntu*" and engenders the view that "I am, because we are, and since we are, therefore I am" (Mbiti 1969 in Teffo 1996: 103). Broodryk (2002: 13) describes it as "a comprehensive ancient African worldview based on the values of intense humanness, caring, sharing, respect, compassion and associated values". According to Letseka (2013: 339), perceived from within indigenous African thought, Ubuntu "can be said to articulate our communal inter-connected-ness, our common humanity, our interdependence and our common membership to a community". Venter (2004) refers to the notion as a philosophy that fosters the collective good of society and embraces humanness as a crucial condition of human development. It is a notion that champions humanism, which finds its manifestation in communalism rather than individualism (Venter 2004; Teffo 1998: 3). Nevertheless, it should be stressed that individuality is neither denied nor repudiated in the African idea of humanity. What is disapproved is the notion that the individual should take priority over and above the community/society (Venter 2004). Since the philosophy with its ideals is central to all African cultures, it has various linguistic manifestations. Different African languages use different expressions for this philosophy, but they encompass its various features including "togetherness, equality, sharing, sympathy, empathy, compassion, respect, tolerance, humanness, harmony, redistribution, happiness" (Compiled from Broodryk 2002: 13).

Ubuntu as a distinctive African philosophy, history, culture, identity, and value of common humanity holds humanness as critical to human development into all its systems, particularly, its formal education systems. Venter (2004) argues that the concept is essential to education in Africa. Certainly, the Ubuntu philosophy and ideals must be made central to Africa's education policy processes, systems, and agents' actions, and must be evoked for an effective re-visioning of Africa's education. This is because, currently, the philosophy and its ideals, which constitute the essence of Africa and its people as well as their indigenous knowledges and history, are lacking in the educational policies and systems of the continent. This absence has culminated in an incongruent link between who Africans are as a people and the educational systems that are meant to help unlock and develop their talents and potential for socio-economic development.

While the nub of this book is on sub-Saharan Africa due to the region's low human development index (AfDB-OECD-UNDP 2016), we define Africans in this context with a deep awareness of the fact that Africans do not represent a monolithic entity. The heterogeneity of Africans is thus acknowledged. However, the study delineates the concept of Ubuntu, which pervaded (and still continues to permeate) the indigenous African cultures in varying linguistic and cultural forms in relation to African peoples, who were indigenously African and lived and practiced this philosophy during the pre-colonial era. This was before the advent of European-styled formal schooling that emerged during the post-/colonial era in Africa and became the hallmark of educational systems on the continent.

The advocacy efforts to rejuvenate African renaissance in post-colonial Africa within society's socio-cultural and educational spheres by Pan-Africanists, the Negritude group, and others yielded negligible results; hence, Africa's educational systems obdurately remained foreign to and alienated from its original context. It is therefore not surprising that educational progress and outcomes in Africa over the years have been nothing but depressing (UNESCO 2015; Nsamenang and Tchombe 2011). Africa's un-/conscious readiness to relegate its indigeneity, essence, and identity to the background in its education and replace (not even blend) it with a foreign alien culture is the bane of its educational systems. Indeed, as the Global Education Monitoring (GEM) Report 2016 rightly notes, "Not all education brings the same benefits to everyone. Time, place, situation and context matter (Harber as quoted in UNESCO 2016: 11)." Hence the need to fundamentally re-vision Africa's education to suit its philosophical, historical, and cultural context by employing the Ubuntu framework in order to produce a well-educated work force whose skills are relevant and deployed effectively toward the continent's socio-economic progress.

THE STRUCTURE OF THE BOOK

This introductory chapter is to provide a summary of the book contents, while outlining its main argument woven around two key questions that relate to: first, the theoretical considerations, which characterize Ubuntu-inspired education for humanity in Africa, and second, some practical solutions that exemplify Ubuntu-inspired education for humanity in Africa. The book aims to highlight these two concerns and their implications for Africa's education and holistic development.

In "The Humanist African Philosophy of Ubuntu: Anti-colonial historical and educational analyses", Ali A. Abdi acknowledges the increasing global popularity of Ubuntu both as an idea that is no longer trivialized and viewed as exotic African term sounding from Africa by some and which is considered as a depth and life-encompassing philosophical platform. In the case of North America with a global component, he refers to the 2015 Comparative and International Education Society (CIES) Conference with the centrality of Ubuntu in its theme. He problematizes the concept and considers that given the educational challenges due to the colonial project, it offers a hopeful broader philosophical and educational framework toward the achievement of humanist and humanizing systems of education.

In "Ubuntu and Pan-Africanism: The Dialectics of Learning about Africa", Tukumbi Lumumba-Kasongo locates Ubuntu in the broader context in connection to Pan-Africanism as two different political philosophies defining historical and contemporary Africa that have been formulated by similar intellectual and political constituents at different historical moments. He articulates the glaring contradictions of Africa characterized by weak solidarity among its people despite the pragmatism of their collective ethos at the communal and institutional levels such as the family. He further argues that in the search for new paradigms of development in Africa, Ubuntu and Pan-Africanism offer some possibilities in reformulating and answering the fundamental questions that model development and the externally defined created nation-states.

Yusef Waghid argues in "On the educational potential of *Ubuntu*" that in the past two decades the *Ubuntu* has been engaged by diverse scholars in many cases in relation to African education. The author aims to offer a different perspective in arguing that the concept of *Ubuntu* is an African notion for education, in the same way that some Europeans describe *bildung* as education, and *ta'dib*, for some Muslims, means education. He offers a critical analysis of the concept and points to the way *Ubuntu* relates to at least three meanings of education, namely, interdependent human action, deliberative inquiry, and socially responsive action. He argues for *Ubuntu* as a cosmopolitan practice and articulates the rationale for *Ubuntu* as a cultivation of dignity.

In "Conceptualizing Gender and Education in Africa from an Ubuntu Frame", N'Dri T. Assié-Lumumba argues that educational and gender inequality are two intertwined areas of critical concern at international levels as reflected in the global consensus of resolutions adopted by the United Nations, its specialized agencies, and as well as by African states. At the continental level, the African Union has adopted the Agenda 2063 in which socio-economic development through education is articulated and gender equality targeted. The author contends that such goals require an overhaul of inherited systems that reproduce inequality and adopting Ubuntu paradigm to harness the values of equal worth and collective well-being, with the potential of becoming a model for the world.

Pai Obanya authoritatively articulates in "Reclaiming the Education that Africa Lost" Africa's loss of its education which occurred with the continent's loss of sovereignty through colonization. Despite some progress in regaining the purely political dimension of its sovereignty, the struggle to regain cultural and socio-economic sovereignty has been a daunting task. Part of the strategy to win this battle requires the integration of key elements of African Traditional Education into present-day educational development efforts on the continent. The author highlights the significance of the benefits of *hindsight* (drawing lessons from Africa's past experience) for clearer *insight* (a deeper understanding of present-day educational development dilemma of Africa) to provide a sound basis for viable *foresight* (projecting for a better future for education in Africa).

In "Ubuntu as humanistic education: Challenges and Perspectives for Africa?", Mohamed Chérif Diarra problematizes the relevance and readiness of Ubuntu-inspired education in promoting economic growth or development in Africa. The author calls for more critical examination, understanding, and practical process for adopting Ubuntu, although the concept is found in different African cultural contexts and languages albeit with different specific words. The author expresses concerns about the possibility that an Ubuntu-inspired education may not necessarily prove to be conducive to expansion of literacy, provision of managerial skills, and education as an investment.

In "Putting the Cart before the Horse? Early Childhood Care and Education (ECCE) in Sub-Saharan Africa", Hamidou Boukary critically examines the development of early childhood care and education (ECCE) in Africa as a key sub-sector which is yet formulated in a cultural and historical vacuum that lacks the capacity to promote education at such a determining and foundational level of educational journey at the upper levels of the system. The author advocates for a necessary foundation that is offered by the Ubuntu-inspired system of education. The author adds that Africa's soul-searching in terms of Africans who realize that their education systems have been inadequate in producing educated individuals who are well positioned in their culture is the result of the process by which Africa missed the opportunity during the early post-independence era to design and implement an ECCE sub-sector rooted in its cultures and value systems. It is possible to redress the loss by embracing Ubuntu-inspired education.

In "Re-visioning Technical Vocational Education and Training (TVET) for the Youth in sub-Saharan Africa (SSA) and the Sustainable Development

Goals' (Sdgs): Prospects and Promises within the framework of Ubuntu Paradigm", Benjamin A. Ogwo employs the Ubuntu lens to make a call for the re-vision of technical vocational education and training (TVET), which is the fundamental means for technically acculturating the youth who will shift the post-2015 development programs toward eradicating poverty, enhancing food security, encouraging gender empowerment, and on the whole improving quality of life and sustainable progress in Africa. The author examines Ubuntu-based soft skills, affective competencies, and ethical re-engineering of TVET programs for environmentally friendly, justice-driven, people-oriented, and communally derived sustainable development of sub-Saharan Africa. A key point is that technical and vocational education and training can help promote progress only if they are not considered void of culture, but rather are located within Ubuntu-centered value system.

With statistical evidence provided by an empirical study, "Ubuntu as a framework for the adoption and use of e-learning in Ghanaian Public Universities" undertaken by Eric Kemeh shows lack of application of the Ubuntu philosophy to e-learning systems in higher education as the policies and practices do not reflect genuine concern for common good. The study revealed that the teaching and learning culture of Ghanaian public universities encourages the adoption and usage of ICT tools as well as e-learning programs, while the integration of technology into teaching and learning processes suffers from lack of e-learning technology, inadequate awareness, and absence of support from the ICT centers in the various public universities. He proposes the adoption of Ubuntu values as an effective pathway for the acceleration of the extensive use of e-learning technologies for teaching and learning in African public universities. The author believes that through this, more youth will gain access to affordable and quality higher education, thereby facilitating the achievement of the SDG 4.

With a focus on higher education in "Addressing the Challenge of Coloniality in the Promises of Modernity and Cosmopolitanism to Higher Education: De-bordering, De-centering/De-peripherizing, and De-colonializing", Jose Cossa tackles the challenge of coloniality in the promises of modernity and cosmopolitanism embedded in the conceptualization and functioning of higher education institutions in Africa as the inherited Western higher education was founded under classical modernism and cosmopolitanism. Such a conceptualization departure does not make room to engage critically coloniality which is the essential fabric of the

African higher education. Thus, there need for engagement toward a "de-bordering, de-centering/de-peripherizing, and de-colonilizing".

In a forward-looking perspective forcefully articulated in "Towards an Alternative Approach to Education Partnerships in Africa: Ubuntu, the Confluence and the Post-2015 Agenda", Emefa J.A. Takyi-Amoako proposes an alternative approach derived from the fusion of the philosophy of Ubuntu and the notion of the Confluence. She argues that a thoughtful consciousness of and sensitivity to people's inter-connectedness, interdependence, shared humanity, and membership to a community, which nurtures the shared benefit of society and holds humanness as an essential pre-requisite of human development, blended with a deep understanding of the Confluence (meeting point) by African national governments, decision makers, education stakeholders, and other agents of change in Africa, and how countries are positioned within this space of power inequalities on the cusp or in the nexus of the global and local is crucial. This is key to the effectiveness and relevance of Africa's current and future educational processes and systems, driving education and training processes to the advantage of Africans and progress in general on the continent.

In the concluding chapter, the co-editors summarize some of the arguments advanced in the different contributions and reiterate the call for the adoption of new philosophy of education as articulated in the Ubuntu paradigm as sine qua non factor of the targeted development goals with integrated levels from pre-school to higher education and from vocational and technical education to academic learning, striving to include all potential learners paying particular attention to gender and equality. Ubuntu is articulated as a unifying force with powerful indigenous agency and vison defining the conceptualization, design, and implementation of relevant and liberating policies. They examine critically the relationship and impact of re-visioned education on socio-economic and political development of Africa, while providing a critique of the current situation from an Ubuntu perspective, and how the Ubuntu philosophy will inspire a new type of education. Overall, the book attempts to instigate and rekindle the debate on the search for new paths for education in Africa and advance fresh thinking and ways of seeing and practicing education in Africa so as to increase its relevance to society and national/regional/continental socio-economic development. Central to all this is the recommendation to the AU to initiate and lead an Ubuntu-Inspired African Continental Partnership on Education to achieve the goals of the AUC Agenda 2063.

NOTE

1. A case in point is that on the website of the University of Oxford Bodleian Libraries, it was once summarily announced that: "Bodleian buys historic ledgers of Oxford Shoemakers Ducker & Son, revealing purchases of literary guests!" It went on to state: "The Bodleian Libraries has purchased the historic customer ledgers of venerable Oxford Shoemaker, Ducker & Son, a unique piece of history which provides a glimpse into the lives of the shop's famous clients such as *Lord of the Rings* author JRR Tolkien and *Brideshead Revisited* novelist Evelyn Waugh. A small selection of the ledgers will be on public display at the Weston Library from 25–26 March, 2017".

REFERENCES

AfDB-OECD-UNDP. (2016). *African economic outlook 2016 sustainable cities and structural transformation*. Abidjan/Paris/New York: AfDB, OECD, UNDP.

AfDB-OECD-UNDP. (2017). *African economic outlook 2017 entrepreneurship and Industrialisation*. Abidjan/Paris/New York: AfDB, OECD, UNDP.

African Union Commission. (2014). *Common Africa position (CAP) on the post 2015 development agenda*. Addis Ababa: African Union.

African Union Commission. (2015). *Agenda 2063: The Africa we want (Popular version)*. Addis Ababa: Africa Union Commission.

African Union Commission. (n.d.). *Continental Education Strategy for Africa 2016–2025 (CESA 16–25): Let's put our heads together for the future of Africa*. Addis Ababa: African Union Commission.

Andrews, N., Khalema, E. N., & Assie-Lumumba, N. (2015). *Millennium development goals (MDGs) in retrospect – Africa's development beyond 2015*. London: Springer.

Assie-Lumumba, N. (2015). Millennium Development in retrospect: Higher education and the gender factor in Africa's development beyond 2015. In N. Andrews, E. N. Khalema, & N. Assie-Lumumba (Eds.), *Millennium development goals (MDGs) in retrospect – Africa's development beyond*. London: Springer.

Broodryk, J. (2002). *Ubuntu: Life lessons from Africa*. Tshwane: Ubuntu School of Philosophy.

Letseka, M. (2013). Educating for *Ubuntu/Botho*: Lessons from Basotho Indigenous Education. *Open Journal of Philosophy 3*(2), 337–344. Published Online May 2013 in SciRes. http://www.scirp.org/journal/ojpp. Accessed 10 Apr 2015.

Mkabela, N. Q., & Luthuli, P. C. (1997). *Towards an African philosophy of education*. Pretoria: Kagiso Tertiary.

Nsamenang, B. A., & Tchombe, T. M. S. (2011). *Handbook of African educational theories and practices: A generative teacher education curriculum.* Cameroon: Human Development Resource Centre (HDRC).

Schiele, J. H. (1994). Afrocentricity: Implications for higher education. *Journal of Black Studies, 25*(2), 150–169.

Takyi-Amoako, E. J. (2015a). Introduction: Education in West Africa: A regional overview. In E. J. Takyi-Amoako (Ed.), *Education in West Africa.* London: Bloomsbury Publishing.

Takyi-Amoako, E. (2015b). *Education in West Africa.* London: Bloomsbury Publishing.

Teffo, L. J. (1996). The other in African experience. *South African Journal of Philosophy, 15*(3), 101–104.

Teffo, L. J. (1998). Botho/Ubuntu as a way forward for contemporary South Africa. *Word and Action, 38*(365), 3–5.

The Economist. (2015). The world is going to university. *The Economist.* http://www.economist.com/news/leaders/21647285-more-and-more-`money-being-spent-higher-education-too-little-known-about-whether-it. Accessed 29 Mar 2015.

UNESCO. (2014). *Education for all global monitoring report 2013/14 teaching and learning: Education quality for all.* Paris: UNESCO Publishing.

UNESCO. (2015). *Education for all 2000–2015: Achievements and challenges.* Paris: UNESCO Publishing.

UNESCO. (2016). *Global education monitoring report. Education for people and planet: Creating sustainable futures for all.* Paris: UNESCO Publishing.

United Nations. (2017). *World population prospects: The 2017 revision- key findings and advance tables ESA/P/WP/248.* New York: United Nations, Department of Economic and Social Affairs Population Division.

Venter, E. (2004). The notion of Ubuntu and communalism in African educational discourse. *Studies in Philosophy and Education, 23*(2–3), 149–160.

CHAPTER 2

The Humanist African Philosophy of Ubuntu: Anti-colonial Historical and Educational Analyses

Ali A. Abdi

INTRODUCTION

The increasing global popularity of Ubuntu, first as an idea for those who positively react to its novelty with the ever-present danger of trivializing it as something exotic and peculiar sounding from Africa, and later for others who appreciate its depth and life-encompassing philosophical platforms, seems to be extending into many corners of the world. In the North American context, for example, the referencing of Ubuntu, again by those who understand it and those who just like it, has massively risen in the past few years, with the first major international gathering, the Comparative and International Education Society (CIES) Conference, which was held in Washington, DC, in March 2015, locating it as its main thematic reference. Interestingly, that conference currently holds the record for the highest number of attendees in CIES' over 60-year history. While I do not need to engage in causal analysis, I will permit myself to assume some attributive correspondence, not necessarily between the thoughtful naming

A. A. Abdi (✉)
Department of Educational Studies, The University of British Columbia, Vancouver, Canada

© The Author(s) 2018
E. J. Takyi-Amoako, N. T. Assié-Lumumba (Eds.),
Re-Visioning Education in Africa,
https://doi.org/10.1007/978-3-319-70043-4_2

19

of the conference and its popularity with people from every continent in the world, my preference is more on the topical interest this has generated from both those who have a discernible understanding of Ubuntu and those who wanted to be exposed to, and know more about it. Having participated myself in the said 2015 conference with a select focus on the conceptual and extendedly epistemological contours of Ubuntu and having used its relational analysis in my writing (Abdi 2013), what I saw in that conference makes me think that a catalyst perspective on learning and, where useful, operationalizing select aspects of the African and as importantly Africanist life philosophy of Ubuntu might be emerging. Based on the dominant and still problematic portrayals of African achievement though, the dangers of trivializing this important thought system as an intra- or inter-epistemic discursive fashionista of the moment are never far away. Indeed, the naturalistic exoticization of this historico-culturally entrenched and pedagogically thick philosophy of inter-subjective living is certainly happening in few places in the world. Indeed, and despite my real concerns with the real trivialization perspective, I prefer to refrain from refuting the good intentions of those who are just uttering Ubuntu as simply something new, or actually misinterpreting it by not critically appreciating its constructively transactional inter-human connections. My concerns and cautionary qualifications about something good that might be emerging here should not surprise those who are either historico-culturally informed or perhaps selectively endowed with some multi-epistemic consciousness. In reality, the monocentric knowledge representations of the world have been anything but either reasonably representational or poly-epistemically inclusive. If anything and especially in the area of either basic philosophy or philosophy of education, the colonialist chorus that ethno-centrically denied anything of that nature to Africa and Africans as well as to some other colonized populations is not a big secret (Said 1978, 1993; Achebe 2000; Abdi 2008). The project of colonialism was itself justified on practically baseless but habitually presumed absence of *mirabile dictu*, history, culture, philosophy, and by extension, viable knowledge platforms from Africa's massive landmass and the people who reside there.

Interestingly, some of the people who were ardently the vanguard for this disparaging, indeed, denying of Africa's philosophical and knowledge achievements were those associated with Europe's so-described high platform thinkers, writers, and philosophers. As I have quasi-extensively discussed in few places (Abdi 2008, 2013), such denials were deliberately orchestrated and, by and large, intended to justify the conquest of foreign lands and the outright, indeed, unaccountable exploitation of their human and natural resources. One of the reasons that understanding this is so important is actually also related to the fact that all lives, all nations, and all continents can be devoid of the foundational philosophical perspective that underpins the way they explain, relate to, and interact with their social and physical environments. To be sure, if philosophy is about, in the most general terms, our thoughtful and reflective inquiry on our historical and contemporary contexts, then how is it possible that we locate some people as devoid of that basic philosophical life tradition? I do not think we need to answer this or similar questions by seeking specific facts that refute the false claims that could instigate in the first place. That is, beyond calling such claims what exactly these are: a deliberate way to lower the achievements of Africans and other colonized populations, they actually had a deep and continue to have further deeper racist foundations that were more or less bent on lowering the assumed full humanity of humans. With entirely Eurocentric and totally unscientific descriptions and methodologies, this process of onto-epistemological dehumanization was intended to pave the way for the aforesaid onslaught on people's lives and environments so as to facilitate their physical and mental colonization. In the following, I will engage limited analyses of the problematic historical constructions and currently increasing discussions of Ubuntu, complemented by a more extensive and multi-critical focus on ways of Ubuntu-izing our educational systems for inclusive epistemologies and more liberating livelihood possibilities. Moreover, and just as an instructive note, while the etymological origins of Ubuntu are Southern African, the humanizing and the knowledge and educational foundations of Ubuntu are fully generalizable to all of sub-Saharan Africa, hence my intention to locate it geographically, historico-culturally, and educationally as such. As such, for methodological intentions, the piece relies exclusively on the review and analysis of contemporary literature and does not engage any forays into fieldwork contexts or related first-hand research platforms; it is, therefore, mainly an analytical and critical treatise of its topical foci.

PROBLEMATIC HISTORICAL CONSTRUCTIONS AND THE CONTEMPORARY EMERGENCE OF UBUNTU

As should be expected, one need not recognize the complete human value of others and then use such recognition to colonize them. To do the latter, one will fabricate—as Said (1993) and Achebe (2000), among others, so cogently noted—new disclaimers on the historical, cultural, and epistemic achievements of the to-be-colonized, thus even advancing the grossly mis-named, so dominantly labeled Mission Civilisatrice project (Missão civili-zadora in Portuguese). That project, beyond its untenable conceptual constructions and anti-humanist (and anti-Ubuntu) practical outcomes (as it actually did the opposite of what is was purporting to do), was responsible, it was worth affirming, for the rescinding of what Cabral (Cabral 1981) termed the deep source of pre-colonial African achieve-ments and life-management systems that represented time-and-space tested ways of living, learning, and advancing. This rescinding of people's achievements was also recorded by, inter alia, Julius Nyerere (1968) and Walter Rodney (1982) who both quite extensively but critically uncovered the false exhortations of colonialism as a developmental project, and more as a well-planned destructive program that canceled so much Indigenous achievement which sustained contextually thriving, complex life systems for thousands of years. Indeed, without a grain of emotions or any biased perspective, and pragmatizing my observations as much as possible, can one imagine or perceive of the lives of people in Africa or elsewhere, think-ing about their life contexts and achieving in their social, political, eco-nomic, and technological contexts over millennia without education, philosophy, and relevant designs of social development? For all sincere intentions, the answer has to be a categorical no, as Africans were always well endowed, not just in their philosophical traditions, but as well in their philosophy of education formulations and implementations (Rodney 1982; Oruka 1990; Abdi 2008). As Rodney (1982) noted in his magisterial research achievement, *How Europe Underdeveloped Africa*, pre-colonial African ways of educating were effectively designed by the concerned com-munities based on the learning and social development needs of such com-munity, thus fulfilling all the things Africa's colonial education currently lacks: culturally relevant and historically connected, as well as linguistically viable and contextually responsive programs of teaching and learning. As has been discussed by, among others, Nelson Mandela (1994) and van Onselen (1996), education was valued qua education and was important in affirming the full humanity of all.

Certainly therefore, such education and its philosophies of learning rep-resented valid categories of knowledge that, as Semali and Kincheloe (1999) noted, contained all the epistemic categories we value today, albeit with hardly any choices for most of us, in our monocentrically structured global schooling systems. In addition, general African philosophies, which categorically answered the main questions of what education the community need, why it needed it, and how such education was to be formulated and implemented, were foundational components of the overall African philosophy of Ubuntu. Here and contrary to the false assumptions about pre-colonial African life with most of those still persistent, it does seem lately that the world has woken up to this humanist way of thinking and constructively relating to one other. With the predatory platforms of neo-liberal globalization (Harvey 2007) and the failure of externally imposed development projects in almost all the countries of sub-Saharan Africa, this late discovery of Ubuntu by the rest of the world seems to be achieving some long overdue crediting of this ancient continent with its rightful claims to what should be the most life-encompassing, humanist philosophy anywhere in the world. By discursively engaging the philosophy of Ubuntu more analytically and critically also, we could expand the circles of its epistemic and epistemological validations and contributions and, by extension, perhaps slowly formalize it as an inter-continentally viable tradition that should be embraced and studied in extra-Africa locations as well, including beyond North America and Europe where the foci and discussions are already expanding.

Still the dangers of a false start with multiple misreadings of Ubuntu and the potential bastardization of the inclusive spirit and practice of this humanist philosophy, and thus misapplied with the wrong outcomes, are never far away. To repeat, the dangers can again be emanating from thick and continuously expansive misperceptions and misconstructions about African ontologies, epistemologies, thought systems, and ways of learning and teaching. That is to say that while historical onslaughts on African cultural, philosophical, and epistemological plateaus are not yet decommissioned, and the needed appreciation of these is not yet fully on the horizon, one has to be hopeful about the global openness to Ubuntu as a well-constructed systemic way of life that can help us all, could only be a welcome moment. This potentially momentous moment in embracing Ubuntu as a global philosophy is actually aided by the emergence of important and timely scholarship in the past 20 or so years (see, inter alia, Swanson 2007; Battle 2009; Carracciolo and Mungai 2009; Sandberg 2010). In addition, and although perhaps not all thematically connected to this, the humanist notations and potential practical outcomes of Ubuntu were foundational to the thinking of South African Archbishop and Nobel Laureate Desmond Tutu's philosophy and political project of reconciliation among former enemies in the tortured history of the South African peninsula. Tutu who was the head of the country's Truth and Reconciliation Commission (TRC) after the fall of official apartheid in 1994 was clear on the need to tell, hear, and forgive. As should be understood though, Ubuntu's project of humanization is not selective; it is for all contexts and relationships.

Indeed, Tutu's TRC, under the presidency and blessing of Nelson Mandela, went beyond just recognizing the humanity of the oppressor but was seeking real ways of forgiving him or her as well. As should be expected, this was exceedingly difficult for the victims of apartheid who rightfully wanted justice to be served. But Tutu, perhaps with his deep spirituality of not missing even the tiny residue of goodness that might reside even in the personhoods of apartheid's most monstrous evil doers, was adamant that the only way forward for multiracial South Africa was forgiveness. In his book, *No Future Without Forgiveness* (1999, p. 2), Tutu notes how his own humanity and, by implied extension, all our humanities are inextricably interwoven and inter-situated within the circle of individual and collective existentialities. That is, we are actually persons only through the personhood of the others. For the TRC confessions and reactions, this connected personhood was to bring together the victim and the torturer, and while one can discern the difficulty of that, no one is actually qualified to cancel off anyone else. Stated with a different descriptive structure, those whose behaviors could be described as worst of human qualities (say members of apartheid's policymakers, jailers, torturers, and killers) would still qualify to be counted in the human family. So, despite the difficulty of his task, Tutu was not in err to refuse denying the basic humanity of the very bad other. Indeed, despite the continuing absence of especially full economic justice for the majority of black South African, Tutu's TRC, with the support and the conscientious leadership of Nelson Mandela, should have majorly contributed to the minimal, functional democracy that is currently at work in South Africa. Beyond the TRC and looking at the individualistic and subjective-centric modes most of us are socialized today, the practice of this noble humanist African philosophy is anything but easy. It at least requires us to modify our historical and contemporary readings of other peoples from near and far, willing in the process, to bridle the intoxicating desire for some measure of superiority over other human beings. Tutu (1999, p. 2) indeed offers us this hopeful depiction of someone who possesses Ubuntu:

> A person with Ubuntu is open and available to others, affirming of others, does not feel threatened that others are able and good, for he or she has a

proper self-assurance that comes from knowing that he or she belongs in a greater whole and is diminished when others are humiliated or diminished, when others are tortured or oppressed, or treated as if they were less who they are (No future without forgiveness).

HUMANIST UBUNTU EDUCATION AND POSSIBILITIES FOR A NEW GLOBAL PERSPECTIVE

With the deeply humanist philosophy of Ubuntu, education in historical Africa was, as stated above and sans condition, valued qua education with the basic and continuing practice of teaching and learning for life being fundamental social development perspective and prospects (Mandela 1994; van Onselen 1996). Indeed, the relevance of such education for life was to be appreciated as a communal project that responded not to the needs of colonial powers and their non-African and radically economized ideas of life, but to the quotidian needs of the Indigenous public that knew, better than any external de-philosophizing or de-epistemologizing hegemonies, what it needed for the well-being of its members and neighbors. This should actually affirm what we saw above from Rodney (1982), Nyerere (1968), and others that on historically retrievable facts, pre-colonial, Indigenous African education was thoughtfully designed for and was robustly fit for the social, cultural, and certainly politico-economic well-being of its recipients. Importantly, this education was constructed upon, and implemented through, the horizontal humanist connections that characterized, indeed, informed, the lives of people from all ages, professions, and contextual positions. This included learners, teachers, acknowledged knowledge experts, and wisdom holders.

In addition, such education was neither too generalistic nor too specialized for its circularly located recipients. As have been partially confirmed by, among others, Semali and Kincheloe (1999), and I have seen myself growing up in the north-easterly corner of semi-rural East Africa, it was not that uncommon to meet Indigenous knowledge experts excelling in multiple fields including but not even limited to medicine (for both people and livestock), agricultural systems, literature, astronomy, and meteorological sciences. The formalized professional labeling here should not sound epistemically extraneous to the informed observations I am engaging as I am actually deliberately elevating natural giftedness and experiential achievements over the current systems of commercialized and elitist credentializations that are, in their harshly rigid categorizations, anti-Ubuntu and work on as a system of winners and losers. To the contrary, Indigenous African education, with expansive Ubuntu foundations, saw only winners who were all capable and uniquely good, but also uniquely connected to the community, its needs, and aspirations. In particlizing the point here a little more, which could descriptively sound contradictory as I am borrowing the term from particle physics, Ubuntu philosophy does not refute or minimize the subjective location or the constitution of the individual and, unlike our old good philosophy of liberal democracy, disavows the supremacy of the individual over the community. As Tutu (1999) noted, learning through Ubuntu advances one's chances of appreciating communalist principles to see, perceive, and relate to others as some extension of our own being and recognizing our livelihood needs as not extricated from the needs of others.

As I have analyzed elsewhere (Abdi 2013), the European systems of learning that do not advance education qua education, but as an extension of the overall radical economization of life created what should perhaps be the most intense onto-epistemological clash between Africans and foreign invaders. The onto-epistemological clash, as critical educational researchers could agree, continues into shaping the schooling formulations and related learning platforms that are henceforward undertaken. Indeed, what has happened in the past 200 or so years, or even before that, as Abu-Lughod (1995) so effectively noted in her study of the longue-durée residence of Eurocentrism in our learning and general epistemic lives, the mundialization of counter-Ubuntu, colonial education systems have been entrenched in almost every corner of the world. To reiterate, this perforce formulated and implemented entrenchment of individualistic, competitively oriented and actually Indigenous-wise, demeaning forms of learning did not take place in analytical or relational vacuum. These were willfully constructed to suppress Indigenous systems of education with the central intention of indoctrinating the so-pejoratively labeled colonized natives across the globe, who were, it is worth repeating, perforce constructed as devoid of any knowledge, educational, and by assumed extension, social development capacities. From there, the abjectly racist argument was attached to the natives' need for everything European. Such claims were not extraneous descriptions to the overall ideologies and philosophies of colonialism, but what we need to challenge now forward is their anti-humanist ways of learning and teaching, which by suppressing the Indigenous expanses of knowledge and education have suppressed and actually diminished potential global epistemic achievements that have been co-created by all continents, all countries, and all peoples (Harding 1998, 2008).

It is on the basis of the realities of not only educational colonization, but as well the thick processes of de-philosophication and de-epistemologization, all complemented by imposed learning systems that actually taught people to devalue themselves, their cultures, and their potentialities that should persuade us to rethink current systems of global education and seriously consider the possible Ubuntu-ization of our diverse and inter-humanly connected learning systems. By so doing, we can also re-issue, for ourselves and for the rest of the world, more humanizing systems of teaching and learning where people's histories, cultures, languages, and related human characteristics, characters, expectations, and aspirational plateaus are considered in inclusive terms accounted for. This does not mean at all that by Ubuntu-izing, not only African systems of education, but at least thinking of doing so beyond the geographical boundaries of the continent with a special focus on previously colonized and epistemically de-indigenized locations, that we will be doing away with all systems of western-style education. For all pragmatic undertakings, we should not, and indeed cannot, disconnect ourselves from the practically constructive attributes of this currently dominant education system as at least partially important and research-based achievements that can relatively benefit the needs of people in our globalized and interconnected world. What we cannot afford to miss henceforward, though, is to collectively devise new platforms that constructively weigh what epistemic achievement credits we could accord to the west vis-à-vis the rest.

As should be known to many of us by now, and I am not at all implicating anything that could go against the collective human achievement of all available knowledge systems, it has to be imperative to note that even in those areas which are so currently associated with western educational and research advancements such as medicine and the physical and mathematical sciences were actually firstly achieved in the East, some of them specifically within the Nile Valley civilizations of Africa. Take the example of medical education and practice where in the west, Hippocrates is affirmed as the father of medicine, while actually medicine was formally and systematically practiced in Egypt around 3000 BC, that is, about 2600 years before the famed Greek physician was born. The same is true of mathematics which is currently hastily credited to the Greek mathematician, Euclid, although sophisticated and complex mathematics was used around 3000 BC by the Babylonians (more or less in present-day Iraq). Granted that people like Hippocrates and Euclid added a lot to the development of medicine and mathematics, the current crediting of these things is certainly problematic and, by and large, emanates from western-centric knowledge and achievement claims that are habitually given to classical Greece. As the claims contain so much more than medicine and mathematics, these also include philosophy, politics, democracy, even partially poetry.

With respect to the needed Ubuntu-ization of global education systems, my above observations on the practically untenable knowledge and learning claims are important in at least two ways. Firstly, these are not detached from the epistemic monocentrization that colonialism used to rescind all other over millennia developed educational programs, thus deliberately stunting the constructive march of knowledge advancement platforms that could have given us so much more in socio-cultural and politico-economic well-being. Secondly, and perhaps equally importantly, knowledge systems and educational programs are, for all ethical and practical intentions, constitutive elements of the lives of the people these represent. Both points here should be constructively responsive to the inter-human and inter-epistemic connections of our lives that are advanced by humanist philosophy of Ubuntu. That is, our lives are not about how we manage our contexts, but as well, how we recognize and relate to others in both our vicinities and extra-territorial faraway places. As a direct and fully discernible extension of its core philosophical and learning foundations, the issue of recognition should especially be to inter-humanizing Ubuntu platforms. In contemporary mainstream writings, the works of the Canadian philosopher Charles Taylor (1992, 1995, 2003), Axel Honneth (1996, 2014), Nancy Fraser and Honneth (2004), and Iris Young (2012) have all critically engaged the social and related issues of recognition. What is apparent from these important thinkers' perspectives is the central importance of recognition and lack thereof, for our personal, national, and global lives.

In Taylor's writings which are perhaps among the most recently referenced perspectives in the area in the past 20 or so years, his observations go beyond our primary need for recognition as fully endowed beings with valuable historical, cultural, and contemporary achievements and rights and point out the damage that could be done when people, especially those who experience negative power differential relations, are either not recognized or, as he puts it, mis-recognized (Taylor 1995). Taylor also understands very clearly that irrespective of how much we are exposed to individualistic tendencies and indoctrinations, we are never just ourselves (1992) and have to be recognized beyond the liberal (neoliberal) democracy assumptions of personal interest and interpersonal competitions (2003).

In analytically agreeing with Taylor, the late Iris Young (2012) asks us to actually enlarge the boundaries of our recognition by assuming responsibility for global justice for all. From her reading, it is clear that she appreciates understanding and recognizing the lives as well as the needs of people beyond our boundaries and willing to engage in efforts of solidarity with them so as to mitigate systems of oppression that spawn political, economic, and overall livelihood marginalizations. The writings of Taylor and Young, among others, which I am extending below into my focus on Ubuntu philosophy, also refuse to miss the historical constructions that have established and entrenched current mis-recognition regimes which are actually not detached from the readings of Africanist scholars like myself who are analyzing the clash between the Ubuntu philosophy of life and the more calculating, profit-driven western thought systems during colonial rule in Africa and elsewhere. As Taylor (1995) so cogently notes, it was actually the west that refused to appreciate the authentic identity (i.e., the subject of identity being the source of such identity) of colonized populations and decided to impose its own biased reading (certainly racist and dehumanizing reading) of people's views of themselves, their histories, cultures, and achievements.

The results of such falsely constructed identity systems are, without a doubt, what has created one of the most enduring and still current outcomes of colonialist, cognitive colonization, which by applying a cluster of perforce distributed demerit points on the psychosomatics of Africans has at least minimally de-patterned their subjective and inter-subjective thought processes and related actions. That de-patterning has produced what the brilliant Martinican duo, Aimé Césaire (1972) and Frantz Fanon (1967, 1968), fully complemented by the deep and culturally attached analysis of what Chinua Achebe (1989, 2000, 2009 [1958]) aptly dubbed the psychophysical deconstructions of the persona Africana. In Césaire's steel-piercing observations, this represented what he described (in paraphrased terms) as men [and women] distilled of their humanity and forced to somehow survive in subhuman servility that they think and act in ways that are counter their dignity, needs, and natural aspirations. What Césaire is first-hand describing here is related to what was also so magisterially analyzed by Fanon in his urgent, anti-cognitive colonization polemic, *Black Skin, White Masks* (1967), where men and women are systematically de-historicized, then de-cultured, then dehumanized, then physically and mentally maximally exploited, then left to die psychosomatically in the debris of destructive, colonialist racism.

It is with these historical realities where global colonialism was predicated on anti-Ubuntu perspective and practice that instead of recognizing people's real lives, it actually chattelized them and established different human categorizations that gave us the first-, second-, third-, and certainly fourth-class citizen situations we are currently dealing with. Especially for the inventors of the most humanist philosophy (Ubuntu) in human history (Africans), the levels of colonialist-driven epistemic and physical dehumanizations unleashed upon them were also unequaled in human history (Van Sertima 1993). In Van Sertima's reading, with much of Africa's social and cultural threads so torn asunder, the complete destruction of the continent's human existence could have been endangered. The fact that Africans survived the holocaust of colonialism (as Van Sertima calls it) should be majorly credited to the deep roots of people's historical, cultural, and undoubtedly philosophical and onto-epistemological blocks that assured us the continuation of pertinent educational and social development categories that also contained in their kernel, the surviving and now tempo-spatially re-endowed fragments of Ubuntu. It is indeed difficult to explain how the people who have been so oppressed in all aspects of their lives have still managed to safeguard the noble and inter-subjectively humanizing philosophy of Ubuntu. With Ubuntu so philosophically and culturally educational, we should be able to safely say that it was actually its learning continuum that assured the survivability in both temporal and inter-generational terms. It is also important to note how the enduring power of Ubuntu is, without a doubt, a gift for humanity; it is indeed an almost cosmological affirmation that irrespective of the onslaughts of de-historicization, de-culturation, and de-philosophication, all complemented by heavy schemes of physical oppression, Africans never disavowed their human connections, even defying the proverbial human logic, as we can read from Tutu (1999) and others, to respond in kind to their torturers.

For me, and I am confident for many others, this refusal to tear up the humanizing prospect could have been only possible through the educational foundations of Ubuntu philosophy as we must clearly understand that this way of thinking and behaving cannot be construed as genetically inherited. It is, therefore, the thick threads of Ubuntu philosophies of education which teach us about the horizontal and unqualified inviolability of all human life that saved us from what would have been the catastrophic loss of our precious philosophy of Ubuntu. It is with this in mind that we can talk about Ubuntu and its educational categories as potentially desirable in global terms. After all, human beings, irrespective of where they reside and regardless of what historical and current living and learning categories they interact with, are capable of goodness, kindness, and benevolence. We could, indeed, safely say that due to the way we are cradled, nurtured, and normatively socialized from birth to adulthood, we are culturally and educationally constructed to act with empathy and can all minimally achieve an aspect or more of Ubuntu-ized living and learning platforms that could lessen the destructions we see around us. We also know that these same people who are so nurtured and taken care of can turn into cruel colonialists who, in repeating Césaire's words above, are willing and can become capable of exactly doing the opposite of Ubuntu: conquering, exploiting, and willfully oppressing others with the intention of political control and economic gain which are almost always undergirded by the refusal to see the full humanity of the other.

It is with these facts and other contemporary global considerations in mind that we need to extend the epistemic and educational boundaries of Ubuntu, so this humanist and ontologically liberating philosophy of life also enriches our lives through its learning and teaching categories which have been both educational and pedagogical in vita Africana over millennia. A propos, every learning and historical survival reference I made in this writing actually leads to what we must reaffirm as Ubuntu philosophies of education which, based on our fully neoliberalized and, by extension, economized structures and arrangements of life, are so needed in learning-wise, marginalized Africa where colonial curricula and languages still reign supreme. In different ideational representations, conceptualizations, theorizations, and intended pragmatizations, we do occasionally talk about systems of education that pretend to be epistemically multicentric, multicultural, and multi-epistemological. In factual terms, though, and as someone who partook in these at best, surface attempts to realign history, knowledge, and social development, myself, I can attest to the triumph of the western global edifice of educational systems that willfully individualize us into de-socialized and fabricated corporate interest-driven citizens who are taught and slowly forced into one-against-all and all-against-one so-called competitions to make sure that some of us are losers in this life. It is for all pragmatic intentions and for any decent claims of multicentric and humanizing learning systems that we need to embrace the humanist African philosophy of Ubuntu in both its inter-subjective and learning-wise, liberating praxes.

CONCLUSION

In this chapter, I have attempted, in quite generalistic terms, to introduce the African humanist philosophy of Ubuntu with anti-colonial historical and extendedly educational analysis. In so doing, I have engaged a critical perspective that attempts to respond to the continuously dehumanizing and cognitively colonizing cultural, philosophical, and learning colonialist projects that were perforce imposed on African populations and on others with quasi-similar historical experiences. By introducing Ubuntu as a sub-jectively liberating and inter-subjectively humanizing platform that refuses to miss the full humanity of all, I was intending to also present the con-trasting ontological and epistemological realities that exist between this philosophy and its contemporaneously operational western thought sys-tems whose most important proponents in colonizing Europe actually attempted to rescind the difficult-to-dilute human value that should be naturally inherent in all of us. It is with that in mind that I see Ubuntu as a hopeful philosophical and educational philosophy perspective that should aid in aiming for and achieving what could be described as humanist and humanizing systems of education. Humanist in that these are inclu-sively designed and implemented by those who have a stake in them, and humanizing with the main philosophical and possible policy trends, hori-zontally and without qualifications, responsive to the immediate needs and aspirational plateaus of those who interact with such programs of edu-cation. This is indeed the opposite of colonial education which still consti-tutes our current systems of learning across the globe, and which was established on exploitative systems of schooling, and currently advances the dominant and globalizing neoliberal programs of education that counter-humanistically and counter-humanely individualize us into quasi-objectified competitive categories that force us to cancel each other out. By heeding the call of Ubuntu's humanizing and inter-subjectively con-necting, not canceling, philosophy of living and learning, we can slowly herald the noble and multi-level humanizing possibilities of something that can be so much better than what we have been hitherto offered.

REFERENCES

Abdi, A. A. (2008). Europe and African thought systems and philosophies of edu-cation: 'Re-culturing' the trans-temporal discourses. *Cultural Studies, 22*(2), 309–327.

Abdi, A. A. (2013). Decolonizing educational and social development platforms in Africa. *Journal of African and Asian Studies, 12*(1–2), 64–82.

Abu-Lughod, J. (1995). *Before European hegemony: The world system A.D. 1250–1350.* New York: Oxford University Press.

Achebe, C. (1989). *Morning yet on creation day: Essays.* New York: Doubleday.

Achebe, C. (2000). *Home and exile.* New York: Oxford University Press.

Achebe, C. (2009 [1958]). *Things fall apart.* Toronto: Anchor.

Battle, M. (2009). *Reconciliation: The Ubuntu theology of Desmond Tutu.* Cleveland: Pilgrim Press.

Cabral, A. (1981). *Unity and struggle: Speeches and writings.* Trenton: Monthly Review Press.

Carracciolo, D., & Mungai, A. (Eds.). (2009). *In the spirit of Ubuntu: Stories of teaching and research.* Rotterdam: Sense Publishers.

Césaire, A. (1972). *Discourse on colonialism.* Trenton: Monthly Review Press.

Fanon, F. (1967). *Black skin, white masks.* New York: Grove Press.

Fanon, F. (1968). *The wretched of the earth.* New York: Grove Press.

Fraser, N., & Honneth, A. (2004). *Redistribution or recognition?: A political-philosophical exchange.* Brooklyn: Verso.

Harding, S. (1998). *Is science multicultural? Postcolonialisms, feminisms and epistemologies.* Bloomington: Indiana University Press.

Harding, S. (2008). *Science from below: Feminisms, postcolonialities and modernities.* Durham: Duke University Press.

Harvey, D. (2007). *A brief history of neoliberalism.* New York: Oxford University Press.

Honneth, A. (1996). *The struggle for recognition: The moral grammar of social conflicts.* Cambridge, MA: MIT Press.

Honneth, A. (2014). *Freedom's right: The social foundations of democratic life.* New York: Columbia University Press.

Mandela, N. (1994). *Long walk to freedom: The biography of Nelson Mandela.* New York: Little, Brown & Company.

Nyerere, J. (1968). *Freedom and socialism: A selection from writings and speeches, 1965–67.* London: Oxford University Press.

Oruka, H. O. (1990). *Sage philosophy: Indigenous thinkers and modern debate on African philosophy.* Leiden: Brill.

Rodney, W. (1982). *How Europe underdeveloped Africa.* Washington, DC: Howard University Press.

Said, E. (1978). *Orientalism.* New York: Vintage.

Said, E. (1993). *Culture and imperialism.* New York: Vintage.

Sandberg, J. (2010). *The philosophy of Ubuntu and the origins of democracy.* https://www.lulu.com/shop/search.ep?keyWords=The+philosophy+of+Ubuntu+and+the+origins+of+democracy&type=

Semali, L., & Kincheloe, J. (Eds.). (1999). *What is indigenous knowledge? Voices from the academy.* New York: Routledge.

Swanson, D. (2007). Ubuntu: An African contribution to (re)search for/with 'humble togetherness. *Journal of Contemporary Issues in Education,* 2(2), 53–67.

Taylor, C. (1992). *Sources of the self: The making of the modern identity.* Cambridge, MA: Harvard University Press.

Taylor, C. (1995). *Philosophical arguments.* Cambridge, MA: Harvard University Press.

Taylor, C. (2003). *Modern social imaginaries.* Durham: Duke University Press.

Tutu, D. (1999). *No future without forgiveness.* New York: Doubleday.

Van Onselen, C. (1996). *The seed is mine: The Life of Kas Maine, a South African sharecropper.* Cape Town: David Philip.

Van Sertima, I. (1993). *Blacks in science: Ancient and modern.* New Brunswick: Transaction Books.

Young, I. M. (2012). *Responsibility for justice.* New York: Oxford University Press.

CHAPTER 3

Ubuntu and Pan-Africanism: The Dialectics of Learning About Africa

Tukumbi Lumumba-Kasongo

INTRODUCTION: ISSUES, OBJECTIVES, AND PERSPECTIVES

People who do not know where they are coming from in terms of their histories, cultures, achievements, and identities are not likely to know where they might go toward (Clarke 1993). Thus, confused nations or people cannot create proper directions to progress for themselves, despite some efforts and their willingness to do so. These premises are behind elements of my problematics in this paper.

This study is essentially a reflective work in which I rethink Africa and her development paradigms through Ubuntu and Pan-Africanism as a normative or a philosophical characterization of Africanness and an approach or intellectual critical category. I do not intend to provide a historiography of both Ubuntu and Pan-Africanism. Although I touch partially on their origins, roots, and some of their histories, I do not expand much on them. This reflection is about the search for the main ideas, thoughts, and theories deriving from them that can explain Africa to herself and Africa in the world system within the context of African education for peace and development with education as a critical social institution.

T. Lumumba-Kasongo (✉)
Wells College, Aurora, NY, USA

© The Author(s) 2018
E. J. Takyi-Amoako, N. T. Assié-Lumumba (eds.),
Re-Visioning Education in Africa,
https://doi.org/10.1007/978-3-319-70043-4_3

What should Ubuntu and Pan-Africanism teach us about Africa? Furthermore, how do we transform her, her institutions and developmental paradigms and programs holistically and structurally for the benefits of her people with an inclusive framework? Thus, my main objectives are to:

1. Examine the concepts of Ubuntu and Pan-Africanism with the main goals of understanding their cultural, social, political, and economic significance/meanings;
2. Compare them as approaches/perspectives to explain Africa; and to
3. Use elements of their philosophical and ideological foundation to project the future of Africa.

I examine the intellectual claims and philosophical and social assumptions of Ubuntu and Pan-Africanism and question their claimed relevancy, in identifying their potential in new regionalist and globalist discourses. Furthermore, I discuss their embodied vision of progress. In this rethinking, I also identify and examine possible contradictions or biases that might be built in them as part of the analysis of the social phenomena. That is to say that my objectives are to reflect on their significance and their policy implications within the framework of the imperatives of nation-states and liberal globalization.

By and large, the study is very much conceptual and theoretical in its content. However, this conceptualization is informed by historical structuralism and political clarifications based on the nature of the current African nation-state, its origins and its functioning, and that of African global political economy. I support intellectual debates on these two concepts as they are contributing to the discourse about unity and change in Africa.

I raise the issues related to the importance of this subject and also make some general assumptions that locate my claims, arguments, and analysis. One of the problems that African nation-states and peoples have been facing in the past 600 years or so is the fact that they have tended to accept without any systematic critique of the European un-historical interpretations of the African world. This implies African nation-states and their people the world over project themselves in the world as institutions and people with a short memory.

Economically and politically, Africa would not have been subjected to the harsh conditions of destructions and humiliation, which are summarized in stand still advanced by transatlantic enslavement, colonialism and neocolonial powers, and her peripheral place and subservient role in international political economy without directly or indirectly her consent. By and large, African people have accepted, to a large extent, consciously or unconsciously, what the European and the American power systems have designed for them as "normal." As manifested in the current dynamics of Africa's international relations, international political economy, and domestic policy frameworks, African nation-states and political elites have internationalized the concept of the "dark continent" as invented by European powers, while they preceded the Europeans in coming to the America long before Columbus (Van Sertima 1976). In this process, many essential aspects of the African identities and histories have been lost.

I argue that Ubuntu and Pan-Africanism based on their particular meanings and their historical configurations vis-à-vis Africa and her multiplicity of cultures (cultural pluralism) can be expected to form a corrective political ideology to change the above descriptive assumptions analytically with a sense of clear direction, as an African-centered transnational ideology.

Historically, the struggles for unity of African people were accelerated during the period of transatlantic enslavement of African people by the hand of Europeans and their descendants in the Americas in the seventeenth and eighteenth centuries. Since then, the resistance to enslavement, colonialism, "savage" capitalism, and imperialism has led to various forms of Pan-Africanism, and its interpretations have been expressed differently in Africa and the African Diaspora.

Although some generalized illustrations are discussed as related to the African Diaspora at large, the paper focuses on political Pan-Africanism. Obviously, Pan-African ideas were born in the Diaspora. The discussion about their significance, both in Africa and in the African Diaspora, attracts scholars and students of African politics and history. It is argued that this significance is shaped by the realities of global capitalism and those of liberal democracy as interpreted or carried by the African nation-states, their civil societies, and diverse social and ethnic groups.

INTELLECTUAL PERSPECTIVES AND JUSTIFICATION

Why and how do I see, analyze, and project things the way I do? My perspectives guide the readers to the content of my worldview and its philosophical assumptions. "The same causes produce the same effects." This reasoning shapes my reflection and recommendations about what should be done with Ubuntu and Pan-Africanism and what should be their place in the struggles for social progress in Africa.

It is necessary that I clarify further where intellectually and philosophically I stand on the issues. Humans embody the germ of the past and build the present on the past. However, the past, the present, and the future have their respective and own specific distinctive moments, spaces, and times. The present should not sacrifice the past. Furthermore, the present is not also the microcosm of the past and the future. Thus, I intellectually value a critical social theory in explaining them. From this perspective, a social progress agenda is considered as being essentially a teleological and dialectically synthesized conscious effort.

I examine the concepts of Ubuntu and Pan-Africanism as two interrelated perspectives upon which national projects can be explored and built. That is to say that Ubuntu and Pan-Africanism are conceived as two complementary political philosophies to guide the direction of the proposed new African systems of governance and the societal values.

How do advocates and supporters of Ubuntu and Pan-Africanism perceive and define Africa? This discussion provides important analytical and methodological elements as well as policy guidelines. However, it should be emphasized that the context of this work has two important dimensions, which are also briefly discussed, namely, the nature of nation-state and its imperatives and liberal globalism, its impact, and its vision of Africa. The global context is as important as the subject matter itself because one cannot understand the subject outside of its context. The relationship between the context and the subject is dialectically defined and projected.

I use a historical-structuralist approach and its philosophical assumptions and claims with a dose of systems analysis (Easton 1965) as articulated by the advocates of the world system. The way social classes, states, and societies function in the world system is a result of the internal and external dynamics of their locations (Gunder Frank 1967). However, these locations are far from being historically fixed or static. The world is a system and an organic whole, whose behaviors are conditioned by the actors' locations and how they came to be in the system (Cardoso and Faletto 1979). The actors and the subsystems do not act similarly because it depends on their specific functions and attributes and their location within the system.

I am consciously avoiding intellectual extremism, historical determinism, and conspiracy theory because they lack a good understanding of the forces of history. I interpret history not simply as a changing event that is not predetermined by any circumstances or forces, but it is also as a moving force that tells us what time it is and where to go from here, a compass (Clarke 1993).

I build my arguments on historical-structuralist assumptions and in finding correlations between historical facts or causations and structures of the African contemporary societies. Historical structuralism raises the question of origins of these phenomena and the nature of the evolution of their structures. Within the structures of the African societies, I put more emphasis on the political institutions or the states and their relations to the world system (Wallerstein 1974, 1980, 1989). Furthermore, my interests in historical causation of social phenomena and critical examination of their structures are shaped by social constructivism. Adler (1997, 2002) and Fearon and Alexander (2002) take social world of agreed upon collective social values as a way of elevating and appreciating the values in a non-material world.

One of the most important manifesting characteristics of the world system at the end of the twentieth century is the movement of nation-states toward some kinds of reformism and people's struggles to redefine themselves. This redefinition has been taking different forms and shapes, some tragically like in the Balkans, many parts of Africa and the Middle East, and others more gradually and peacefully. However, the substance of the content of this redefinition and its intellectual quality depends on the dynamics of the local political configurations, how a given people and state have become part of the world system, the location of these actors in the international political economy, what they are bringing into the global market, who the actors are, and who their alliances are. This process of redefining themselves is facilitated by the following attributes of globalization:

1. The level of solidarity, which is being characterized as anti-nation-state, among institutions, grassroots organizations, and professional organizations across nation-states, has been increasing. This solidarity is partially due to the relatively high level of consciousness or awareness about the relevant issues. The rising consciousness is the product of the level of interdependence among the actors.
2. Search for new identities: In most parts of the world, people are struggling to redefine themselves by using history and culture, while others are attempting to reconstruct new ideologies or even mythologies through accommodation to the global system. This struggle and processes it creates lead to the various types of clashes of values between what can be or are perceived as the nationalistic values and those which may be considered either as chosen or imposed global values by the global market forces. Since the

Westphalia Treaty of 1648 in Europe, the transatlantic enslavement on a large scale, and the colonization of the world, especially Africa, the common policy of the dominant powers has been to make and redefine national identities in ideological, geo-political, and ethnic-linguistic terms protected by the new nation-states. Their policies have been the instruments used for systematically weakening individual and collective cultural and ethnic values, as they were often perceived as "pre-modernist" and "irrational" or primordial forces, the impediments to the building of nationhood.

3. The nature of new information and communication technologies and the role of the media and the Internet diplomacy in challenging the old national and individual identities and creating new ones in a new international relations context.

4. The domination of liberal politics in the forms of liberal and illiberal elections.

5. Finally, the nature, level, and quality of the world's distribution of resources, which are characterized at the same time by new opportunity, unequal competition, and social inequality, are essential elements of the discourse of globalization.

Another dimension or manifestation of the global context is regionalism. Although its economic content cannot be neglected as capitalism itself is defining its self regionally, regionalism in its pragmatic form is more associated with geo-politics and history than globalism, which has claims and tendencies of promoting "universalism" from a perspective of a world without borders. Regionalists are more sympathetic to economic protectionism even if the actors who advocate globalism like the United States also use protectionism as an instrument of advancing their national or class interests.

While capitalist regionalists accept the existence of other poles of influences in other parts of the world as they are defined politically, economically, or culturally, the globalists emphasize universal human values as defined by the market and individualism. This global context not only influences how we perceive Africa but also why we perceive her as we do. Furthermore, in advocating Ubuntu and Pan-Africanism it is necessary to take into account the imperatives of liberal globalism as reflected in the value given to individual rights, free market, free movement of labor, transnationalism, centrality of science, monopoly capitalism, and liberal democracy. They should incorporate them into their discourses: claims, arguments, and policy analysis either in rejecting them in order to operate outside of the dominant social paradigm or in appropriating their dogmas as a necessity for thinking about reformism.

LEARNING FROM UBUNTU

Literally, the expression Ubuntu as a Zulu word means a 'unifying vision' or 'a worldview.' This expression is enshrined in the Zulu maxim: "umuntu ngumuntu ngabantu," that is, "a person is a person through other persons" (Shutte 1993, p. 46). Whether it means African communitarian (Eze 2008) or a collective disposition about forgiveness and reconciliation based on African humanism according to Bishop Desmond Tutu (Battle 2007), Ubuntu in South Africa has been defined as a moral theory (Metz 2007). In its ancient African form, it means "humanity to others." In its meaning, Ubuntu is part of the efforts in the search for new paradigms to explain Africa in the world and the world in Africa and imagine a new world.

In my view, the word Ubuntu is not a generic expression that applies to universalism of the humanity according to the principles and politics of the so-called civilizing mission that came with Europeanization and subjugation of the world from a unilinear perspective. Its meaning captures specific realities of various Bantu and African philosophies in general, customs, and traditions that are located in many parts of African societies. It is about the essence of being human (Tutu 2013). Its usage and pragmatic implications have to be appreciated within the logic of the principle of "I am because you are."

It is argued that the Ubuntu's ontological dependency is vital to both survival and progress mood of Africans because the nature of this relationship is not based on selfishness. It is different from individualistic dependency associated with the contemporary capitalism, which is the invention of the West. While this type of dependency leads to schism, Ubuntu's kind of dependency leads to ideal and ideas of "cultural and social harmony" or social solidarity. However, it should be noted that within the extreme level of economic and social poverty in many parts of Africa, the practices of Ubuntu at the family or ethnic groups' levels have also been very much abusive and as such have led to distortions of its meaning and intended social function.

It is emphasized that the coexistence of self and collective self described above is deeply rooted in African way of life even between and/or among Westernized and non-Westernized Africans. It tends to transcend social class interests, gender rigidity, ethnic imperatives, religious absolutisms, political fragmentations, and physical borders. In the dualist economies of rural versus urbanized Africa, this way of thinking and doing characterizes how Africans in general have been responding to human demands and conditions domestically and internationally. However, exceptions and unique cultures and conditions must be noted and recognized.

Other attributes which are related to Ubuntu include "community life," "friendship," "ethics of social justice," "open-ness," "collective solidarity," "common human bond between us," "new understanding of socio-economic and political relations," "struggle against poverty in schools," "ethical and humanist goals of the great religions of the world," "a multiplicity of worldviews," "new partnerships between nations without monopoly," and "placement of the human conditions above everything else" (Tutu 2013; Broodryk 2002; Teffo 1994; Shutte 1993).

Within Ubuntu these attributes are not abstract. They are not intellectualistic. They shape social relations within communities rooted on the concept of "Oto" (*untu* or *muntu*), for instance, which means human being in many languages spoken in Central Africa. In Tetela, a language spoken in Sankuru, Oriental Kasai, Umuntu means a woman. Thus, she represents the whole humanity. The mentioned attributes are derived from practical and functioning worldviews or ways of life. Ubuntu in Africa has also its equivalences in other cultures. Although the concept of Ubuntu is not exclusively African, it is essentially part of the African cosmology and ethos. As such, it can be projected both as an approach or methodology and established African social value.

Thus, it is necessary to take into account the contexts in which these attributes have developed and where they have been used and how they might be projected into policy frameworks. In the context of this chapter, I address them at the level of critical thinking, research, and perspective. They represent a perspective or worldview.

However, the contexts in which Ubuntu is critically examined, recovered, and reclaimed in Africa are colonial, political decolonization, and post-colonialism with their immense contradictions as reflected in the rate of poverty, levels of social injustices, magnitude of unemployment, and gender inequality, despite some improvements in some countries.

Furthermore, for several decades, Africa has been suffering from the effects of appropriating irrelevant or inapplicable development paradigms conceived and defined mostly by the interests of the global North in the name of "unified," internationalized, and universalized liberal globalization.

It should be clarified that Ubuntu is a critical notion that challenges the African systems of governance and their policies. The national context in which Ubuntu as a social value is being reflected upon is projected in the discussion. I argue that given their Western legalistic and political origins and their evolutions within liberal globalism with free trade, free market, and competition, the post-colonial African nation-states in general are not capable to conceptualize and formulate policies and device practices from Ubuntu perspectives. It is so because these states are essentially artificial Western constructs with concrete role to protect the major interests in the international capitalism. It should be noted that the African nation-states were created without any participation of the African political elites and/or any African for that matter. Even the then non-formally colonized political African country of Liberia was not invited to participate in the deliberations of the Berlin Conference of 1884/1885, where the Western monarchs, under the leadership of von Bismarck of Germany and the United States and Russia as observers, divided Africa without her consent.

Kenneth Kaunda's African humanism (1966) and Julius Nyerere's African socialism (1968) were close to the notion of Ubuntu as defined in this chapter: collective solidarity, independence, and self-reliance. The slogan of "Uhuru" (freedom) was met with "Tupendani" (love to one another).

However, one of most acute weaknesses of African humanism or African socialism as ideological foundation of the African nation-state was its philosophical incompatibility with the structures of the African nation-states that both Kaunda and Nyerere decided to maintain (though strategically) and later reform it from within. Political decolonization process stopped short the actualization of independence or freedom that was expressed in both Kaunda and Nyerere and other African political figures as well.

Since the time of formal/nominal political decolonization, the post-colonial African nation-states have not fundamentally and sufficiently been decolonized and, thus, have not acquired political skills and ideological visions to define clearly their national priorities and their positions in relation to those of their peoples and their needs. In many aspects, these states are mimics or caricatures par excellence of the colonial states, which could not have any agenda about development. This is why most of them are structurally and historically neocolonial states. They have approached progress mainly from selfishness, individualism, materialism, militarism, and territorial security perspectives at the expense of the people.

Thus, Ubuntu is a profound corrective philosophy (African collective solidarity), which should embody elements of methodologies, approaches, and policy framework. Its origin is into explaining collective self without rejecting self-being. Some of the interpretations of this origin are elaborated in the works of, for instance, Placide Tempel's *Philosophie Bantu* (1959); V. Y. Mudimbe's *The Invention of Africa: Gnosis, Philosophy, and the Order of Knowledge* (1988); Vincent Mulago's *Théologie Africaine et Problèmes Connexes* (1972); John Mbiti's *African Religions & Philosophy* (1969); and Guy Martin's *African Political Thought* (2012).

Ubuntu is claimed through a new decolonization movement, which includes indigenous knowledge systems and acquisition, decolonization of the mind (neo-Fanonian concept of consciousness), historization of what is being learnt (curriculum), interconnectedness, and a critique of "anthropocentricism."

LEARNING FROM PAN-AFRICANISM

As African people and their social institutions are struggling to look for development options, the study of Pan-Africanism is very justified. The faulty universal historical premises as articulated in the American and European foreign policies at the end of the Cold War politics and their social and political implications provide us an opportunity to revisit Pan-Africanism (Lumumba-Kasongo 2003).

Pan-Africanism is not new in terms of its intellectual positions as to what directions Africa should take and the kind of projects that should be developed to allow Africans to set up institutions of societal transformation. But at the policy and political levels, Pan-Africanist advocates have not seized or created any real opportunity for its actualization. Pan-Africanists have not succeeded in capturing state power and in actualizing Pan-Africanism in public policies and development. It should be noted that the need to rethink Pan-Africanism has significantly been expanding. African engaged scholars have increased their visibility in their discourse in African learning institutions about Pan-Africanism. As stated elsewhere (Lumumba-Kasongo 2003, p. 4):

> Pan-Africanism has been instrumental in the achievement of nominal political independence, but so far economic independence has eluded African peoples. This is because the alliance between black labour and black capital has not materialised due to the fact that the black world controls very little of the world monopoly capital. Hence Pan-Africanism needs an economic component in its ideology. Africans, who are the most exploited groups in

the capitalist system, need to construct a theory of economic emancipation rooted both in economics and in the ethnic experiences of the black world.[1]

Literature on, and/or about, Pan-Africanism is immense. The discussion about its significance, both in Africa and in the African Diaspora, continues to attract scholars, students of African politics, education and history, and also political figures. From scholars and political figures such as Edward Blyden (who did not use the word Pan-Africanism), Frederick Douglass, Harriet Tubman, Marcus Garvey, Amy Garvey, W. E. B. Du Bois, Shirley Graham, John Henrik Clarke, Gamal Abdel Nasser, Kwame Nkrumah, Patrice Lumumba, Julius Nyerere, George Padmore, Muammar Gaddafi, Laurent-Désiré Kabila, Ali Mazrui, Tajudeen Abdul-Raheem, Georges Nzongola, James Turner, Sékou Touré, Kwame Touré, and Thomas Sankara, to cite only a few, much has been said, written, and published about classical Pan-Africanism.

As indicated earlier, as an ideology and intellectual discourse among African scholars and political activists, Pan-Africanism is not new within the framework of the search for new directions that Africa should consider to allow Africans to set up institutions of societal transformation. But at the policy level, Pan-Africanist advocates have not seized or created any real opportunity to take over power locally. Pan-Africanists have not been able to capture nation-state powers and actualize Pan-Africanism into national public policies and development projects. They have not been creative and innovative enough to transform local politics and its interests, in part amidst the global power system.

From W. E. B. Du Bois, known as the father of Pan-Africanism, to Kwame Nkrumah, the guru of Pan-Africanism, Pan-Africanism has generally embodied the following aims: the search for common cultural specificities and affinities among African people, and for intellectual connections among them based on "race," ethnicity, geography, and history. All these objectives were supposed to lead toward fostering an understanding and appreciation of African culture. Thus, in general terms, Pan-Africanism embodies an ethnic/racial, cultural, or continental unity of some kind.

With few exceptions, Pan-Africanists have mostly articulated in intellectualistic abstraction, ahistorical, and apolitical fashion the issues of unity across geo-political boundaries of the citizens of many nation-states with different political realities and identities, social class base, and levels of economic development. Furthermore, definitions of Pan-Africanism and their interpretations have produced various meanings which, within the context of the world of the nation-states, have been difficult to actualize as policy frameworks. An effective policy formulation requires a high level of political realism. Thus, some common characteristics of Pan-Africanism must be further identified and their meanings explored.

A summary of institutional Pan-Africanism is necessary to localize the pragmatism of this ideology. Historically, various forms of nationalistic policies have been explored, tried, and implemented by the African nation-states and people. Pan-Africanism, one of them, has not been fully understood and implemented.

While political Pan-Africanism, especially the interpretations by Kwame Nkrumah, Ahmed Sékou Touré, and Gamal Abdel Nasser, called for the establishment of a federal African state in early 1960s, cultural Pan-Africanism has focused on the search for common cultural symbolism and historical linkages.

On May 25, 1963, with the participation of all independent African countries, the Organization of African Unity (OAU) was finally formed in Addis Ababa, Ethiopia. It was created as an ideological and institutional compromise among various political tendencies that developed among African nationalists in the 1950s and early 1960s.

What kind of compromise was it? What were the intended objectives of the political actors and leaders involved at the time? And how was Africa perceived in the OAU? Because much has been said about the OAU, only a brief comment is needed here to clarify my position and support my perspective on institutional Pan-Africanism.

I restate the point that, with the creation of the OAU, Kwame Nkrumah's ambition to realize the formation of a continental union government as a political reality and a monumental dream was defeated by the other African heads of state. The OAU became, rather, a symbol for unity and a basis for articulating functional economic cooperation. Prior to the creation of the OAU, several political blocs were formed on the continent. In December 1959, for example, Kwame Nkrumah convened the first All-African People's Conference in Accra, Ghana. This conference called for a commonwealth of all African states, a commonwealth that was going to transcend ethnic, linguistic, ideological, and colonial or nation-state boundaries. The most important resolution adopted in the conference was the drafting of the constitution, which included a provision for a United States of Africa or union government. All the independent African states were present, and most African nationalist political organizations sent their delegates as well, including those from the Belgian Congo.

After this conference, three different ideological and pragmatic blocs emerged before the formation of the Organization of African Unity, which were the Monrovia bloc, the Brazzaville bloc, and the Casablanca bloc. The Monrovia and Brazzaville blocs strongly rejected the idea of the union government or the political integration of sovereign states that they considered to be premature at that time. For instance, the Brazzaville bloc's position opted for a functionalist approach, namely, cooperation in economic and military relations. The Casablanca bloc was mainly formed of the North African countries under the strong influences of Nasser of Egypt, Kwame Nkrumah of Ghana, and Ahmed Sékou Touré of Guinea-Conakry. In East Africa, Tom Mboya (Kenya) and Milton Obote (Uganda) were strong supporters of the union government approach as well. It also should be said that the solidarity of the Casablanca group was not based only on a common ideology but also on strategic preference. For instance, Morocco was not a progressive state, but it joined the group to seek its support for its territorial dispute with the Western/Spanish Sahara.

Bloc politics weakened the organization and its policies, and this did not allow state members to see clearly the degree of seriousness of the economic, political, and social problems with which Africa has been faced. However, concerning the OAU's behavior in international fora, it attempted, sometimes successfully and other times not so, to formulate common positions. On the positive side, the position of the OAU against the apartheid was firm and consistent. It supported the freedom fighters in Southern Africa militarily, financially, politically, and morally through the establishment of a special committee of frontline states in Tanzania.

In the 1981, the Lagos plan of action was created as a genuine progressive program for regional development. It was never implemented. It was replaced with the structural adjustment programs (SAPs) of the World Bank and stability programs of the International Monetary Fund (IMF).

In the 1990s, especially with Salim Ahmed Salim, a nationalist Tanzanian and General Secretary of the OAU, most debates in the organization took on a strongly Pan-Africanist tone rather than a sub-regional one. On the debates concerning the African economic crisis and how to deal with it, the position taken by the OAU in Addis Ababa, with a strong initiative and directive from the United Nations Economic Commission for Africa (UNECA) under the leadership of Adebayo Adedeji, comprised a collective and determined effort.

One of the most important decisions was taken on June 3–5, 1991 at the OAU summit in Abuja, Nigeria, with the participation from 34 African political leaders, which was the signature of the treaty for the establishment of the African Economic Community (AEC). This initiative was the most important ideal to have been ever initiated by the OAU and the UNECA. It came as a result of the individual failures of most national economic policies to deal with the conditions of underdevelopment. This option was an effort to approach African social and economic problems collectively from an African perspective.

Between May 1993, when a Pan-African Conference on Reparations was organized by the OAU together with the Nigerian Government in Abuja, Nigeria, and the July 2001 summit in Lusaka, Zambia, where the African leaders agreed to form an African Union (AU), the Pan-African project took on a different perspective and form.

With an agreement of the African heads of state in Lusaka, Zambia, in July 2001 to form the African Union (AU), and the subsequent creation of the AU in 2002, which led to the dismantling of the disabled Organization of African Unity (OAU), these leaders made a statement to try to actualize a higher political order, which was defeated at the formation of the OAU in 1963. In 2017, 55 African states are members of the AU, and the African Diaspora has been created as the equivalent of an African region, hence embracing elements of Pan-Africanism. What does that mean for the African people, the African nation-states, and the African Diaspora?

CONCLUDING REMARKS

Pan-Africanism is essentially an international phenomenon described in multicultural linguistic expressions. Its based relationships are international and federalist. To actualize such a federalist system, it is necessary to rethink African nation-states and restructure them within large cultural and economic regionalisms on history, culture, and linguistics (Martin and Muiu 2009) as the most important engines of new re-mapping. National project of each African nation-state has to be part of African regional planning. From a realist perspective in international relations, nation-states pursue mainly their own "national" interests. How to transform these "national" and narrow interests into Pan-African ones with the focus on unified collective benefits?

For this ideology to be actualized, it has to transform the African institutions, including education, and African people ways of thinking and doing with new knowledge about their assets. Although we do not have

Pan-African barometers yet, in this chapter I tried to demonstrate that African progress is not and cannot be sustained without a strong unified regionalist cultural and ideological project. Its politics and policy base should positively change the Africans' ways of defining themselves, their local socio-economic and political conditions, and knowledge about themselves. It must be pragmatic and realistic.

I contend that it is through education first, both political education and formal education, that the transformative process would be possible. In terms of institutions, the nature and structures of the African nation-states must be transformed to allow Pan-African international cooperation and humanism to be translated into policies and collective actions.

I argue that Pan-African sets of rights should be developed and debated within the existing African institutions. It is only when and if these rights are pragmatically protected that Pan-Africanism will make firm inroads into people's life.

In my viewpoint, Pan-Africanism can be a political philosophy of change only if it is able to promote the following elements: a strong sense of self-determination, wisdom of belonging to a larger political unit, knowledge of one's objective conditions and constraints, a progressive agenda with bottom-up guidelines which should be permanently a critical assessment of one's role in the international political economy and the division of labor, and a strong common cultural basis.

Economic independence has eluded African peoples. This is because the alliance between African labor and African capital has not materialized due to the fact that the African world controls very little of the world monopoly capital. Hence, Pan-Africanism needs an economic component in its ideology. Africans, who are the most exploited groups in the capitalist system, need to construct a theory of economic emancipation rooted both in economics and in the ethnic experiences of the black world.

The openness among African nation-states, countries, and people is the prerequisite for this new reshaping of African conditions and policies. This cannot be done randomly. Félix Houphouët-Boigny of Côte d'Ivoire lost his leftist radicalism straying in the 1950s through nominal independence as compared to Kwame Nkrumah of Ghana. However, he strongly supported an openness that could promote needed economic linkages among African peoples through coordination of national policies and social and political organizations. But an economic argument alone, whether it is a free market, trade, capital, or bank arrangement, is not sufficient to deal with the African crisis or the crisis of the African state and African nationalism. The African crisis cannot be dealt with only technically or by sector analysis. Indeed, I deal with it as a structural political problem that requires decolonization through education.

The existing political and economic structures are not conducive to the creation of structures in which Ubuntu and Pan-Africanism can be fully developed because their actualization requires genuine people's participation in their local political process and collective leadership which can transcend the imperatives and constraints related to political territoriality, national sovereignty, and local citizenry to promote contemporary meaning of caring for collective well-being.

The way Africa will be able to progress will depend much on the abilities of her people and their political organizations to restructure their existing political systems and establish their policy priorities in the international political economy. This has to be based on the local needs and priorities toward collective well-being, the energy of the local culture, renewed confidence in the capabilities of African culture, and the participation of the African community in the global economy from a position of strength.

The exploration of Ubuntu and Pan-Africanism requires a new remapping of Africa. No democratic principles, neither comparative advantage theories in laissez-faire economics nor preferential trade relationships would successfully operate as long as Africa as the whole is still an extremely dependent economic and cultural unit of the dominant world economy, which is primarily managed by the former colonial powers, their local extensions, and multinational corporations with no interest in the advancement of the African people.

The questions of democracy and of economic independence must be dealt with simultaneously keeping making a priorities to transform the ways of thinking and doing through education using and promoting Ubuntu and Pan-Africanism. Without that, even the progressive nationalists will not be able to be democratic and free in a world dominated by power and national interests. Democracy and freedom are prerequisites for Ubuntu and Pan-Africanism to be developed.

Pan-Africanism, as a political realist ideology, requires that one becomes aware of who one is, where one stands in international politics, what one possesses, what one is capable of producing, the way to consume cultural or material production, and where one plans to go from here. International relations and politics are strongly influenced by these factors, but to participate productively in these relationships, the major decisions must be made at the local or regional level. Though I am underlining the need for focusing on the implications of Pan-Africanism on regional conditions and its potential solutions to social problems, an important point is that all solutions also must be part of a larger political unit. Pan-Africanism is, above all, an international phenomenon and, as such, it should deal with power and interest and their dynamics in the international arena: international political forums and international political economy.

To move away from the existing old designed world system, Pan-Africanist ideology articulates the need for delinking of Samir Amin (1990) which I call rethinking and a selective approach to development organizations. It should be noted that delinking does not mean autarky.

Another important element in the debate deals with the potential contribution of the African Diaspora, which includes African people who live and are citizens of countries in continents other than Africa. New international cooperation that is based on culture, education, economics, and science and technology, consolidation of collective solidarity, fight against poverty, and social and gender injustices and inequalities and people's genuine participation in their local politics should be in the national agenda that is either missing or is very weak in most parts of African political landscape. The advocates of Ubuntu and Pan-Africanism should contribute to establish and advance social Africa.

How to incorporate Ubuntu in the discourse of the nation-state ideology or a philosophy upon which policies can be formulated for the benefits of all? Democratic education and education for development and peace should continue to be part of the discourse in order to find consensus about humanist progress. This is possible if Africans take their rights seriously in peacefully and democratically challenging undemocratic practices of the nation-states and multinationals, which monopolize most resources.

Democratizing educational curriculum in schools, for instance, is a path toward creating dialogue between the teachers and students. On the above issue, I stated elsewhere:

> The Pan-African curriculum should put an emphasis on multiculturalism and respect of unity in diversity. Unity in diversity cannot be promoted without inter-cultural dialogue among various social groups. Democracy and consensus are important values of this inter-cultural dialogue.[2]

Ubuntu is inspirational philosophy upon which a new model of education for all can be rooted. Utopianism is still relevant if we believe in building a society based on social justice, gender equality, and freedoms. Thus,

Ubuntu should be a new utopianism inspired from the past and still interwoven in disconnected part of African reality in the post-colonial era. The discourse for transforming Pan-Africanism as an ideological alternative to the existing systems of governance should include inventing out the repository of the culture, new theories and practices of diplomacy, and international cooperation among the African people, their states, and the rest of the world. Pan-Africanism should pave the way toward building genuine political dialogue, which is needed to advance and establish Pax Africana (Mazrui 1967, Lumumba-Kasongo 2017, p. 44). For the *Agenda 2063: A Living and Dynamic Framework for Africa's Development* to be effectively and gradually implemented, the African collective solidarity must be consolidated in the programs of eradication of poverty with social policies; in people's participation in national projects; in promoting unity of rights, including those of citizens; and in Pan-African institutional building.

NOTES

1. http://cies2015.org/response-lumumba-kasongo.html
2. Tukumbi Lumumba-Kasongo, "Exploring Pan-African Curriculum and Philosophy in Higher Education in Africa: A Reflection," In Michael Cross and Amasa Ndofirepi (Eds). *Knowledge and Change in African Universities,* A W Rotterdam, The Netherlands: Sense Publishers, 2017, p. 60

REFERENCES

Adler, E. (1997). Seizing the middle ground. Constructivism in world politics. *European Journal of International Relations, 3*(3), 319–363.

Adler, E. (2002). Constructivism in international relations. In W. Carls-naes, B. Simmons, & T. Risse (Eds.), *Handbook of international relations.* London: Sage Publications.

Amin, S. (1990). *Delinking: Towards a polycentric world.* Atlantic Highlands: Zed Books.

Battle, M. (2007). *Reconciliation: The Ubuntu theology of Desmond Tutu.* Cleveland: Pilgrim Press.

Broodryk, J. (2002). *Ubuntu: Life lessons from Africa.* Pretoria: Ubuntu School of Philosophy.

Cardoso, F. H., & Faletto, E. (1979). *Dependency and development in Latin America.* Berkeley: University of California Press.

Clarke, J. H. (1993). *African people in world history.* New York: Black Classic Press.

Easton, D. (1965). *A system's analysis of political life.* New York: Wiley.

Eze, M. O. (2008). What is African communitarianism? Against consensus as a regulative ideal. *South African Journal of Philosophy, 27*(4), 386–399.

Fearon, J., & Alexander, W. (2002). Rationalism v. constructivism: A skeptical view. In W. Carlsnaes, T. Risse, & B. Simmons (Eds.), *Handbook of international relations.* Thousand Oaks: Sage Publications.

Gunder Frank, A. (1967). *Capitalism and underdevelopment in Latin America: Historica studies of Chile and Brazil.* New York: Monthly Review Press.

Kaunda, K. D. (1966). *A humanist in Africa.* London: Longmans.

Lumumba-Kasongo, T. (2003, December 10–12). *Can a 'realist Pan-Africanism' be a relevant tool toward the transformation of African and the African diaspora politics?: Imagining a Pan-African state.* Paper prepared for, and read at, the CODESRIA 30th anniversary grand finale conference and celebration held in Dakar, Senegal.

Lumumba-Kasongo, T. (2017). Exploring Pan-African curriculum and philosophy in higher education in Africa: A reflection. In M. Cross & A. Ndofirepi (Eds.), *Knowledge and change in African Universities.* Rotterdam: Sense Publishers.

Martin, G. (2012). *African political thought.* New York: Palgrave Macmillan.

Martin, G., & Muiu, M. w. (2009). *A new paradigm of the African state: Fundi wa Afrika.* New York: Palgrave Macmillan.

Mazrui, A. A. A. (1967). *Towards a Pax Africana: A study of ideology and ambition.* Chicago: University of Chicago Press.

Mbiti, J. (1969). *African religions and philosophy.* New York: Praeger.

Metz, T. (2007). Toward an African moral theory (symposium). *South African Journal of Philosophy, 26*(4), 331–335.

Mudimbe, V. Y. (1988). *The invention of Africa: Gnosis, philosophy, and the order of knowledge.* Bloomington: Indiana University Press.

Mulago, V. (1972). *Théologie Africaine et Problèmes connexes: Au fil des Années 1956–1992.* Paris: Editions L'Harmattan.

Nyerere, J. (1968). *Uhuru Na Ujamaa: Freedom and socialism.* London: Oxford University Press.

Shutte, A. (1993). *Philosophy for Africa.* Rondebosch: UCT Press.

Teffo, J. (1994). *The concept of Ubuntu as a cohesive moral value.* Pretoria: Ubuntu School of Philosophy.

Tempel, P. (1959). *La Philosophie Bantoue.* Paris: Présence Africaine.

Tutu, D. (2013). *Who we are: Human uniqueness and the African spirit of Ubuntu. Desmond Tutu, Templeton Prize 2013.* https://www.youtube.com/watch?v=0wZtfqZ27lw#t=162. Downloaded 16 May 2017.

Van Sertina, I. (1976). *The came before Columbus.* New York: Random House.

Wallerstein, I. (1974). *Modern world system, vol. 1: Capitalist agriculture and the origins of the European world-economy in the 16th century.* New York/London: Academic Press.

Wallerstein, I. (1980). *Modern world system, vol. II: Mercantilism and consolidation of the European world-economy.* London/New York: Cambridge University Press.
Wallerstein, I. (1989). *Modern world system, vol III: The second great expansion of the capitalist world-economy, 1730–1840s.* San Diego: Academic Press.

CHAPTER 4

On the Educational Potential of *Ubuntu*

Yusef Waghid

Introduction: Revisiting the Notion of *Ubuntu*

After having taught a course on African teaching and learning for change through a massive open online course (MOOC) on the Future Learn/ Stellenbosch University platform for two one-monthly sessions during 2016 and 2017, I gleaned from several of the comments offered by course participants that *Ubuntu* could provide many non-African communities epistemological spaces to reconsider human engagements. In other words, I learned from the comments of participants that *Ubuntu* might also be a concept that can be used to remedy community problems other than those that show their faces on the African continent. This gave me the idea to expand talking about and thinking through the concept of *Ubuntu* in relation to other global contexts. In other words, unlike some of my critics who lament about *Ubuntu's* apparently local relevance, it seems from the comments of some of my MOOC participants that *Ubuntu* might not just

---

Yusef Waghid is a distinguished professor of philosophy of education in the Faculty of Education at Stellenbosch University in South Africa. He is coeditor of *African citizenship education revisited* (New York: Palgrave Macmillan, 2018).

Y. Waghid (✉)
Faculty of Education, Stellenbosch University, Stellenbosch, South Africa

© The Author(s) 2018
E. J. Takyi-Amoako, N. T. Assié-Lumumba (Eds.),
Re-Visioning Education in Africa,
https://doi.org/10.1007/978-3-319-70043-4_4

have a local relevance. Hence, I wish to argue for a plausible conception of *Ubuntu* that can impact any form of human engagement, most notably, associative, deliberative and responsible human encounters.

As it has already been mentioned in the brief introductory section to this chapter, I shall not revisit an analytical exposition of the concept *Ubuntu* on the grounds that the latter philosophical activity has already been taken up extensively in the literature on African thought and practice. Drawing on my own seminal thoughts on the concept of *Ubuntu*, I infer that human interdependence and co-existence seems to be the most appropriate way in which the concept can be articulated (Waghid 2014). In the main, the concept is most poignantly depicted in reference to an isiXhosa[1] dictum: *Ubuntu ngumuntu ngabanya abantu*—that is, a person is a person through other persons (Letseka 2000). When an individual in African parlance is only considered as human on account of his or her relations with other individuals, then such an association is referred to as a community of persons. The latter implies that *Ubuntu*, in the first place, is concerned with the co-existence of individuals in some form of community. The point is a community is representative of an association of individuals whose individuality is collectively expressed through the aspirations of the collectivity. Hence, *Ubuntu* is also literally depicted through the phrase, 'I am because we are' (Mbiti 1969). Simply put, a human being cannot lay claim to his or her humanity without engaging with other humans. What makes an individual uniquely human is his or her encounters with other individuals. The question is what does an encounter entail?

Firstly, when humans engage in an encounter, they present themselves to one another on the basis of one another's speech acts, that is, articulation and listening. Individually, they give an account of their perspectives about their conceptions and perceptions of the world in which they live— that is, they offer some understanding of their cultural, rational and ideological attachments to their social contexts. By presenting themselves in such ways, others get to have some idea of who they are—that is, their encounters determine their very being and actions in relation to one another. In this way, humans are said to be in association with one another—a matter of enacting *Ubuntu* on the basis that humans are attentive to one another through sharing and the cultivation of relations of trust—as Steve Biko aptly reminds us of (1978: 42):

[Through *Ubuntu* we are] … a community of brothers and sisters jointly involved in the quest for a composite answer to the varied problems of life.

Hence in all we do we always place [wo]man first and hence all our action is usually joint community oriented action rather than the individualism.

Secondly, an encounter among humans is considered as a moment of empathy and compassion humans have for one another. This implies that, in an encounter, humans recognise the vulnerabilities of one another with the aim to contribute towards modifying one another's condition of vulnerability, considered by Ifemesia (1979: 2) as acting humanely. When humans engage in an encounter, they encourage and stimulate one another to develop a sense of self- worth and dignity together with harnessing their accountability to family, neighbours and other members of the community—a matter of living their *Ubuntu* (Waghid 2014: 61).

Thirdly, in an encounter, the younger ones are obliged to show respect for elders. However, such a form of respect is not synonymous with an uncritical adherence to the thoughts of elders. Rather, respect through *Ubuntu* means that humans are expected to listen to the views of elders before proffering their own judgements. In other words, showing respect for authority in African communities implies that humans must first equip themselves with wisdom and guidance before making moral claims themselves about what is good for society. This makes sense because without listening and contemplation, humans would not be in an authoritative position to proffer plausible rational judgements. Rational judgements are most tenable on the grounds that such judgements can be defended, albeit morally, judicially or epistemologically. By implication, listening to the views of elders even without offering any kind of response is an enabling activity in the pursuit of making sense of what elders have to say. Of course, listening in itself is not a sufficient condition for making judgements because the latter later on require that humans (say, younger ones) proffer some sort of response to others' thoughts. However, the latter cannot occur meaningfully if listening to others' thoughts has not been internalised, in this instance, by younger persons. Thus, showing respect is conditional upon listening before any meaningful rational judgement can be offered in response to what has been heard. This makes sense on the grounds that human encounters remain subjected to what is heard before people can offer any kind of rational responses.

In brief, *Ubuntu* is a form of human encounter through which humans can nurture relations of sharing and trust, compassion and respect towards one another. I shall now examine the educational potential of *Ubuntu*.

On the Educational Potential of *Ubuntu*

What emanates from the aforementioned discussion is that the concept of *Ubuntu* signifies the occurrence of human encounters whereby individuals engage in association—that is, community, with one another. It is not that individuality is abandoned in association, but rather that humans' individual potential is engaged with through attentive relations of sharing and trust, compassion and accountability towards one another, and mutual respect through listening and the acquisition of guidance and wisdom. In this section, I examine some of the educational implications of *Ubuntu*.

Firstly, when humans encounter one another and do things on the basis of sharing and trust, they are engaged in some form of practice whereby they learn from one another. They are not merely an aggregation of individuals but are intricately engaged in some form of social practice which allows them to become associated with one another through the understandings and ways of seeing the world. Of course, some of them share commonalities, and others experience one another's differences. Although they are equal in humanity, they potentially differ on account of having had different experiences and connections to their respective social arrangements or contexts. This is what *Ubuntu* means for them: being engaged on account of the similarities and differences in particular social settings. And, as has been mentioned previously, their association in a community of individuals is determined by their relations of trust and sharing they embark on. Put differently, their association together is a manifestation of their learning from one another.

Yet, following Seyla Benhabib's (2011: 79) enunciation of education as a public sphere of living in which humans encounter moments of hospitality and hostility, it can be inferred that *Ubuntu* is a way in which education's hospitable dimension can be enacted on the grounds that *Ubuntu* relates to caring, trust, respect and compassion—all virtues that constitute hospitality. However, to care for others does not mean that one cannot evoke their potentialities or even provoke them to think differently and anew. Maxine Greene (1995) makes the point that provoking students to think anew is a matter of stimulating them to discover unexpected truths—an important dimension of educational experience. In this way, *Ubuntu* can also lay claim to cultivating positive hostility. Benhabib (2011: 76) describes this positive hostility as 'hostipitality'—that is, 'a dangerous indeterminacy or mutual suspicion' through which participants in the encounter are initiated into becoming mutually suspicious of undesirable speech acts, or actions, and are prepared to speak out against it. In this sense, participants or students are encouraged to reconsider particular beliefs and are critical of simply accepting taken-for-granted ways of seeing the world in which they live.

Secondly, a human encounter, such as showing respect for elders, does not imply that *Ubuntu* is remiss of an important educational aspect, namely, deliberation. Mutual respect in the first place implies that people listen attentively to the views of one another before making up their minds in relation to the ways they should respond. Mutual respect does not imply accepting views of another for fear of showing disrespect. Quite legitimately it can be argued that *Ubuntu* obliges young minds to listen to the views of elders. However, this does not mean that elders' views should be endorsed uncritically as if young people do not have anything to contribute to such a human encounter. The point is that listening respectfully is a precondition for judgement. One would not be in a position to judge amicably and fairly if one does not have the wisdom and insights to offer any form of rational response to elders' views. So, even listening and making sense momentarily without immediately responding to elders and then later on reflecting about the guidance and wisdom acquired is in itself a mode of inquiry that potentially leads to taking more informed decisions. In a way, listening to elders and reflecting on their perspectives is tantamount to taking their views into some sort of controversy as it could be that one might either agree or disagree with another's perspective in a deliberative way. And, as it happens in African indigenous communities, someone else can communicate the views and perspectives of younger ones to elders. In turn, elders and or sages would invariably be exposed to views that they potentially act on. In other words, not being able to offer counter views in the presence of elders does not mean that deliberation does not occur.

Deliberation stands the best chance of being realised if different and/or contending views are conceived by one another in light of what can also retrospectively be considered albeit in the absence of those younger ones who offered initial critiques. The upshot is that enacting *Ubuntu* whereby elders' views are more reflectively considered by young minds and when perspectives and counter views are proffered even through the agency of others considered more authoritative is not a denial of deliberation. Instead, deliberation takes on a more reflective and insightful agenda when communication about differences is enacted via the agency of those considered as more thoughtful than perhaps younger impetuous minds. For this reason, *Ubuntu* as respectful action has the potential to engender deliberative action—a significant educational virtue.

Thirdly, a human encounter is a form of engagement whereby people from perhaps different socio-economic and cultural backgrounds face up to one another. In doing so, they encounter one another in their otherness and differing ways of being. And, it could be that some in the encounter present themselves in divergent ways which others might find disagreeable. For the encounter to continue, one would expect some people to perhaps recognise someone else's vulnerability in say, articulating himself or herself about a particular matter of interest. If this does not happen, the possibility is always there that someone would be treated with disdain as if such a person does not have any useful contribution to make. However, for the encounter to last, some people ought to act with compassion such as to recognise the vulnerable speech of others. But, for the sake of avoiding the encounter from perhaps remaining unresponsive, people are encouraged to recognise the vulnerabilities of one another—that is, to act compassionately towards one another. And, when people act with compassion towards others in relation to which they recognise one another's vulnerabilities, they can be said to be acting in a spirit of *Ubuntu*. Thus, an encounter framed through *Ubuntu* is a responsible action in the sense that people recognise one another's vulnerabilities and actually do something about changing what people experience. Put differently, enacting *Ubuntu* involves recognising people's vulnerabilities and subsequently endeavouring to change it. In this way, people would be acting responsibly in the sense that such an activity is intertwined with doing something that would positively modify reprehensible action. Humans acting with *Ubuntu* would then act with compassion—that is to say, they would act responsibly.

In relation to education, Stanley Cavell (1979: 441) posits that humans act responsibly on the basis that they respond to an undesirable situation which they envisage to change. In an educational encounter, humans act responsibly towards one another when they conceive what others have to say from others' points of view with which they (humans) engage afresh (Cavell 1979: 441). Acting responsibly towards one another implies that humans acknowledge one another for who they are and not always what they want one another to be. They acknowledge one another on the basis that they enact their humanity—that is, they acknowledge one another as humans deserved of respect (Cavell 1979: 435). When the latter happens, humans would then act with compassion towards one another—a situation in turn which enhances their responsibility and by implication humans' education. In a different way, educated humans act responsibly by virtue of their humanity and *Ubuntu* situatedness. When humans act without Ubuntu, they could become irresponsible which would invariably undermine their education.

In sum, human encounters are educational on the grounds that such encounters are constituted by *Ubuntu*. *Ubuntu* or human interdependence and connectedness can effect hospitable and hostile encounters that are both respectful and compassionate. Such encounters make humans what they are on the basis that their educatedness and hence their humanity would impact the way they acknowledge one another, provoke one another to see things differently and stimulate one another to act with responsibility. Next, I examine as to why *Ubuntu* with its educational impetus has a uniquely cosmopolitan agenda.

ON THE COSMOPOLITAN OUTLOOK OF *UBUNTU*

Thus far, I have argued that *Ubuntu* has an educational potential on the grounds that the former is linked to the cultivation of associative, respectful and responsible human encounters. I shall now show how *Ubuntu* connects with the cultivation of cosmopolitanism as espoused by David T. Hansen (2011). Hansen (2011) offers an account of cosmopolitanism which situates people in the presence of the world. In others words, when people are present in the world they are both reflectively loyal to what they know and simultaneously show a reflective openness to what is not yet known or what is still to come (Hansen 2011: 7). In relation to African indigenous practices, to be a cosmopolitan implies that people do not just abandon their practices but rather show a willingness to reflect on what is familiar to them and then to reconsider these familiarities with the possibility of embarking on the unfamiliar. The latter implies that people would be willing to listen, even to criticism of their traditions and cultures with the intent to rearticulate their understandings of such traditions and cultures. Yet, they are not closed to any new understandings that might in future impact their traditions and cultures.

Now considering that *Ubuntu* privileges, the cultivation of associative, respectful and responsible encounters, such forms of human engagements cannot happen without reflection and openness. It is inconceivable that people engage in a responsible encounter without reflecting openly in and about the encounter. Likewise, it can also be that human encounters are constituted by particular rules of engagement which people can openly reflect about for the sake of improving the interactions among people in such encounters without simply abandoning the encounters. In addition, reconsidering the unfolding of human encounters in light of what can still unexpectedly emerge is tantamount to being reflectively open to the new. Bearing in mind that practices of *Ubuntu* are open to such forms of reflections which involve maintaining a loyalty to the known and showing an openness to what is still to come, traditions and cultures within African communities cannot remain oblivious of a cosmopolitan outlook. It is such an outlook that potentially brings local traditions and cultures into conversation with often global understandings without necessarily abandoning such traditions and cultures. Similarly, adopting and *Ubuntu* approach to human understanding could also open up local traditions and cultures to unexpected and perhaps unimaginable developments that may enhance human engagement rather than stunting it. Therefore, I am in agreement with Marianna Papastephanou's (2015: 88) take on cosmopolitanism that is firstly, 'about enriched cultural choice[s] and the hybridization of the self' and, secondly, 'about the complexities [of encounters] yet to come'. Developing 'enriched cultural choice[s]' goes along with showing a reflective openness to the known and contemplating about 'complexities [of encounters] yet to come' is commensurable with exercising a reflective openness to what remains in becoming.

Ubuntu, Education and Dignity

Thus far I have shown that *Ubuntu* has an educational record and potential with a cosmopolitan outlook. I shall now examine as to what underscores such an understanding of *Ubuntu* in relation to the cultivation of dignity. Thus far, I have examined understandings of the notion of *Ubuntu* and have particularly highlighted its educational and cosmopolitan potentials. However, the question needs to be asked: what is it about *Ubuntu* that gives it its distinctive form? In reference to the extermination of Jews at Auschwitz which is associated with the term 'holocaust' literally meaning ('completely burned'), Giorgio Agamben (2002: 69) reminds us that the aforementioned act of 'horror' 'marks the end of every ethics of dignity …'. That is, the atrocious and appalling debasement and degradation of human life at Auschwitz for Agamben (2002: 72) constitute a 'horror' during which 'corpses were produced' associated with extermination of humans at the hands of the Nazis. To act with *Ubuntu* is to never act without 'dignity and decency beyond imagination'—a phrase coined by

Agamben (2002: 69). Thus, dignity implies, firstly, having respect for human autonomy and, secondly, preserving human existence at all costs. *Ubuntu*, with its emphases on education and cosmopolitanism, inherently connects with the cultivation of humanity. This implies that humans' dignity has to be preserved and defended at all costs. Hence, *Ubuntu* means that humans should always be treated with dignity which rules out degradation, debasement, genocide and terror of humanity.

Of course, my potential critic might claim that despite *Ubuntu's* connection with African human practices, there are persistent instances of terror and violence on the continent, most notably nowadays the terror perpetrated by Boko Haram in the northern parts of Africa. Agreeably, like in other parts of the world, there are perpetual outbursts of terror most significantly in the UK, Europe, the USA and, on a larger scale, in the Philippines and Middle East (in particular the 'jihadist' operations of ISIS in Iraq, Syria and countries of the Levant). Because of the overt terror perpetrated by Boko Haram or AQMI (*Al-Qaïda au Maghreb islamique*, Al-Qaeda in the Islamic Maghreb) against their fellow human beings in various parts of West and Northern Africa, it can be assumed that human rights violations are on the upsurge. By implication, such often heinous terror does not mean that *Ubuntu* is absent on the continent.

Rather, like in many parts of the world, *Ubuntu* or honour for human life is undermined, and decency towards humans is constantly receding. If *Ubuntu* were to have been completely absent, not more than 50 per cent of African nation-states would have adopted democratic forms of political governance and, neither would an African Union with its vision of uniting the continent against crime, corruption and violence have gained priority. So, the sporadic absence of *Ubuntu* in several parts of the African continent is not a vindication of its ubiquitous absence. It is merely a confirmation that on some parts of the African continent, human life and dignity are degraded and conformity to *Ubuntu* is discontinued. Yet, because of *Ubuntu's* educational and cosmopolitan potential, the possibility is always there for humans to engage and be openly reflective about their traditions and cultures and that unexpected and unimaginable stability and non-violence might yet ensue. Being open to new insights implies in the first place that people are not uncritical towards their cultural traditions. They are willing to take their cultural traditions into critical scrutiny and in this way invariably remain open to the unexpected—that is, what might still ensue.

CONCLUSION: *UBUNTU* AND ITS IMPLICATIONS
FOR TEACHING AND LEARNING

Teaching and learning in post-apartheid South African university class-rooms are expected to be engaging, deliberative and responsible considering the legacy of both apartheid and colonialism whereby students were con-strained to speak their minds. The democratic transformation of several universities on the African continent, most notably in South Africa, is a testimony to the democratic aspirations of communities of thinking. Such communities in the post-colonial and post-apartheid periods were intent on resolving their societal malaises on the basis of freedom and the uncon-strained articulation of speech acts. And, universities with their democratic intent were committed to producing graduates who could serve the demo-cratic ethos of their respective communities. By implication, students had to be taught what it means to deliberatively engage with one another, question the assumptions of their respective thoughts and becoming attuned to unexpected and improbable truths that might arise. It is here that *Ubuntu* offers much for the cultivation of teaching and learning on the grounds that the former considers dignified engagement, deliberative attunement and moving towards encounters that are reflectively open to new insights and perspectives.

When university educators and students treat one another dignifiedly, there are always pedagogical opportunities for them to become more insightful and resolute about their optimism to look at things anew. This implies that they would be more open and reflective for that matter on what they produce together rather than just being concerned about their own autonomous reflections and/or articulations. Similarly, being attenu-ated to *Ubuntu* would instil in them the propensity to engage with one another's views more engagingly, that is, more deliberatively. Educators and students would not be indifferent towards one another's divergent and perhaps underdeveloped thoughts as through deliberation they remain open to one another's views even if such views might be incongru-ent with their own. They would continue to engage deliberatively on the grounds that they remain open to what is new and unexpected without prematurely rebuking one another's perspectives—a matter of acting with *Ubuntu*.

Finally, as with many democratic communities, universities that insist on students and educators learning together on the basis of reflection and openness—much in the same way *Ubuntu* requires—also engender opportunities for educators and students to think about ways as to how their societies can be more democratically transformed. It is in the latter regard that *Ubuntu*, with its emphasis on a reflective openness to what remains in becoming, offers much opportunity for educators and students to see things differently and to proffer ways in which societal advances can be made more politically, economically, culturally and educationally. In the main, *Ubuntu* affords educators and students opportunities to transform societies vis-à-vis engaging and reflectively open processes.

NOTE

1. IsiXhosa is an indigenous language spoken by many Africans in the Western and Eastern Cape provinces of South Africa. It is also the language spoken by the late President Nelson Mandela.

REFERENCES

Agamben, G. (2002) *Remnants of Auschwitz: The witness and the archive* (trans: Heller-Roazen, D.). New York: Zone Books.

Benhabib, S. (2011). *Dignity in adversity: Human rights in troubled times.* Cambridge: Polity Press.

Biko, S. (1978). *I write what I like.* New York: Harper and Row.

Cavell, S. (1979). *The claims of reason: Wittgenstein, scepticism, morality, and tragedy.* Oxford: Clarendon Press.

Greene, M. (1995). *Releasing the imagination.* San Francisco: Jossey-Bass.

Hansen, D. T. (2011). *The teacher and the world: A study of cosmopolitanism as education.* New York/London: Routledge.

Ifemesia, C. (1979). *Traditional humane living among the Igbo: An historical perspective.* Enugu: Fourth Dimension Publishing Company.

Letseka, M. (2000). African philosophy and educational discourse. In P. Higgs, N. C. G. Vakalisa, T. V. Mda, & N. Assié-Lumumba (Eds.), *African voices in education* (pp. 179–193). Cape Town: Juta.

Mbiti, J. (1969). *African religions and philosophy.* London: Heinemann.

Papastephanou, M. (2015). *Thinking differently about cosmopolitanism: Theory, eccentricity and the globalized world.* Boulder: Paradigm.

Waghid, Y. (2014). *African philosophy of education reconsidered: On being human.* New York/London: Routledge.

CHAPTER 5

Conceptualizing Gender and Education in Africa from an Ubuntu Frame

N'Dri Thérèse Assié-Lumumba

INTRODUCTION

Conceptualizing the interface of gender and education from an Ubuntu framework requires referencing the fundamental idea of inalienable rights in equality and responsibilities of all citizens based on their inescapable common humanity in any given society (Teffo 2000; Kunnie 2000; Odora Hoppers 2002; Wiredu 1998; Coetzee 1998). It follows from this idea that the perceived or actual interests of one individual or social category ought to be shared concerns.

The role of education in any given society is to promote, enhance, and develop capabilities of individuals and groups toward the fulfillment of their responsibilities and interests that are individual as well as collective. The term Ubuntu captures "the underlying principles of interdependence and humanism" (Letseka 2000). In essence, it advocates for providing equally enabling and liberating power of education to all individuals and groups in society for their own rights and the sheer interests of all linked by the humanist web of interdependence. Thus, the biological differentiation between males and females (or any other ground for social differentiation) ought not to constitute a determining factor in access to education of all levels and types and qualification for socio-economic attainment.

N. T. Assié-Lumumba (✉)
Africana Studies and Research Center, Cornell University, Ithaca, NY, USA

© The Author(s) 2018
E. J. Takyi-Amoako, N. T. Assié-Lumumba (Eds.),
Re-Visioning Education in Africa,
https://doi.org/10.1007/978-3-319-70043-4_5

67

In *Development as Freedom*, Sen (1999) articulates the notion of freedom as a facilitator for development. In *Sex and Social Justice*, Nussbaum (1999) argues that there are three intertwined types of capabilities: (1) basic capabilities that are the natural tools of individuals necessary to develop more advanced capabilities, (2) internal capabilities which provide the sufficient conditions needed for applying abilities in real-world activities, and (3) combined (external) capabilities that are facilitated by external powers, mainly the policymakers.

The thrust of this chapter is to critically examine the gender-gap factor Africa, from colonial to post-colonial policies of education in the different countries and the continent as whole, and demonstrate that they have been devoid of Ubuntu values. Sen (1999) contends that it is the role of public action to provide the means by which humans pursue and desire for the collective interest. Hence, this chapter aims to propose that there is a need for an Ubuntu-based public policy of education that organically encompasses gender equity as a sine qua non for social progress in Africa.

The first section provides an overview of the global advocacy to promote equality of educational opportunity and gender equality and the persistent gender inequality endemic in African education systems. Yet, post-independence official commitments throughout Africa have been articulated to achieve the repeatedly missed target of gender equality at even the basic primary school level. The second section discusses the basic tenet of Ubuntu which, I contend, has been missing in policies and practices of African countries and sustain, albeit unofficially, the institutional apparatus for the reproduction of gender inequality in education, despite the shared African values imbedded in Ubuntu and its enduring presence in other sectors and spheres of contemporary African societies. The third section, followed by the conclusion, presents Ubuntu as a preventive and lasting corrective framework for educational policies promoting equality that can support sustainable social progress.

THE GLOBAL ADVOCACY AND THE STATE OF GENDER IN/EQUALITY IN AFRICAN EDUCATION

A full appreciation of the contours of the state of gender in/equality in African countries, and globally, necessitates reflection and a historical approach in examining critically the various forms, types, and levels of educational systems to understand the contributing factors at every historical moment considered. The structures, criteria, and mode of transition between levels of each education system vary from society to society. However, in the contemporary world, there are worldwide similarities in the ideas and practices of hierarchy and differential values in the systems with regard to the various levels and types. In many parts of the world, the shared organizations whose structures and modus operandi and values are similar were purposefully and carefully established with European colonial policies in the form and degree of transfers and legacies. Notwithstanding the current reproduction of Western models through colonial legacies globally, there are cases of "colonization by choice" whereby countries that were not formally colonized "willingly" establish and maintain systems that reproduce those Western models. On the African continent, the Ethiopian case is a good illustration of this "voluntary" transfer of Western models.

In the post-World War II context of the establishment of the United Nations with its stated goal of promoting advocacy for a more just world within and also between nation-states, the central UN system and its various specialized agencies have been making the case for the need to advance equality and equity in both education and the gender. African countries were still firmly under the colonial yoke when grand ideas about equality and justice were articulated in the Charter of the United Nations signed on June 26, 1945. It stipulated its commitment to promote "social progress and better standards of life" and "respect for human rights and for fundamental freedoms for all without distinction to race, sex, language or religion." Subsequently, its specialized agencies and programs focusing on education and/or gender re-affirmed this broad commitment.

For the purpose of the topic in this chapter, it is worth mentioning that since the creation of UNESCO in 1948, the idea of education as a human right has consistently been re-affirmed in subsequent international declarations and agreements. Numerous resolutions, programs, and projects focusing on education have been adopted since then, including year-long focal points and longer-termed resolutions. For instance, 1990 was declared the year of literacy, and in 1990 in Jomtien and 2000 in Dakar, the resolution of Education for All (EFA) was adopted, and in 1998 UNESCO held its World Conference on "Higher Education in the 21st Century." More recently, as part of a general global commitment to social advancements, some aspects of broader resolution have focused on education. For instance, the second of the eight Millennium Development Goals (MDGs 2000–2015) was to "Achieve universal primary education," and the fourth among the 17 Sustainable Development Goals (SDGs 2015–2030) is geared to "Ensure Inclusive and Equitable Quality Education and Promote Life-Long Learning Opportunities for All." Additionally, Africa as a world region also has had decades of stated focus on education. For instance, the seminal seminar titled "the Development of Education in Africa" that was held in Addis Ababa in 1961 (UNECA UNESCO 1961) was a forerunner of the African ministerial regular conferences on education. At this meeting, education was declared "the priority of priorities," considering its centrality to all aspects of life and societal development.

Similarly, during the launching of the United Nations, the fundamental question regarding the glaring gender inequality in the world found in all the domains of society including education was expressed. Granted that in the beginning of the preamble of the UN Charter, a gender-insensitive term "mankind" was used as an acceptable generic term for humanity, of critical importance was the stipulation, in the same text, of the UN commitment "to reaffirm faith in fundamental human rights, in the dignity and worth of the human person, in the equal rights of men and women and of nations large and small … ." Thus, the Commission of the Status of Women (CSW) was established in 1946 and started holding annual conferences, of which the 61st was held in March 2017. Numerous resolutions have been adopted since then such as the International Women's Year (IWY) in 1975 and the 1976–1985 the United Nations Decade for Women that started with the inaugural international conference of the decade held in Mexico City in 1975 followed by the mid-term Copenhagen conference in 1980. Of particular significance was the end of the decade celebration at the Nairobi conference in 1985, flowed a decade later by Beijing 1995 conference and the Beijing + every five years thereafter. It is also worth mentioning the seminal Convention on the Elimination of All Forms of Discrimination Against Women (CEDAW) which was adopted in 1979. Also articulated in third goal of the MDGs to "Promote gender equality and empower women" recapped in the fifth of the SDGs which expresses the need and commitment to "Achieve Gender Equality and Empower All Women and Girls" as universal policies. Although gender has been addressed in many international and national documents as a cross-cutting domain, its interface with education has been more specifically articulated.

Global proposals voted by international bodies, especially the United Nations, are only recommendations appealing to the moral conscience of leaders of nations. The concrete design and implementation of policies actualizing the global call for equality, justice, and human rights as sine qua non for social progress have been purely voluntary. However, since the mid-1950s when African countries began to acquire their independence and formally joined the United Nations, they have officially voted for the UN official resolutions on education and gender equality in promoted through the UN global activism.

Gender, as a social construct, has been recognized as a universal ground for potential and actual inequality, specifically in education. While factors of inequality such as social class, race, ethnicity, religion, area of birth, residence, and rural-urban divide, gender is the only factor that is inevitably and intrinsically part of the existence of human societies across the globe. The state of gender in/equality can be aggravated or lessened by its interface with a single or a conjunction of several effects of the aforementioned factors among others.

In most parts of the African continent, there has been persistent gender inequality and under-representation of the female population in the systems of education. The inequality issue has a dimension of human rights violations. Of equal importance is the fact that the marginalization and lack of equality for girls and women in education as the persistent under-representation are a great loss to society with partial participation and difficulty in contributing to socio-economic progress of their respective countries.

The expectation has been that formally educated girls and women would acquire necessary skills that would position them well enough to earn a living and acquire socio-economic attainment in terms of job distribution and social mobility. However, empirical evidence shows that there are persistent social structures and values that tend to be mainly reproduced through the educational systems and hindering institutional cultures that prevent education from being an effective instrument for breaking the cycle of gender inequality and poverty/powerlessness (Meena 2007; Eholié 2007).

Since the 1950s, when African countries began to gain their independence from the colonial powers, only a few localities and countries have achieved gender equality in access to education. There have been promising legal frameworks as a critical dimension of any policy designed to eliminate gender inequality (Higgs 2002). However, there have been persistent gaps between the most progressive laws and the enactment of policies and the negative impact of institutional and social cultures that reproduce structural inequality from primary to higher education (Assié-Lumumba 2000). The various legal amendments enacted toward more progressive pronouncement, and after the euphoric period of the Millennium Development Goals and EFA targets, universal enrollment at the primary school level has not been achieved. Subsequently, the widening gaps from the lower to the upper levels of education systems persist.

Strides have been made in general enrollments and female representation, specifically in the first post-independence decade of each country. However, there seems to be a plateau that few have been able to overcome and reach the remaining 20–5%. Furthermore, some externally driven policies from global organizations that draw their policy framework from the former colonial powers have contributed to major setbacks experienced by African countries. Thus, in addition to failing to reach their 1961 Addis Ababa Conference (UNECA UNESCO 1961) goals of universal enrollment up to the 1980s, the economic crisis during the same period had a direct and indirect impact on Africa's ability to pursue its policies of increasing enrollment.

Of particularly negative impact was the structural adjustment programs (SAPs) of the World Bank and International Monetary Fund (IMF) which led to major negative repercussions. Many countries experienced stagnations and outright decline. As female enrollment was lagging behind even during the first period of steady increase, the prospect for gender equality in most countries became bleak with declining enrollment, retention, promotion, and transition rates from the lower to the upper levels, leading to even more severe female under-representation. Interestingly, even a study conducted and published by the World Bank (Subbarao et al. 1994) revealed the devastating impact of the gender policies in Africa imposed by the financial international organizations. According to the findings of this study, the proportion of the World Bank's higher education projects and investment in Africa which included a gender component experienced a major decline. As they stated, "total investment in higher education projects acknowledging gender in the Sub-Saharan African region during the 1980s decreased to a mere 6 percent from 16 percent in the 1970s" (Subbarao et al. 1994, p. 32).

Some progress was visible following the period of decline and the resurgence of education enthusiasts. High female enrollment was emerging after the 1980s up to the 1990s. Nevertheless, according to global statistics, patterns of female enrollment and representation especially in higher education in many countries of sub-Saharan Africa show persistent gender imbalance with the female population lagging behind, in most cases representation only one-third of the enrollment (UNESCO Institute for Statistics-UIS 2017; Bloom et al. 2006). The general trend at the tertiary level continues to show an even smaller percentage of female students in the fields of science, technology, and particularly engineering. While this is a common trend worldwide, the representation of female students in the fields of sciences in African institutions of higher learning is particularly dismal. It is clear that educational policies in Africa are still built on the roots of colonial systems that they inherited and which have been advised by and international financial organizations, such as the World Bank, despite the more progressive messages and resolutions of the United Nations and some its specialized agencies.

The low proportion of girls and women at every level of the formal education system is not the only problem. Broader philosophical and political issues of the nature of education itself exist. In the rush for expanding general education in the post-colonial era, African policymakers failed to pay attention to the fundamental question regarding the nature and content of education that would be relevant for the African societies and populations and an effective instrumental for development. Therefore, the search for a development model that would make use of all human resources is produced in inclusive educational systems.

Based on the past and current statistics and the patterns established, it is quite revealing to note that in the forward-looking "Gender Agenda in Agenda 2063" of the African Union, Mwebaza (n.d.) makes a statement about the dismal achievement today despite the official commitment:

> Africa is addressing the gender gap in Primary Education. However, the continent is below the average for the group of LDC's.
> Gender parity at secondary and tertiary levels is however less promising, though women's enrolment at the tertiary level is growing faster than men.

In beholding a brighter future, a new philosophy and policy framework, namely, Ubuntu, articulated in this chapter of the book, is necessary to guide relevant education that strives for excellence and gender balance. Thus, in the next section, the main tenet of the Ubuntu is recapped.

Ubuntu: An Overview of the Tenets

As a signifier, Ubuntu is a specific term derived from the Bantu/Nguni language of Southern Africa. Re-centering Ubuntu is a paradigm shift from the inherited western archetype. The meaning, philosophical representation, and worldview that Ubuntu captures are shared by the African continent and in fact exist in other societies beyond Africa. For instance, Native Americans, in the fight for the protection of their lands and in the protection of the environment, have a similar concept of Ubuntu, in articulating to the concept of *Pachamama* (Mother Earth) that embodied the spiritual being and material representation of the Earth. In terms of the signified/ meaning, Ubuntu is found in all societies in Africa, even though variations of the concept exist and are specific to culture and language.

Conversely, the actualization of the concept has been under threat of being diluted by the modern and contemporary intrusion of Western colonial policies and practices. To Africans, the essence of the Ubuntu worldview articulates essential "oneness of humanity, a collective, community, and a set of cultural practices and spiritual values that strive for respect and dignity for all humanity" (Goduka 2000, p. 72). Ubuntu acknowledges and emulates shared humanity in its complexity encompassing an interdependent ecosystem of humans, nature, and the planet (Letseka 2000; Wright and Abdi 2012; Waghid 2014). V. Y. Mudimbe (1988a, p. 1) articulating the essence of Ubuntu argues that it is a belief system that embraces a collective ethos asserting that "to be is necessarily to be in relation" to others and the "center is a human being who is free and at the same time highly dependent upon others, on the memory of the past, and on emphasizing the balance between nature and culture" (Mudimbe 1988a, p. 1). In this conception, there is an affirmation of equality and existential worth among human beings and the broader environment and the totality of its constituents even the ones that may appear to the humans or specific cultures and societies as unimportant or outright "irrelevant." Every human being has a unique contribution to the society and we are co-dependent on each other.

The core of the Ubuntu worldview is the recognition that every human is equal regardless of the differences of which gender is included. This notion of equality and human worth requires an equal disposition in society to develop the respective potential toward achieving the actualization of active and productive membership in the human community and broader ecosystem. An important tenet of the Ubuntu is interdependence and complementarity. However, it is important to differentiate between negative and positive complementarity. Negative complementarity characterizes situations in which different contributions create a whole web of structural inequality, whereas positive complementary recognizes and promotes the important roles of the different parts of the whole which are interconnected. Positive complementarity is essentially empowering and gives meaning to the notion of equal worth. In these conditions, this interdependence assumes equal worth regardless of gender.

In the realm of languages and their social roles, in Africa the interface of gender and language is a component that cannot be overlooked. African languages across the African continent try to emulate the idea of gender parity and equal worth. As human beings, it is an ultimate expression of their collective importance and a reference to humankind. In the various parts of the continent, languages provide an unequivocal historical and continued testimony of the centrality of the idea of equal human worth on the basis of gender. By and large, African languages have a gender-neutral term that refers to humanity of the human/person. In addition, two separate, parallel, and distinct terms designate the female and male genders, respectively. One of the criticisms inherent in Western feminist literature is the lexicon found in European languages. In most cases, the term referring to the male gender is the prevalent norm and has been used as a generic term for humankind. Historically, it has been the norm for languages such as English, French, and Spanish to use the words man, *l'homme, el hombre* as generic for humankind. While some progress has been made in the English language, in French, for instance, the old habit persists. Indeed, it is only recently that "Human Rights" translated as "*Droits de l'Homme*" has shifted to "*Droits Humains*" or "*Droits de la Personne.*"

The imposition of colonization on African lives was embroiled with policies designed by colonial powers to destroy, eliminate, and radically change African institutions. Formal education was used to further inculcate African peoples and perform social surgery on societies and social institutions. Colonial ideas were to be imprinted on the minds of Africans through formal education. The use of European languages in African education systems contributed to create and consolidate conceptions of gender hierarchy, and male terms were adopted as generic for humankind, which ignored African languages and its social implications.

Ubuntu as an ideology was/is designed to empower African peoples from the colonization gaze; thus, it is well positioned within a world inundated by an ecosystem that is complex and hierarchal in the realm of gender. Ubuntu embraces the idea of interdependence and embodies humility and a collective bargaining power which acts as a symbiotic relationship that is mutually reinforcing and from which strength emanates. Ubuntu's principles mean recognizing and living by mutuality upholding positive and constructive power, whereas disengaging from the empowering bond of interdependence, the disconnected elements of dissonance produces weakness. In essence, "Ubuntu" captures the productive power of collective ethos (Assié-Lumumba 2016) which is much needed in African peoples.

I use the term social surgery to refer to the profound changes that colonization undertook to re-invent Africans (Mudimbe 1988b) and women (Oyěwùmí 1997) in totality. The colonial system used the three types of education, namely, the formal/schooling, non-formal, and even informal education, toward its goal of creating new Africans and African societies. Colonial education, reinforced by changes in other social institutions, created new structures designed to perform a radical transformation of the African with the intention of stripping her/him of the essence of her/his being and worldview. The imposition of a new foreign Western paradigm aimed at restructuring the African society according to a colonial hierarchical vision including gender hierarchy. This hierarchy is connected to the broader organization of society within a public sphere where power lies and where men are in charge and women are relegated to the private sphere, voiceless, and devoid of power (Paulme 1971).

In the post-Westphalian model of nation-states and the mapping of Africa with the creation of the new nation-states emblematic of the control of Africa by European powers, the power distribution on the global stage reflected the restructuring. Indeed, the power to create and name these countries and their artificial borders was accompanied by European unilateral conceptualization and design of education for the colonized Africans. Indeed, the prevailing modernist epistemology that has been spread across the globe with the trajectory of colonial empires has shaped contemporary education systems in various corners, with a special implication in Africa, the continent that was colonized nearly in its entirety, with the exception of Ethiopia and Liberia with a modified version. As a reflection of their own societies marred in century-old rigid social classes, the world and especially the African continent, the Europeans conquered by military means were restructured on the ground of fundamental inequality in order to further oppress and disempower the peoples to exert their hegemony and totally control the colonized masses.

Colonial systems that were set up were remolded and reproduced colonized subjects that were to their own liking (collaborators) different from the combative Africans (both women and men) across the entire continent who resisted colonization and fought for their rights and freedom. Many of the resistance movements up to the initial colonial settlement/administration included male and female leaders (Sweetman 1984). Their level of consciousness and capabilities was the result of African indigenous education. The colonial designed education was deliberately meant to create a new hierarchy and preparation for the economic and social life according to the new structure with the colonizers as the supreme leaders holding all the power, while African men stripped of their power even though they operated in the public sphere. The new African women were relegated to the private sphere where they were expected to become voiceless and powerless, under the yoke of a European-brand patriarchy.

A hierarchy of identification ascended, and there was a tug of war between the colonizers and the colonized. The colonial regime in place was designed to produce and manufacture powerless colonial "pacified" by the newly designed education for the colonial subjects deprived of critical thinking and therefore expected to be happy to accept their colonial condition. The system proved less effective than planned since many of the formally educated with minimal curriculum for colonial subjects challenged and resisted the system vehemently. However, even with formal decolonization, the marks of the colonial system are still resolute and the colonial remnants still linger on. The formal education in Africa inherited institutions that were colonial in essence and purpose. Ubuntu paradigm calls for a new system that will contribute to promoting social progress with education as a crucial instrument.

Ubuntu Paradigm as a Preventive and Corrective Framework in Rethinking Education and Gender Equality in Africa

In the "Gender Agenda in Agenda 2063" of the African Union (Mwebaza n.d.), it stipulated:

> The vision of Africa expressed in Agenda 2063 is one of an Africa whose development is people-driven, especially relying on the potential offered by its women and youth;
> Under this vision, it is envisaged that there will be gender equality in all spheres of life and an engaged and empowered youth.

In three specific components highlighted, it is further articulated (Mwebaza n.d.) that:

1. By 2063, all forms of violence and discrimination (social, economic, political) against women and girls would have been eliminated, and they would fully enjoy all their human rights. This means an end to all harmful social practices and that all barriers to access to quality health and education for women and girls would be non-existent.
2. The Africa of 2063 would see fully empowered women with equal access and opportunity in all spheres of life. This means that the African woman would have equal economic rights, including the rights to own and inherit property, sign a contract, and register and manage a business. Over 90% of rural women would have access to productive assets, including land, credit, inputs, and financial services.
3. The Africa of 2063 would see attainment of full gender parity. It would see women occupy 50% of elected offices at state, regional, and local bodies, and 50% of managerial positions in government and private sector would be women. The economic and political glass ceiling hindering women's progress would finally have been broken.

The year 2063 in *Agenda 2063* (African Union Commission 2015) is in reference to the centennial of the Organization of African Unity (OAU) which was created in 1963, before it was renamed African Union (AU) in 2001. In *Agenda 2063*, gender inequality which includes dimensions of human rights and investment in human capabilities is some of the main objectives. However, the stated goals will not be achieved without a new type of education. Indeed, the immediate and long-term social progress in Africa requires that the persistent gender inequality be effective addressed with consistent resolve. Effective solutions call for questioning and revisiting the colonial legacy and critical examination of the ways in which education has been conceptualized, designed, and applied with colonial legacy in the content and pedagogy.

For instance, the hitherto conception of education and ongoing global emphasis on the quantitative outputs of educational processes and competition reveal a disconnection. The ability to measure quantitative outputs and promote quality education and excellence should not be conceived as mutually exclusive with cooperation and values that are imbedded in Ubuntu philosophy. Some of the cultural elements in Ubuntu ideology cannot be quantified, but Ubuntu offers the framework for conceptualizing and operationalizing relevant education for collective well-being in symbiosis with the broader ecosystem. Quantitative analysis guided by competitive motives should not be the bona fide narrative whereby if concepts are not quantifiable then it is not valid. Indeed, deep philosophical questions regarding the model of formal education in the local, national, and global society ought to be beneficial and sustainable. A significant question is: what will it take to have all children learn skills and values that will promote cooperation, deep understanding of the positive, and necessary respect for the ecosystem, including humans, other beings, and the environment in general? Gender-equity approach in policy conceptualization, design, implementation, and evaluation (for adjustment) becomes a sine qua non for such empowering education that will contribute to achieving the goals of Agenda 2063 as well as, on the global scale, SDGs. Ubuntu and its inclusive philosophy that guarantees gender equity constitute an effective preventative and permanent corrective measure.

It is important to highlight that the type of gender equality expressed herein implies substantive and positive equality at all levels of the education system and the entire societies when taking into account outcomes of education. The search for gender equality is intrinsically linked to the quest for positive change in individuals' and collective attitude toward life, lived experience, and social progress at the level of families, local communities, countries, and the global community. It is imperative for the continent of Africa to play a leading role with a successful, collective, empowering, and human-centered model to inspire the world. Achieving gender equality does not mean to have just any type of equal enrollment figures and representation. For instance, in the context of the aforementioned economic crisis and subsequent SAPs policies, the enrollment rates declined in some countries and some cases hitherto higher rates of enrollment for boys dropped and reached the same level of the stagnating rates for girls. The resultant equal gender enrollment rates can be referred as negative equality because the financial barriers created negatively impacted boy's enrollment in schools that declined to the unsatisfactory enrollment rate levels of the girls.

This type of state of affairs can be referred to as negative homogenization whereby the positive situation is eroded and reaches the unfavorable level. The lowering of male enrollment rates is not an achievement and ought to be of equal concern just as the lower female enrollment rates. The ultimate objective in adopting a gender-equity approach inspired by Ubuntu is to promote the development of the comprehensive human capacity in the entire society. Ubuntu-inspired gender equality must encompass positive equality whereby everyone has the same opportunity to develop their capacity, aspiration, and contribute to social progress.

Amidst the major challenges of liberal globalization since the end of the twentieth century and the ever-competitive context of "knowledge economy," African countries have earmarked their respective development agendas expressed in visions targeting specific decades in the first half of the twenty-first century to achieve their goals as "emerging economies" with competitive capacities to reckon with on the global scale. The continent of Africa must pool its resources and advance its agenda and provide a global leadership single-handedly as a world region or in partnership with regions/people who espouse similar values and/or appreciate and make a commitment to emulate their liberating capacity toward global social progress. The values imbedded in Ubuntu position the continent favorably for its social progress aspirations. At the level of the entire continent, Agenda 2063 has set goals, all of which require acquisition of cutting-edge knowledge that emphasizes the preeminence of science and technology for optimal economic performance.

For nation-states, leverage in the competitive world is determined by powerful human capacity with Ubuntu-based values. Instead continuing to be the targeted beneficiary of the call for global engagement for Education for All, gender equality, eradication of poverty, and so forth, with Ubuntu values education, Africa can provide a new local and global leadership for social progress for all. Boubou Hama (1968, p. 376) states that all (starting with the Africans) should consider that "Old Africa" has something to offer despite its "old bottlenecks that are entrenched in our old society" as also argued by Abdou Moumouni (1968) and Ki-Zerbo (1990), among many other African scholars and practitioners. Education conceptualized on the framework of Ubuntu essentially promotes humanism and inclusiveness (Kaunda 1968; Waghid 2014). Such values embrace education that promotes learning outcomes geared toward contributing to actualize and appreciate a common collective well-being (Assié-Lumumba 2017).

In search for a solution to the gender imbalance, there is a need to understand the complexity of the explanatory factors that must be taken into account. The functional illiteracy is expected to have worse effects in the context of the current digitization of farming, increased trade liberalization, and international competition, in which the rural women are in conflict with industrial/commercial farming. Despite the successes of a few women in trade, some who are involved in transcontinental trade have inadequate skills and face challenges and are inhibited from competing on a fair level in part owing to their illiteracy in the languages of trade in the global context.

In this era of the expansion of information and communication technologies (ICT) and the emergence and dominance of the disciplines of science and technology being adopted and privileged by African governments in their proclaimed visions for what they view to be progress, profound gender imbalance must be eradicated by empowering all learner to excel in disciplines regardless of gender. It is important to clarify that an Ubuntu-inspired education philosophy is not mutually exclusive with the scientific, technological, and engineering disciplines. For the arguments of this paper, Ubuntu aims to ground the education process and different disciplines in values that foster a collective well-being for the human and the entire ecosystem.

CONCLUSION

Since the onset of the end of formal colonial rule over the African continent in the mid-1950s, many engagements advocating for education and promotion of socio-economic development in Africa have been expressed by African governments as well as the United Nations and its various specialized agencies. From the Addis Ababa Conference in 1961 to the 2015 Agenda 2063 and the numerous resolutions of the United Nation system including the most recent ones such as EFA, MDGs, and SDGs, the centrality of education and the imperative of achieving gender equality have been articulated with an established consensus. Yet, one of the main and persistent characteristics of African education has been the entrenched gender inequality in enrollment in basic education, survival, transition from the lower to the upper levels of the system, and skewed distributions in the different post-secondary disciplines, with subsequent occupational clusters with women at the lower levels of the ladder. With a few exceptions, the gender imbalance is evident with persistent under-representation of the female population.

In this chapter, it is argued that the gender inequality is intrinsically related to the inadequacy of the existing systems of education which is, in essence, set to produce inequality with the female population as the primary group that was historically left at the periphery and under-represented. To eradicate these entrenched patterns of gender inequality, it is necessary to adopt a new philosophy of education that is essentially inclusive and egalitarian.

Ubuntu is in alignment with African cultures, and the philosophy of inclusiveness is rooted in African collective ethos and forward-looking resolve

(Mazrui 1992). This empowering philosophy that can offer a breakthrough in reshaping the conceptualization, design, planning, implementation, and all the dimensions of education that promote positive and enabling equality in part requires recovery of the lost memory (Mazrui 2013), innovative capacity (Assié-Lumumba 2004), and a certain degree of fusion (Assié-Lumumba 2005, 2016). Ubuntu embodies the values of interdependence, mutuality, and connection to the social and the broader environmental ecology, as articulated in both the SDG and Agenda 2063. Solutions to problems emanating from various and inter-related contradictions including gender hierarchy produced by ill-conceived education can be harnessed with Ubuntu-inspired education that is essentially inclusive and fosters collective advancement and social progress.

REFERENCES

African Union Commission. (2015). *Agenda 2063: The Africa we want.* Addis Ababa. https://archive.au.int/assets/images/agenda2063.pdf. Accessed 30 June 2017.

Assié-Lumumba, N. T. (2000). Educational and economic reforms, gender equity, and access to schooling in Africa. *International Journal of Comparative Sociology, XLI*(1), 89–120.

Assié-Lumumba, N. T. (2004). Sustaining home-grown innovations in higher education in Sub-Saharan Africa: A critical reflection. *Journal of International Cooperation in Education, 7*(1), 71–81.

Assié-Lumumba, N. T. (2005). African higher education: From compulsory juxtaposition to fusion by choice-forging a new philosophy of education for social progress. In Y. Waghid, B. v. Wyk, F. Adams, & I. November (Eds.), *African(a) philosophy of education: Reconstructions and deconstructions* (pp. 19–53). Matieland: Stellenbosch University.

Assié-Lumumba, N. T. (2016). Harnessing the empowerment nexus of afropolitanism and higher education: Purposeful fusion for Africa's social progress in the 21st century. *Journal of African Transformation, 1*(2), 51–76.

Assié-Lumumba, N. T. (2017). The Ubuntu paradigm and comparative and international education: Epistemological challenges and opportunities in our field. *Comparative Education Review, 61*(1), 1–21.

Bloom, D., Canning, D., & Chan, K. (2006). *Higher education and economic development in Africa.* Washington, DC: World Bank, Development Sector, Africa Region.

Coetzee, P. H. (1998). Particularity in morality and its relation to community. In P. H. Coetzee & A. P. J. Rioux (Eds.), *The African philosophy reader* (pp. 275–291). London: Routledge.

Eholié, R. (2007). Ivorian women: Education and integration in the economic development of Côte d'Ivoire. In N. T. Assié-Lumumba (Ed.), *Women and higher education in Africa: Reconceptualizing gender-based human capabilities and upgrading human rights to knowledge* (pp. 233–275). Abidjan: CEPARRED.

Goduka, I. N. (2000). African/indigenous philosophies: Legitimizing spiritually centred wisdoms within the academy. In P. Higgs, N. C. G. Vakalisa, T. V. Mda, & N. T. Assie-Lumumba (Eds.), *African voices in education.* Kenwyn/Johannesburg: Juta/[Distributed by] Thorold's Africana Books.

Hama, B. (1968). *Essai d'Analyse de l'Éducation Africaine.* Paris: Présence Africaine.

Higgs, P. (2002). Nation building and the role of the university: A critical reflection. *Southern Africa Journal of Higher Education, 16,* 2.

Kaunda, K. D. (1968). *Humanism in Zambia and a guide to its implementation.* Lusaka: Zambia Information Service.

Ki-Zerbo, J. (Ed.). (1990). *Educate or perish.* Dakar-Abidjan: UNESCO–UNICEF.

Kunnie, J. (2000). Indigenous African philosophies and socioeducational transformation in 'post-apartheid' Azania. In P. Higgs, N. C. G. Vakalisa, T. V. Mda, & N. T. Assie-Lumumba (Eds.), *African voices in education* (pp. 158–178). Kenwyn/Johannesburg: Juta/[Distributed by] Thorold's Africana Books.

Letseka, M. (2000). African philosophy and educational discourse. In P. Higgs, N. C. G. Vakalisa, T. V. Mda, & N. T. Assie-Lumumba (Eds.), *African voices in education* (pp. 179–193). Kenwyn/Johannesburg: Juta/[Distributed by] Thorold's Africana Books.

Mazrui, A. A. (1992). Towards diagnosing and treating cultural dependency: The case of the African University. *International Journal of Educational Development, 12*(2), 95–111.

Mazrui, A. A. (2013). Cultural amnesia, cultural nostalgia and false memory: Africa's identity crisis revisited. In Assie-Lumumba, N. T., Mazrui, A. A., & Dembélé, M. (Guest Eds.), *The owl of minerva on a baobab tree, schooling, and African awakening: Half a century of post-colonial education for development in Sub-Saharan Africa, African and Asian Studies, 12*(1–2), 13–29.

Meena, R. (2007). Women's participation in higher levels of learning in Africa. In N. T. Assié-Lumumba (Ed.), *Women and higher education in Africa: Reconceptualizing gender-based human capabilities and upgrading human rights to knowledge* (pp. 75–108). Abidjan: CEPARRED.

Moumouni, A. (1968). *Education in Africa.* New York: F. A. Praeger.

Mudimbe, V. Y. (1988a). *Liberty in African and western thought.* Washington, DC: Institute for Independent Education.

Mudimbe, V. Y. (1988b). *The invention of Africa: Gnosis, philosophy, and the order of knowledge.* Bloomington: Indiana University Press.

Mwebaza, R. (n.d.). *The gender agenda in agenda 2063.* https://webcache.googleusercontent.com/search?q=cache:w37NSwOQ0uQJ:https://au.int/web/

sites/default/files/newsevents/workingdocuments/14606-wd-gender_
agenda_in_agenda_2063.pptx+&cd=1&hl=en&ct=clnk. Accessed 26 July 2017.
Nussbaum, M. (1999). *Sex and social justice*. New York: Oxford University Press.
Odora Hoppers, C. A. (2002). *Indigenous knowledge and the integration of knowl-
edge systems: Towards a philosophy of articulation*. Claremont: New Africa Books.
Oyěwùmí, O. (1997). *The invention of women: Making an African sense of western
gender discourses*. Minneapolis: University of Minnesota Press.
Paulme, D. (Ed.). (1971). *Women of tropical Africa*. Berkeley: University of
California Press.
Sen, A. (1999). *Development as freedom*. New York: Alfred A. Knofpf.
Subbarao, K., Raney, L., Dunbar, H., & Haworth, J. (1994). *Women in higher
education: Progress, constraints, and promising initiatives*. Washington, DC:
The World Bank.
Sweetman, D. (1984). *Women leaders in African history*. London: Heinemann.
Teffo, L. J. (2000). Africanist thinking: An invitation to authenticity. In P. Higgs,
N. C. G. Vakalisa, T. V. Mda, & N. T. Assie-Lumumba (Eds.), *African voices in
education* (pp. 103–117). Kenwyn/Johannesburg: Juta/[Distributed by]
Thorold's Africana Books).
UIS-UNESCO Institute of Statistics-UIS. (2017). http://uis.unesco.org/en/
topic/higher-education. Accessed 28 July 2017.
United Economic Nations Economic Commission for Africa-UN ECA and the
United Nations Educational Scientific and Cultural Organization –UNESCO.
(1961, May 15–25). *Conference of African states on the development of educa-
tion in Africa*. Addis Ababa. http://unesdoc.unesco.org/images/0007/
000774/077416e.pdf. Accessed 2 July 2017.
Waghid, Y. (2014). *African philosophy of education reconsidered: On being human*.
Abingdon/New York: Routledge.
Wiredu, K. (1998). The moral foundation of an African culture. In P. H. Coetzee
& A. P. J. Rioux (Eds.), *The African philosophy reader* (pp. 306–316). London:
Routledge.
Wright, H. K., & Abdi, A. A. (Eds.). (2012). *The dialectics of African education
and western discourses: Counter-hegemonic perspectives*. New York: P. Lang.

CHAPTER 6

Regaining the Education That Africa Lost

Pai Obanya

Africa lost its Education the very moment she lost her sovereignty through being colonised. The continent has made some progress in regaining the purely political dimension of its sovereignty, but regaining the cultural and socio-economic dimensions has remained an uphill task. Education would be an essential ingredient in tackling the daunting task involved. This chapter emphasises the point that Education has always been with us, whatever the form of organisation and the state of evolution of our societies. It then goes on to show the defining characteristics of Education in primary (traditional) African societies, ending up with suggestions for injecting key elements of African traditional Education into present-day educational development efforts on the continent. The chapter relies principally on the benefits of *hindsight* (drawing lessons from Africa's past experience) for clearer *insight* (a deeper understanding of present-day educational development dilemma of Africa) to provide a sound basis for viable *foresight* (projecting for a better future for Education in Africa).

P. Obanya (✉)
Institute of Education, University of Ibadan, Ibadan, Nigeria

© The Author(s) 2018
E. J. Takyi-Amoako, N. T. Assié-Lumumba (Eds.),
Re-Visioning Education in Africa,
https://doi.org/10.1007/978-3-319-70043-4_6

NATURE OF AFRICAN TRADITIONAL SOCIETIES

As Box 6.1 shows, African societies had evolved in different forms before the continent's shock contact with a wider world. The box distinguishes six main types of societies, each of which had its organised social structure, a model of governance and what can conveniently be called an economy. To a very large extent, geography was the major determinant of the dominant social structure and of the economy.

Box 6.1   African Traditional Societies

Six major types of societies developed in Africa before colonial rule in the nineteenth century. They were hunting and gathering societies, cattle-herding societies, forest dwellers, fishermen, grain-raising societies and city/urban societies.

The hunting and gathering societies were those whose livelihood was based on hunting wild game. Whenever game was scarce, they relied on roots, herbs and berries. Few of these societies still exist, and the Khoisan of the Kalahari Desert is an example.

Cattle-herding societies have developed around the herding and trading of beef cattle. They include the Fulani of the Sahel region of West Africa, the Masai of Eastern Africa and the Zulu of South Africa. They have a division of labour: men herd and hunt, while women garden and build houses. People of the tropical forest societies live in scattered villages. The villages were bound to one another in tightly knit, dependent groups. Together, they cleared the dense forests for cultivation, and in times of trouble, they assisted one another.

On the coasts and along the rivers are societies of fishermen whose life centred on fishing, usually with nets. They traded the fishes for their daily necessities. The high quality of these peoples' diet was a major factor in their producing large and dense populations. The granary societies developed on the open plateau, using the slash and burn technique to grow maize, millet, rice, sorghum and cassava. They had more settled lifestyles with the attendant order and stability, which guaranteed each family adequate land for farming.

© *1997 Compton's Interactive Encyclopaedia.*

These societies were never static. They evolved as they continuously adapted their structures to the demands of changing times. There is every reason to believe that social change occurred slowly, at a considerably slower rate than our current period that is witnessing the acceleration of history.

THE EDUCATION THAT AFRICA LOST

'In the beginning was Education', so say the early theorists of the discipline. This is because Education exists, and has always existed in human societies, irrespective of the level of complexity of organisation of each society.

Traditional African societies had their educational systems, and whatever the form that Education took, it met the requirements of social cohesiveness and regeneration of society. Above all, traditional African had a lot in common with Education everywhere else, in that it had a philosophical underpinning, a socio-cultural foundation, a psychological intent, an organisational setup and societally determined outcomes.

Philosophical Underpinnings

The philosophical underpinnings of African traditional forms of Education are directly linked with the community's worldview. First, there is the belief in a supreme being, as well as in an afterlife. Thus, the earth is considered a mere marketplace while the true home is heaven. Second, the ultimate goal of our stay on earth is the good life, and failure to lead the good life is punishable by our forebears, to who we all return at death. Related to this is the belief that Nature (the Earth) has to be respected, and the Earth shall swallow up anyone who fails to respect Nature. Life and death are inseparable: the two constitute a continuum. Therefore, children are brought into the world to lead the good life and at old age return to their ancestors clean. Traditional educational systems, for this reason, place a priority on preparing children for the good life: morality, adherence to societal norms, group solidarity, and so on.

Culture as Cornerstone

Each generation makes it a bounding duty to transmit its cultural heritage to the next one. This inter-generational transmission of cultural heritage is in fact the primary meaning of Education. In traditional African societies, culture was the cornerstone of education, and like in all other societies, the educated person was also the cultured person.

All-Inclusive Lifelong Learning

The educational system is mapped out to fall in line with the development stages of life. Thus, children receive primary socialisation, adolescents consolidate this and add on life skills, while adults consolidate these two and add on organisational and social skills. In doing this, special needs are taken care of, as communal life did not allow for exclusion.

Even the gender perspective was not neglected. Girls and women received education: a common core socialisation in the early years of life, and gender-role-appropriate life skills in adolescence and adulthood (Table 6.1).

Articulation Among Diverse Routes to Learning

To say that education in African traditional societies is largely informal amounts to telling only a part of the story, telling the whole story requires that we emphasise the fact that formal, non-formal and informal approaches

Table 6.1   Organisational setup for traditional African education

Phase of life	Educational goal	Place of education	Agencies of education
Childhood	Primary socialisation	The home The extended family The community	Parents All older relations Elders in the neighbourhood The age grade Community-based organisations
Adolescence	Life skills acquisition	THE COMMUNITY (all places of work, recreation, religious observance, etc.) The initiation ground	Parents Community elders The age grades The guilds Secret societies Games and sports clubs
Adulthood	Social and organisational skills development	The community	Community rulers and elders Community special service groups Special interest groupings The guilds

to education are not dichotomous entities. The three approaches are most of the time inseparable, as there is informal (or incidental) in the process of formal learning. So much formal learning also comes into non-formal learning.

Emphasis of Life Skills

The society sets the goals, its normal and organisational patterns determine the mode and its expectations of a cultured person are the yardstick for the outcomes of education. In principle, this is (or should be) the case in all human societies. Thus, Africa's philosophical worldview and cultural heritage expect the following traits in the educated (or cultured) person.

- Spirituality (and leading the good life in order to be accepted in the life hereafter),
- Full integration into the community, by imbibing its cultural norms.
- Acquisition of the life skills necessary for earning a living and contributing to societal life
- Social and organisational skills, for interpersonal relations

High Regard for the Educator

The third column of Table 6.1 shows that at every phase of life someone (some group) is learning and someone (or some group) is guiding the learning process (i.e. TEACHING).

There are three very important points about persons who guided learning in traditional African settings: they were knowledgeable; they were skilled; and they enjoyed social recognition. The 'curriculum' was the cumulative social and technical knowledge and resources of society, and those who taught the 'curriculum' (as parents, community leaders, elders, leaders of various organised groups in society) lived that 'curriculum'. Such teachers actually lived the culture that was the cornerstone of the 'curriculum'. Therefore, they were usually deeply versed in what they transmitted to the next generation (in the case of childhood and adolescents) as well as in life skills they transmitted to youth and adults.

Teachers in traditional African societies were generally older than those to whom they transmitted knowledge. Since age carried respect, persons playing the teaching role enjoyed automatic respect. In addition, skills of a certain specialised nature (music composition, playing of musical instruments, the practice of traditional medicine, hunting, animal husbandry, etc.) have strong magical beliefs around them. The mastery of such magic also conferred respectability on the practitioners of various arts, who also had to teach these to children, adolescents and youth.

Socially Accepted Pedagogy

Traditional education also had its un-codified but socially accepted pedagogy. This is intimately linked with oral (pre-literate) culture and socially accepted personal interaction modes. Broadly speaking, the pedagogy of African traditional education consisted of the following seven elements:

1. *Oral communication*: traditional story telling by grandparents around the fire place, public performance by the Griot, and so on.
2. *Instructing*: assigning tasks along with the socially accepted rules for executing such tasks (using oral communication)
3. *Demonstrating*: physically showing the step-by-step process of producing a product (as in artisanal work) of getting things done (as in sowing and harvesting, in food processing and cooking, etc.)—a process that encourages learning to do by actually doing
4. *Encouraging and admonishing*: reinforcement of socially approved behaviour or actions; reprimand for whatever is considered socially unacceptable
5. *Repetition*: saying, illustrating, demonstrating, over and over again (over a period of time) until rules, skills, processes are mastered
6. *Team teaching* and collaborative learning: adults collaborating to transfer skills to groups of children; older children teaming up to take care of the socialisation of younger children
7. *Internship and apprenticeship*: exposure (often for prolonged periods) to skilled and knowledgeable practitioners (craftwork, traditional medicine, music and dance, etc.) to allow for mastery of the technical and social aspects of a trade.

Mastering these unwritten but widely applied pedagogical principles was an essential aspect of 'growing up' in African traditional societies. It is therefore virtually automatic for anyone who found themselves in teaching relationships with others to apply them as and when appropriate.

CONTEMPORARY DILEMMA OF EDUCATION IN AFRICA

This presentation recognises the incontrovertible fact that the world has changed and that Africa must be carried along with the change. We are therefore not advocating that Africans should be educated to remain itin-erant food gatherers and club-wielding hunters of wild animals. We are not advocating that Africans should be indoctrinated to opt out of modern science and technology and the knowledge economy. Our stand is that the transformation of Africa should not lose sight of the deep roots of Education: its being seriously anchored on the people's culture, so that we do not make the people extinct by destroying their culture.

What Africa lost with colonisation was that which it shared with every other society in the world—an Education that keeps you psychologically in your socio-cultural frame. With colonialisation, Education became equated with mere schooling. In traditional societies, Education for All was taken for granted; in a colonial setting, Schooling for All became a problem. The result is that Africa entered the twenty-first century with a huge education deficit, the hard facts of which are captured in Table 6.2.

Failure of Meaningful Access

The figures are for the year 2014, and they show sub-Saharan Africa lagging behind world average and even developing countries' attainments on primary and secondary school net enrolment, as well as on youth and adult literacy rates. These figures do not however tell the whole story, as

Table 6.2   Africa's attainment on selected basic education indices in comparable terms

Index	World	Developed countries	Developing countries	Sub-Saharan Africa
Primary net enrolment	91	90	90	80
Secondary net enrolment	84	96	82	66
Youth literacy	91		89	71
Adult literacy	85		82	60
Females in youth literate population (%)	59		59	65
Females in adult literate population (%)	63		61	61

Source: UNESCO Global Education Monitoring Report: 2016

the source had a great deal of missing data. The real issue in Africa's educational development has remain *the failure of meaningful access.*

The global post-2015 Education Agenda, as proclaimed in the May 2015 Incheon Declaration, envisages 'inclusive and equitable quality education and lifelong learning for all'. That is the true import of EFA, as intended (though not achieved) by the Jomtien (1990) and Dakar (2000) declarations. Meaningful access occurs when the emphasis rises beyond mere physical access. It is a situation in which

- enrolment covers virtually the entire catchment population
- virtually every child who enrols in school participates
- virtually all who participate progress
- virtually all those who progress successfully complete the cycle
- virtually all those who complete the cycle transit to the next cycle

The phenomenon is one in which there is hardly any cohort depreciation. It is a hallmark of education systems that promote equitable access, along with quality and efficiency within an over-arching context of a responsive policy environment. Figure 6.1 is a further illustration of the phenomenon.

Gross depreciation ratio is the difference between the cohort population (the ideal in Fig. 6.2) and the proportion of the cohort transiting into the next cycle, while the net cohort depreciation is the difference between

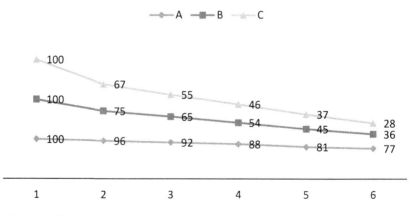

Fig. 6.1   Three degrees of meaningful access

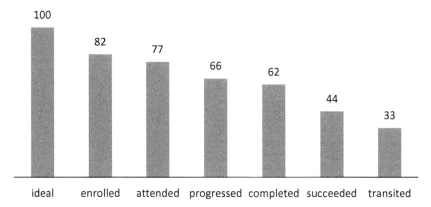

Fig. 6.2 Cohort depreciation—17 Nigerian states: 2009/2010. Source: UNICEF-Nigeria

those transiting and those initially enroled (out of the cohort total population). Table 6.3 makes this distinction clearer. All the three cases are illustrative of non-meaningful access, though to varying degrees, and cases B and C show some similarity with the general situation in African countries' situation.

Figure 6.2 (combined data from 17 states in Nigeria) shows a gross cohort depreciation rate of 67 and a net depreciation of 49, thus demonstrating clearly that there is no meaningful access. This point (for which Nigeria is simply an illustrative example) will be fully supported as we later discuss factors responsible for non-meaningful access.

A RIGHT-ABOUT TURN IN EIGHT DIRECTIONS

The big question then is, *how best can borrowing intelligently from the education that Africa has lost to be harnessed to bring about an education scenario that ensures that Africa has gained, thus moving from a situation of an education loser situation to an education win-win situation?* A viable way forward would be to borrow a leaf from the distant past (pre-colonial era) to right the wrongs of the immediate past (colonial and post-colonial years) in matters of Education. This would require a right-about turn in eight directions, as summarised in Table 6.4.

The eight points cover a wide range from our conception of Education (what we think education should do), to our conceptualisation of the

Table 6.3   Three illustrative examples of non-meaningful access

Cases	A=Ideal	B=Enrol	C=Tansit	Gross dep (A minus C)	Net dep (B minus C)
A	100	96	77	23	19
B	100	75	36	64	39
C	100	67	28	72	39

Table 6.4   The way to go in eight points

Prevailing notions and practices	Desirable new directions
1. Education equals schooling	Education with a capital E Synergy among the four routes to Education
2. Education for THEM	Education for ALL, with ALL and by ALL
3. Restricted access with high cohort mortality	All our children learning
4. Marketable skills	Integrated 3-H education
5. Acculturation-enculturation	Inculturation as the foundation
6. Teaching without teachers	Teaching with genuine teachers
7. Examinations mistaken for Education	System assessment for system development
8. Education as dead end	Education for employability and productive work

concept (how to go about educating), and our picture of the educated person. The persistent wrongs that would need to be put right are listed on the left-hand side of the table, while the *turnaround goals* are on the right-hand side. The rest of the discussion discusses each item on the table in some detail.

Education Is Not Simply Schooling

Education in Ancient Africa was a whole-society undertaking, even though people could meet in specially designated places (in an open field, on the farm, the field, under a tree, in a village square, in a family compound, etc.) to learn and practise specific skills. With the advent of schooling, Africans have redefined education to mean simply a formal institutional affair.

Most post-colonial education reforms have simply restructured the school system, while policy documents simply accord back room space to out-of-school education. If Education for All must become a reality, instead of a mere slogan in Africa, our compass should move from *education equals schooling* to *Education with a capital E*, as illustrated in Fig. 6.3. The diagram shows four major routes to Education—incidental, informal, non-formal and formal. It also shows that in-school and out-of-school education do co-exist. More importantly, they are both a lifelong undertakings, as they do cover all phases of life. It would therefore be helpful for Africa to reconceptualise Education along the Capital E model and create learning opportunities for both school-age and outside the school-age population. School-based education can also borrow from the cultural tenets of out-of-school education to enrich the process of teaching and learning (learning by doing, harnessing environmental resources for teaching and learning, etc.).

In the same vein, non-formal education programmes in Africa should rise above initial youth and adult literacy programmes (that often lead to a relapse into illiteracy) and ad hoc skills acquisition activities for adults (that are often not sustained). We should instead adopt a more holistic view of

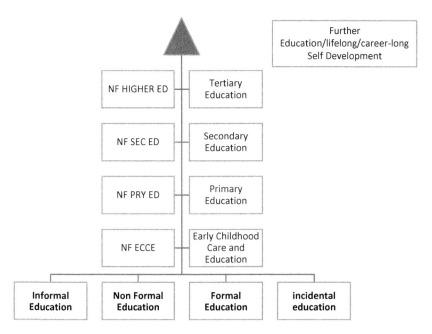

Fig. 6.3   Education with a capital E

out-of-school (mass) education that caters for large populations of people and responding to a variety of learning needs in a lifelong perspective, as detailed in Table 6.5.

There are two important points about the model presented in Table 6.5. First, it covers all phases of life and if vigorously pursued should contribute to ensuring that no one is left behind or swept aside. Second, the ideas in the Purpose and Emphasis columns of the table, if ploughed into contemporary education systems in Africa, would contribute to addressing the skills gap challenge that employers often complain about. This is because of the importance attached in the model to *SOFT SKILLS*, the real skills that make a difference in today's knowledge economy.

Education for ALL, with ALL and by ALL

Table 6.6 shows a broad spectrum of education sector stakeholders. Category one represents the most deprived groups in African society, who are the real *need bearers* since they live in circumstances of huge human development deficits. Classes four and five are equally important, but not only are they fewer in society, they are also living in conditions of relative privilege. Class two represents organised groups in grassroots civil society, while class three represents the day-to-day implementers of education policies. In Africa's post-independence education reform efforts, classes one and two have remained relatively unseen and unheard, category three has had token representation, mainly at the 'sensitisation' stages, while classes four and five have played a dominant role in the policy-making process.

This policy imposition methodology has often resulted in education policies being dead on arrival. A major reason for this is the neglect of the need bearer in the policy process. Table 6.7 shows three different approaches to what is commonly referred to as educational reform in Africa. Imposition is seen in most cases.

Government decides and calls on the system mangers to implement and sensitise the people to buy in. As the table shows, the result is often antagonism (quiet grumbling or loud protests) on the part the beneficiaries and mishandling by the mangers.

With the consultation approach, the initiators of reform would *occasionally* hold working sessions with selected groups of stakeholders and would sometimes accept new ideas, but every attempt is made to keep persons and groups that can upset the establishment cart at bay. The result

Table 6.5 Forms and levels of out-of-school education

Level	Target audience	Purpose	Emphasis
Basic education	ALL persons (children, adolescents, youth and adults) without basic education	Laying the foundation for lifelong learning	Literacy and numeracy fundamentals Fundamentals of life skills Lifelong learning skills
Secondary education	ALL adolescents, youth and adults who have acquired the basics of literacy, numeracy, life skills and are internalising learning and self-development skills	Consolidating the gains of basic education Broadening the scope of experience Preparation for the world of work Preparation for a life of continuing learning	Literacy and numeracy Exploration of the physical and socio-cultural life skills Practical/vocational skills Entrepreneurial skills Communication skills
Tertiary education	ALL youth and adults who have been through formal or non-formal secondary education	Consolidation of skills acquired at the secondary level Preparation for life Sustained interest in learning	Consolidation of literacy and numeracy Analytical and logical reasoning skills Interpersonal skills Knowledge/information search skills Communication skills Leadership skills Entrepreneurial skills Exploration of the physical and cultural/social world
Further education	ALL persons who have been through tertiary education— formal or non-formal	Sustained interest in learning Enhanced ability to cope with rapid social change Re-skilling and re-tooling	Knowledge/information search skills Self-management skills Communication skills Entrepreneurial skills

Table 6.6   The broad spectrum of stakeholders in education

Class one	Class two	Class three	Class four	Class five
Rural dwellers	Women groups	Practising	Education	Government
The urban poor	Youth	teachers	sector	agencies
Traditional	organisations	Teacher	technocrats	Legislature
institutions	Organised labour	associations	Academics	Education
Grassroots-based	Small-scale	Parent-teacher	Organised	ministry
organisations	economic	associations	private sector	Education
	operators	Political parties	Professional	Sector
	Local government	Religious	bodies	Parastatals
	agencies	bodies		Other
				government
				ministries

Table 6.7   Characteristics and results of different approaches to educational reform

Approach	Characteristics	Results
Imposition	Reform already decided; no questions; no going back; government knows what is good for the stakeholder	Antagonism
Information	Reform packaged; key elements revealed to *peripheral stakeholders* before sensitising the real stakeholders	Apathy
Consultation	A series of discussion sessions with *selected stakeholder groups* as you go along	Lethargy
Involvement	Side-side work with *veritable stakeholders* all through the process	Enthusiasm

has always been that the real stakeholders keep asking 'what is this really about?' and worse still; they never show any enthusiasm for the reform initiatives.

Whenever the involvement methodology is used, stakeholders and their ideas are accommodated right from the inception and conceptualisation phases of reform. They become genuinely implicated in it as the process goes on. They end up internalising the underlying philosophy of the reform initiative. They tend to speak more of 'our reform' than of 'government's reform'. Such a situation is often more likely to breed enthusiasm for reform because the process has involved groups that are likely to be affected by the process.

CONSULTATION is therefore the way to go, involving a modern-day adaptation of old Africa's village square gatherings in which every social group and age grade was fully involved in major decision-making.

The prevalent elitist approach to education policy development has created a mentality of *EDUCATION FOR THEM* (the ordinary people) *BUT NOT FOR US* (the select group that cooked up the education programme). As Table 6.5 shows, consultation engages all segments of the population all through the process. Every group consequently internalises the spirit behind the programme, takes ownership and radiates the acceptance that makes programme implementation to go on smoothly. The bottom line is that consultation most likely creates a phenomenon of *EDUCATION FOR ALL, BY ALL AND WITH ALL.*

All Our Children Learning

Figure 6.2 has shown a cohort depletion of over 50% in the basic education cycle in Nigeria (not an isolated case in sub-Saharan Africa). Pre-colonial education did not know exclusion. All persons passed through the socialisation process appropriate to their age and socio-geographical circumstances and carried on the social responsibilities linked with their age, gender and place in society. Exclusion has however become a fact that we have had to live with in colonial and post-colonial education.

Table 6.8 shows six zones of exclusion from basic education. These range from inability to gain access to basic education to inability to transit into post-primary education after scaling all hurdles. For every one of the 'zones', there are demand-side and supply-side bottlenecks. The former relates to personal and environmental factors, while the latter is concerned with institutional obstacles. These are the issues to be addressed in turning Education around in African countries. First, poverty and poor living conditions would have to be tackled. Then, the real people must be the key actors in development-related decision-making. Third, education opportunities must go beyond the provision of schools and classrooms to the deployment of quality inputs (funding, responsive curricula, quality teachers for quality learning and learner psycho-social support). A combination of these steps would go a long way in creating a situation in which children go to school (in which youth and adults acquire life skills outside the formal school) and be assist to stay on and learn.

Integrated 3-H Education

The 3-H refers to the Head, the Heart and the Hands. Traditional African societies emphasised this whole person (overall personality development) view of education, but colonial and post-colonial education in Africa has

Table 6.8 Bottlenecks causing exclusion from basic education

Zones of exclusion	Demand-side bottlenecks	Supply-side bottlenecks
0. Unable to access primary education	Resistance to/wrong conception of 'western' education Poverty Opportunity cost syndrome	Poor school mapping; impossible physical distance between home and school Deceptive politics; not backing government promises with concrete action
1. Enroled in primary, failed to complete cycle	Poverty Poor performance Loss of interest and motivation	Hidden financial costs of 'free' education Poor/in-adaptive teaching Non-responsive curricula
2. Complete primary, unable to transit to junior secondary	Poverty Poor performance Loss of interest and motivation	Hidden financial costs Poor teaching/teacher shortage Strict selection examinations Limited absorptive capacity at the junior secondary level
3. Enrol in junior secondary, unable to complete the cycle	Poverty Learning getting increasingly difficult Attraction of moneymaking possibilities out of school	Hidden financial costs Poor teaching/teacher shortage/poor quality of teaching-learning materials Poor level of learner psycho-social support Non-responsive curricula
4. Complete junior secondary, unable to transit to senior secondary	Poverty Learning getting increasingly difficult Perceived irrelevance of schooling	Hidden financial costs Poor learning environment in schools Poor learner psycho-social support Low absorptive capacity at senior secondary level Strict selection examinations
5. Transit into senior secondary, unable to complete that cycle	Poverty Learning getting increasingly difficult Perceived irrelevance of schooling Early marriage customs (in case of girls)	Hidden financial costs Poor learning environment in schools Poor learner psycho-social support Low absorptive capacity at senior secondary level Lack of job opportunities for persons with secondary education
6. Complete senior secondary but without the requisite certification	Declining interest and motivation School and learning tasks becoming more and more difficult	Hidden financial costs Poor learning environment in schools Poor learner psycho-social support

accorded heavyweight attention to the Head, with consequent neglect of the Heart and the Head. It is no wonder then that more and more Africans are questioning the relevance of education, with the economic sector deploring the unemployability (i.e. socio-economic usefulness) of the products of the school system.

Today's knowledge economy happily has shifted emphasis solely from how much you know to how well you have learned (and continue to learn) how to learn. Learning through a process of Education is expected to transform lives. 'Knowing book' is not a sufficient condition for transforming lives. The quality of what you know is the deciding factor, and this reflected in the extent to which learning has effected positive personality changes (re-shaped the character) of the learner, as well as the extent to which the learner is able to do things (thinking and acting and performing) differently. It is this all-round development view of Education (as preached by modern thinkers and as intimately wound into traditional systems) that today's education policies in Africa should return to (if the educated African is ever to be of enhanced value to society).

Figure 6.4 is an attempt to show that the three dimensions of what you know (knowledge or hard skills), what you are (character or soft skills) and what you can do (competences or innovation-creativity skills) are not discrete (isolated) elements to be treated in an either/or manner. They form an integrated whole that should guide our thinking and doing Education in the Africa region. That has the double advantage of bringing us back to the basics (a major guiding principle of traditional education) and also helping us to push forward (as the tripartite-integrated 3-H idea is in sync with modern ideas on education and in keeping with the demands of today's knowledge economy).

Inculturation-Acculturation-Enculturation

These are three terms that refer to different approaches to socialisation, which is the primary function of Education. *Inculturation* is the process of learning one's own culture, while *Acculturation* is the process of taking on another group's culture, and *Enculturation* distinctively refers to exchanges of cultural features with foreign cultures. Traditional Africa educated its populace through Inculturation, colonial education operated mainly through Acculturation—teaching in a foreign language, based on foreign content and learning materials. While there has been a good deal of 'Africanisation' of curricula in the post-independence era, the language of instruction is still foreign (often called a second language), while African culture has not been

Fig. 6.4 A tripartite view of the transformational potentials of learning

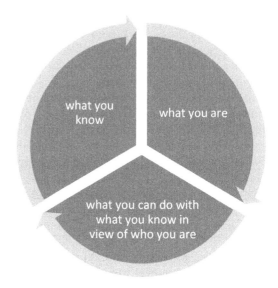

explicitly built into the curriculum. Thus, unlike the situation in other climes, the educated African is not synonymous with the cultured person.

Culture is dynamic everywhere in the world. We are living in a period of rapid change and in a world in which physical barriers are progressively being broken by the wonders of ICT and the consequent wider opening of the door to outside influences. Thus, we expected people to be world citizens, able to share knowledge and information with persons in faraway places with the seat of light. In such a world, Acculturation and Enculturation become desirable. However, the wider horizons that should come from these must be built on a solid foundation of 'know thyself first'. The prevailing situation is one in which the educated African is not well-entrenched in African culture and at the same time unable to fully acquire the eternal cultures. Regaining the education that Africa lost would require concerted efforts to address this *culture vacuum challenge*.

Turnaround education policies would be needed, with the following culture-related provisions:

- A commitment to the development of indigenous languages for use in Education.
- The development of national authorship, and publishing of educational materials

- Commitment to the development of other cultural industries that can impact on Education (film, the media, traditional medicine, music/dance, etc.)
- Mobilisation of other societal resources (cultural events and practices, crafts, farms, workplaces) for enriching teaching and learning.
- Development of school architecture and classroom environments that conform with local climate and culture
- School calendars that blend neatly with local work and leisure programming
- Building of strong school-community ties

Africa's contemporary education dilemma (the factors that should be addressed to ameliorate the failure of meaningful access) can also be addressed through the instrumentality of culture, as shown in Table 6.9.

Table 6.9   Culture-routed solutions to Africa's major education sector challenges

Challenge area	Culture-routed solutions
ACCESS: Schools physically, socially, psychologically, economically inaccessible to children	Strong community involvement, relying on culturally accepted structures Use of traditional structures (homesteads, playgrounds, etc.) for schooling
GENDER EQUITY: Poor participation of GIRLS (their entry into school, retention, progression, completion)	Adapting schooling to local realities Using culturally acceptable mobilisation strategies Attending to the special needs of girls
RELEVANCE: Aligning educational processes to the perceived needs of communities and learners	Use of local culture/local activities as the substance of Education Use of methods, materials and content appropriate to the environment Community language for laying the foundation for learning
QUALITY: The extent to which Education makes a permanent positive impact on the learner	Learning based on activities and socially acceptable skills and competences (instead of rote learning) Use of the learners' language for deep understanding
EFFICIENCY: Elimination of wastage through a judicious mix and use of resources	Community involvement in school management Active and culturally imbued teaching-learning activities that make schooling interesting Activities that enhance relevance and quality (as already outlined)

Going down from the realm of policy to that of institutional-level activities, it should be possible to bring culture into schools and classrooms, as a subject to be promoted consciously on its own, as well as a set of activities permeating all school activities, as outlined in Table 6.10.

Teaching with Genuine Teachers

In pre-colonial times, and in traditional African societies, teachers were usually respected persons in society—elders, persons with special skills (hunting, art work, traditional medicine, etc.). Teachers also enjoyed social respect in early decades of colonisation, as they were relatively well educated and also practised the new ways of life of the period, thus serving as role models to children and youth. Islamised societies in Africa use the learned man (the Mallim) as teacher. Such a person was usually well versed in Islamic theology and was regarded as authority figures by devotees (*the Talibés*).

By early independence times (the 1960s), there had been an expansion in sedentary education, and this had a toll on primary teacher training institutions that became less prestigious in the eyes of the people. At the same time came increased opportunities for white-collar jobs in the expanding public sector as well as in the emergent private enterprises, and working in offices was a good deal more attractive than sweating it out in

Table 6.10   Suggested place of culture in the curriculum

Level of education	Culture education strategy	Main features
Primary and pre-primary	Implicit in the entire process	The local environment and local culture (including community language) should pervade this cycle of Education
Junior secondary	Integrated into ALL disciplines	A step ahead of the implicit curriculum organisation strategy. Culture is specifically mentioned, and there is reference to it in all forms, but it is not treated as an examination subject
Senior secondary	Distinct discipline	Raising a conscious awareness of culture, building upon work at lower levels of Education and making culture a compulsory, examination subject
Tertiary	Core discipline	More detailed, more analytical studies, some comparative studies of other cultures, culture-related practical/field project

the classroom. Post-independence educational reforms have not seriously address these issues. The result today is that we are *teaching without teachers*.

This is so primarily because teaching has long lost its social recognition in Africa (see Box 6.2). Teacher education programmes no longer attract the brightest and the best motivated. Young persons go into teaching only as a temporary, stopgap measure. Serving teachers are ill-motivated as career-long teacher development programmes are almost non-functional (even where they exist on paper (see Table 6.9)). Schools (the teacher's workplace) are in a sorry state and they hardly exert any educative influence on children.

The following true life story is very illustrative of societal perceptions of teachers and teaching. The effect of such perceptions on Education can best be imagined than described. The occasion is one in which a family has gone with its son (who happened to be a teacher) to the prospective in-law family to ask for the hands of their daughter in marriage. A most revealing interaction takes place in the process, as presented in Box 6.2.

The conversation shows the future bridegroom talking about what he does for a living (teaching) timidly. This portrays the lack of self-esteem highlighted in the story of Akka and Akko below. We should also notice the future father-in-law's conditions for giving out his daughter in marriage. The young man's family lineage is an advantage, but he must 'look for a job', implying that teaching is seen as something below the level of a job.

Box 6.2   Get Out of Teaching and Look for a Job

- *Suitor's family spokesman*: A-salama-leikun, my people. May I introduce my young man, Ahmadu Tijani. Stand and be seen, Tijani
- *Tijani* (standing): A-salama-leikun, my elders
- *Spokesman*: As you are well aware, we have come to ask for the hands of your daughter, Amina, in marriage
- *Amina's father*: La-kuli-lai! Tijani has grown so big! Looks every inch like his grandfather. What does he do for a living?
- *Tijani* (timidly): I teach at Government Secondary School, Azare.
- *Amina's father*: Huuum! Well, you are from a good family. I'll give you my daughter, but....*LISTEN CAREFULLY Promise me that you'll look for a job!*

The African teacher's plight in the form of lack of career-long development opportunities is illustrated in the following life story involving twin brothers, both of whom graduated from university with identical qualifications and at the same time. One of them went straight into marketing as salesman, while the other continued his formal education to post-graduate level to qualify as a professional teacher.

A look down the six rows of Table 6.11 reveals the following:

- The teacher continues with formal tertiary education with formal qualifications
- The salesman goes through a variety of job performance-related programmes on a continuous basis.
- Ten years after graduating from university, both brothers have made progress in their chosen careers

Then comes the major difference in the lives of the twin brothers. The teacher is meek, humble, timid, has had very limited exposure to new ideas, and has a limited intellectual horizon. The salesman, on the other hand, has had wide exposure to new ideas, has accumulated a variety of skills, and he is cosmopolitan. The end product is that the teacher has low self-esteem, while with the salesman high self-esteem is the case. As a corollary, society would likely have more respect for the brother who has been marketing than the one who has been teaching.

To ensure that teaching is done by genuine teachers, Africa would have to undertake a two-pronged task, as follows:

1. a value-reorientation programme that returns respect for service to community
2. bringing back the teacher to the school system

African traditional societies rewarded and recognised people for service to their immediate communities and persons so recognised served as role models to the younger generation. Traditional politics was for service to society, but this day and age politics is largely concerned with what you can squeeze out of society. Persons who are able to squeeze society and amass material wealth tend to be highly respected, while non-material wealth (morals, integrity, selfless service, learning, etc.) tend be generally undervalued. The undervaluing of the teaching profession in today's Africa is a product of values being turned upside down in wider society.

Table 6.11 The tale of Akka and Akko

Life path	Akka	Akko
1. Formal qualification at age 18	Senior secondary school certificate	Senior secondary school certificate
2. Choice of university course	Mathematics/physics	Mathematics/physics
3. Career choice on graduation	Teaching	Marketing
4. On-the-job further education opportunities	Post-graduate diploma in education (2nd year of career) Master's degree in education (6th year of career) Two-week integrated science workshop (7th year)	Basic marketing course (1st year) Annual marketing seminars (1st year onwards) Overseas attachment (2nd year) ICT applications in marketing (4th and 5th years) New product development seminar (6th year) Finance in marketing (7th year) Fellowship of the institute of marketing (8th year) Study tour of Asian emerging markets (10th year)
5. Position ten years after graduation	Secondary school principal	Executive director (client services)
6. Personality features ten years after graduation	Meek and humble Timid Limited exposure to new ideas Limited social and intellectual horizon Low self-esteem	Wide exposure to the world and to new ideas Accumulated skills in a variety of areas Cosmopolitan High self-esteem

That phenomenon is also responsible for high social acceptance of occupations that are perceived as capable of yielding instant material wealth. Value reorientation is therefore an undertaking that goes beyond the Education sector and would have to be undertaken by all for the benefit of all. The other task of bringing back the teacher to the African school may not succeed if it is not carried along with value reorientation.

Ensuring the return of the teacher to the African school would require teacher development programme that should produce

(a) the *EDUCATED* teacher
(b) the *HUMANE* teacher
(c) the *EFFECTIVE* teacher, and
(d) the *LEARNING* teacher

To produce *the educated teacher*, African teacher education programmes would need to move away from the 'subject and method' paradigm (master the discipline and learn how to pass it on to students) to one that assures that the teacher has the skills needed for functioning in today's knowledge society.

Figure 6.5 shows how the emerging trends in a knowledge-propelled world have meant additional requirements and qualifications for the teacher. These rely on a solid foundation of lifelong/life-wide learning

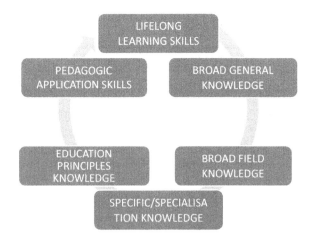

Fig. 6.5   The multi-layered intellectual skills set of today's teacher

skills on which other layers of knowledge are to be built: broad general education, broad-based subject area knowledge, in-depth knowledge of a specialised area of knowledge (with emphasis on ways of knowing), broad knowledge of the foundations and principles of Education and practical skills in effective teaching to foster effective learning.

To ensure that the system is served by *the humane teacher*, African teacher education programmes must recognise that intellectual knowledge and technical skills alone do not make a teacher. To be successful in empathising with learners, motivating them and bringing about the best in them and to enhance the teacher's social acceptance, additional skills of the 'soft' type are required. These are:

(a) Love of learning and knowledge—an important trait for persons in the front line of promoting learning, the knowledge profession
(b) Love of children—the work of every teacher centres on facilitating learner development; thus love of learning should be mainly for the interest of learners
(c) An eye (as well as an ear) for community signals—the ability to follow the evolution of society as a means to ensuring that school work derives from societal dictates as much as possible
(d) Grooming (appearance, clothing, speech, interpersonal relations, etc.)—a means by which the teacher teaches by personal example
(e) Gender sensitivity—with particular emphasis on ability to remove obstacles to the full participation of girls in schooling
(f) Acceptance of differences (racial, ethnic, gender, religious, political/ideological, etc.)—implying the avoidance of prejudice and stereotyping
(g) Team play, as school work is team activity among teachers, while helping the child to grow involves team work with parents and communities
(h) Professionalism—familiarity with education policy, curricula, examination requirements, commitment to continued professional development, maintenance of high standards, and so on.
(i) Role model for integrity, morality, work habits, and so on.
(j) Key emotional intelligence competences—self-control, patience, temperance, empathy, and so on.

The system should also place emphasis on having *the effective teacher*. Governments and most employers of teachers tend to place emphasis on the *TRAINED* teacher. Education statistics on teachers used to be limited to computing TPR (teacher-pupil ration), but there has since been a move towards QTPR (qualified teacher-pupil ratio). The rationale seems to be that all that a teacher needs to be a high-performing professional is for him or her to be qualified, according to official/national prescriptions. However, the reality is as follows:

- A qualified teacher is not necessarily a competent teacher
- A competent teacher is not necessarily an efficient teacher, and
- An efficient teacher is not necessarily an effective teacher.

No play on words is intended here, as there are clear differences among the four categories of teachers.

- A qualified teacher is one who possesses the minimum accepted qualifications to function as a teacher
- A competent teacher is one who has mastered the principles of teaching
- An efficient teacher is the one who can apply the principles of teaching to the letter, as learned
- An effective teacher possesses all the above attributes, but is able (most importantly) to teach creatively, in such a way that results in most—if not all—students learning.

In summary, the teacher should not simply be qualified, she or he must in addition be competent, efficient and, on top of it all, be efficient. A teacher is not a teacher until she or he attains the effectiveness level of competency.

People, institutions and systems grow through continuous learning. In a knowledge-driven world, schools need to be manned by *the learning teacher*, and African nations can produce such professionals through systematic, career-long professional, academic and professional development of teachers. A viable approach would be to inst;tionalise institutional-level mentoring for young teachers followed by the provision (system-wide) of programmes with appropriate, needs-based areas of emphasis at different points on the career ladder; teachers' learning needs would likely witness shifts at different points in their careers, as illustrated in Table 6.12.

Thus, teachers early in their career will concentrate more on professional (task skills) and academic improvement (updating knowledge). Middle and

Table 6.12   For each level of teacher, a different emphasis in focus of career-long education

Career Level	Professional improvement	Academic improvement	General Education	Management Related Skills
Interns	⬭	⬭		
New Entrants	⬭⬭⬭⬭⬭⬭⬭⬭			
Mid-Career Teachers	⬭ ⬭	⬭ ⬭	⬭ ⬭ ⬭	
Top Career Teachers				
Teachers in Supervisory/Management Positions	⬭ ⬭		⬭	⬭⬭⬭

top career teachers will have opportunities for general education with introduction to management-related programmes, while teachers in supervisory and management positions will have adequate exposure to management skills development (process and strategic thinking skills).

Education Is Not Examination

In traditional Africa, children and youth as the go through the Inculturation process are systematically followed, monitored, admonished, praised and counselled as and when necessary. They move from fewer complexes to more complex tasks and from easier to more difficult engagements according the stage of mastery of the easier and less complex undertakings. They take on responsibilities as determined for their age grade by the norms of society. Children advance in societal and family-assigned functions in whole age cohorts, with hardly any dropouts or cohort depletion (except because of death or incapacity).

Colonial education popularised formal examinations, mainly for selective purposes, as schooling was not universal. Post-colonial reforms have not been able to reverse the trend, and the result today is that the African child in school is over-examined, as illustrated in the following example of the Nigerian high school student.

- Competitive entrance examinations for movement from primary to secondary school
- Terminal examinations twice in an academic year
- Promotion examinations at the end of every academic year
- Basic Education Certificate Examinations (BECE) in Ghana
- JSSCE (Junior Secondary School Certificate Examination) in Nigeria
- Qualifying 'mock examination' instituted by schools and now institutionalised by a few Nigerian states
- WASSCE (West African Senior Secondary School Certificate Examinations) by WAEC
- NECO (National Examinations Council) senior secondary examinations
- London/Cambridge external IGCSE by candidates in some private schools
- The International Baccalaureate Examinations—also by students in private schools
- American SAT (Scholastic Aptitude Tests)—also largely a private school and privileged students affair
- All along, a series of continuous assessment procedures that has turned continuous assessment to continuous testing, if not continuous harassment of students.
- Two additional examinations for access to tertiary education

  - UTME (Unified Tertiary Matriculation Examinations), by the Joint Admissions and Matriculations Board (JAMB)
  - Post-UTME screening at the institutional level

This climate of stress and drudgery may produce good examination results, but it is doubtful whether they present desirable education results. The situation aptly justifies the observations by an American educator reported below (Box 6.3).

Examination failure in Africa seems to herald doomsday, and children and parents devote so much effort (both fair and foul) to ensure success. Examinations drive the curriculum instead of the curriculum driving the examination. Even in cases where continuous assessment has been introduced, its practice is often reduced to continuous testing, as the guidance-counselling and remediation aspects are often not practised by schools and teachers. On the release of the results of public examinations (usually at the end of the secondary cycle, people decry the phenomenon of mass failure. In considering candidates for positions, examination success (sanctioned by a form of certification) takes precedence over personal qualities, and employers keep complaining of the mis-fit nature of students certified by the examination system.

We just have to pay attention to addressing the problem at its roots, bearing in mind that examination failure cannot occur in a situation in which there has not been education failure and that in itself is predicated on system failure. We should therefore be looking at failure at three levels, as illustrated in Fig. 6.6.

Box 6.3   An Education System or an Examination System?

An American educator on a tour of Nigeria had visited schools in a poor state of disrepair. He had seen empty libraries and laboratories with broken down equipment. He had observed teachers at work and concluded that learning never occurred since what he saw was not his idea of teaching.

On his way back to his hotel, he noticed an imposing building not far from the old Yaba Roundabout. 'What's happening in the magnificent building over there'? He asked. 'That's the West African Examinations Council' replied his host.

'I see', continued the American visitor. 'You don't seem to have an education system. What you have is an examination system'.— *A popular anecdote from Prof. Babs Fafunwa, a foremost Nigerian educationist*

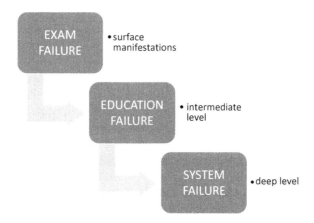

Fig. 6.6   The root of exam failure lies with the system

We therefore need a society that supports education (through involvement in its development and social recognition for the educator), a system of education that genuinely promotes learning and a rigorous promotion of quality teaching for quality learning (with in-built continuous assessment and learner counselling, along with continuous development opportunities for all categories of teachers). That would nip examination failure in the bud and ensure that diplomas awarded by the education system really testify to genuine educational attainment.

Education for Employability and Productive Work

In traditional Africa, the youth was educated (*INCULTURED*) to fit into the society in which virtually everyone was engaged in socio-economically productive activities. Today, school education seems to be leading to a dead end of unemployment, compounded by unemployability. While the former refers to the state of lack or insufficiency of job opportunities, the latter describes a condition in which young persons are not able to fit into existing job opportunities, and cannot create enduring opportunities on their own.

While unemployment is a worldwide problem, it is particularly acute in the shaky political and socio-economic conditions of most African countries, and the youthful population is particularly hard hit, as captured in Fig. 6.7. While the youth aged between 15 and 24 make up just 20% of Africa's total population, they constitute 40% of the total work force, and an amazing high proportion of the unemployed (60%)!

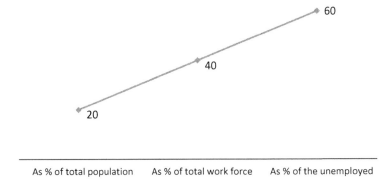

As % of total population   As % of total work force   As % of the unemployed

Fig. 6.7   African youth aged 15–24. Source: ILO

Unemployability has in fact become a hydra-headed monster, considering its multiple manifestations. As shown in Table 6.13, unemployables are a combination of persons who cannot be helped as well as persons who cannot themselves.

Therefore, unemployment would require political and economic management-type solution, while unemployability is a mentality/behaviour/attitudinal challenge which is best addressed through Education in the true sense of the term.

This in effect recalls a point earlier made in the course of this discussion: an education system that is not limited to *what you know* but goes to emphasise *who you are* and *what you can do* with what you know in view of what you are. Translated into what one should gain from education to avoid falling into the dead-end trap, this boils down to inculcating and developing the tripartite skills set outlined in Table 6.14 in all forms (non-formal, formal) and levels (basic, secondary, tertiary) of Education.

These are transversal skills to be promoted in all teaching-learning activities (across disciplines and across education levels and forms). They are not intended as additional content areas; they are that new blood that must be infused into school curricula to bring about the regenerative knowledge (the type that predisposes one to continuous learning), personality/character development, and an abiding thirst for creating and leveraging on opportunities. This goes beyond mere vocationalisation of education and ad hoc entrepreneurship development programmes.

Table 6.13   Who is the unemployable?

The ill-prepared	Persons that cannot find employment
The ill-informed	Cannot grow in and adapt readily to the workplace
The ill-equipped	Nor possess the drive, the initiative, the creative mindset
The ill-suited	and the resiliency needed for self-employment
The ill-adapted	
The ill-disposed	
The ill-conditioned	
The ill-motivated	
The unable	
The unwilling	

Table 6.14   A tripartite skills set for twenty-fist-century needs

Hard skills	Soft skills	Go-getting skills
Cognitive intelligence	**Emotional intelligence**	**Imaginative intelligence**
What you know	*Who you are*	*What you can do*
Self-expression skills	Character formation skills	Creative thinking skills
Logical reasoning skills	Intra-personal skills	Ideational fluency skills
ICT/computational skills	Interpersonal skills	Opportunity-seizing skills
Design/manipulative skills	Lifelong learning skills	Experiential learning skills
Conceptual skills	Perseverance skills	Idea-to-product (or ideas conversion) skills

CONCLUSION

We are not going back to the bygone past. Our emphasis is on a bright future full integration of Africa into a fast globalising world that is advocating education for an innovation economy. Drastic education reform is the key, but this should go beyond mere surface features to the fundamentals. Africa's philosophical values and cultural wealth are key elements of these fundamentals, and should therefore be embedded in future education reforms for a win-win position in a globalised world.

One major education dream of the current century is that curriculum need not be truncated. Narrow specialisation should give way to broad-based exposure to various ways of apprehending reality.

African traditional education had this holistic, integral personality development notion of education. This was lost when schooling replaced education and when educating for adaptation to life was replaced by education (narrowly defined as examination success) for paid employment.

Conventional formal education was restricted almost exclusively to the inculcation of the hard skills that emphasised cognitive intelligence. Modern-day concerns are more in the domain of soft skills that build up emotional intelligence and the go-getting skills for imaginative intelligence. The three 'intelligences' are expected to be combined to produce today's flexible, creative/innovative person capable of coping with change and uncertainty.

NOTE: *This chapter has drawn heavily on ideas canvassed by the author over the years, as in the following:*

Obanya, PAI 2006: "Historical Hints for Futuristic Studies of Education" *African Journal of Historical Sciences in Education*, 2/2 (November 2006), 5–13
Obanya, PAI 2008 "Developing Education with a Capital 'E' "Boucouvals and Aderinoye (Eds.) *Education for Millennium Development* (Essays in Honour of Professor Michael Omolewa): Spectrum Books Limited –Vol.II – 349.367
Obanya, PAI 2008: 'Reforming Educational Reforms' –Lawal, A R et al. (Eds.): *Education Reforms in Nigeria.*, Faculty of Education, University of Ilorin, 24–46
Obanya, PAI 2010: Bringing Back the Teacher to the African School, UNESCO/IICBA Series on Teacher Education, Number 1
Obanya, PAI 2011: Politics and the Dilemma of Access to Education: The Nigeria Story, CREATE-Pathway to Access No.56, Centre for International Education, the University of Sussex.
Obanya, PAI 2011: "Re-profiling Teachers and Teacher Educators", *The Moulder: Journal of School of Education, Alayande College of Education, Oyo-Nigeria*, 3/1, 1–18
Obanya, PAI 2012: Looming Threats to Teachers, Teaching and Education. *ICET 56th Yearbook on Teacher Education*, ICET/University of Cape Coast, Ghana, 15–32
Obanya, PAI 2012: Nipping Examination Failure in the Bud (17th Annual Endowment Lecture)-West African Examinations Council –WAEC-, 37 pp.
UNESCO. (1990, June 5–9). *World conference on education for all-declaration and framework for action.* JomtienThailand.
UNESCO. (2000, April 26–28). *World forum on education-Dakar declaration and framework for action.* Dakar-Senegal, Final report.

CHAPTER 7

Ubuntu as Humanistic Education: Challenges and Perspectives for Africa?

Mohamed Chérif Diarra

INTRODUCTION

The western model of education, a legacy of colonialism, brought in nearly a couple of centuries ago, has existed side by side with the African traditional form of education that underscores values and philosophies not fully integrated in the formal education curriculum of numerous African countries. One of such philosophy examined in this chapter is Ubuntu and Maaya/Hadama de ya (its sister philosophy in Mali).

When examining the re-visioning education in Arica thematic or Ubuntu as humanistic education discourse, the theme of this book, a number of key questions come to mind. To what extent do Ubuntu and Maaya/Hadama de ya inspire education for humanity? Do traditional African philosophies impact in any way the western model of education? What are the effects of this influence and how does it manifest itself in the education systems of African countries? Does this existence percolate in the formal education curriculum or is it present in other components and processes of the educational systems?

M. C. Diarra (✉)
Educational Research Network for West and Central Africa (ERNWACA), Dakar, RP, Senegal

© The Author(s) 2018
E. J. Takyi-Amoako, N. T. Assié-Lumumba (eds.),
Re-Visioning Education in Africa,
https://doi.org/10.1007/978-3-319-70043-4_7

119

The main purpose of this chapter is to examine the assumption that Ubuntu may inspire education, and that its educational tenets and principles may, in turn, influence the economic development and growth perspectives of African countries. So how and in what ways can this happen? Naturally, it goes without saying that they are pros and cons to claim or disclaim this assertion and to accept or reject it. In any case, in the current African education discourse, this debate, although in its infancy, is drawing a lot of attention as Ubuntu and other similar philosophies are gaining more and more recognition and impetus. As such, they are inspiring numerous scholars, researchers, and policy makers around the African continent.

This chapter, basically an essay, is based on a qualitative research design that focuses primarily on uncovering secondary data sources such as historical sources, research journal articles, personal experience, and traditional knowledge base to thoroughly examine the topic at hand by comparing and contrasting, analyzing, and synthesizing its major components. To achieve this objective, the chapter comprises two main parts: Part 1 is the introduction including a conceptual and theoretical framework and Part 2 that deals with Ubuntu/Maaya Hadama de ya as humanistic education.

Conceptual and Theoretical Framework

Interestingly, among the wide spectrum of educational philosophies in Africa, Ubuntu which originates in the South African Nguni Bantu ethnic group believes human beings are, by nature, self-developing creatures. It is a theory of humanness whose transformational virtues and power are transcendental. In fact, at this time, Ubuntu as a term overshadows other similar philosophical constructs that are illuminating the lives and daily practices of numerous communities and societies across Africa. These concepts and Ubuntu are similar in many respects, notably in their semantic constitution, conceptual meaning, social and cultural dimensions, as well as the vision and perspectives they project.

The gamut of philosophical concepts similar to Ubuntu in Africa is extremely wide. Its counterpart exists in many African countries. Understandably, the term goes by different labels in different countries and communities around Africa. For example, in the Shona community of Zimbabwe, it is known as "Unhu". In the Mandingo/Bambara society of Mali and Guinea, the Dioula communities of Côte d'Ivoire and Burkina

Faso, and other West African counties such as the Gambia, Sierra Leone, and Liberia, among others, it is called "Maaya" or "Hadama de ya". In Malawi, the same philosophy exists and is called "Munthu". Elsewhere in Africa, the philosophy exists, and like in South Africa, Mali, or Malawi, it constitutes the central pillar around which the communities' beliefs, ethic values, traditions, and customs have been strongly rooted and articulated for centuries.

In fact, an in-depth analysis of the semantic structure of the "Maaya" concept reveals a striking similarity with Ubuntu. Maaya also means humanness and is composed of the prefix "maa" meaning human and the suffix "ya" meaning ness, which combine to give "Maaya". As for "Hadama de ya" (the synonym of "Maaya"), it is composed of Hadama, "de" (child), and "ya" (ness) or "Adam ness". Hadama is a corruption of Adam the way the Mandingo/Bambara people call Adam who, according to biblical and koranic sources, is the father of humanity. He begets Cain and Abel. The terms constitute the solid bedrock on which the philosophical, social, cultural, moral, and educational principles of the Mandingo/Bambara society are profoundly rooted. "Maaya" or "Hadama de ya" further provides the guiding principles, the modus operandi, the educational philosophy, the social orientation, the moral direction, the interpersonal, as well as the inter- and intra-social relationships, rules, customs, and traditions that govern the day-to-day running of these communities at various stages of their social and historical development.

Interestingly, the definitions of Ubuntu in South Africa, Unhu in Zimbabwe, Maaya/Hadama de ya in Mali, and Munthu in Malawi are strikingly similar. This makes one think that they all belong to the same African macro culture, despite the fact that there are many different, not always compatible, definitions of what Ubuntu is in South Africa. There is though one core definition on which the different people of South African descent tend to agree according to which Ubuntu asserts that society, not a transcendent being, gives human beings their humanity, an assertion that underscores the fact that human beings are first and foremost a social product that is shaped by society. Numerous African scholars have extensively researched the Ubuntu concept and have come up with interesting findings. According to Onyebuchi Eze (2011), the core of Ubuntu can best be summarized as follows:

"A person is a person through other people" strikes an affirmation of one's humanity through recognition of an 'other' in his or her uniqueness or difference. It is a demand for a creative intersubjective formation in which the 'other' becomes a mirror (but only a mirror) for my subjectivity. This idealism suggests to us that humanity is not embedded in my person solely as an individual; my humanity is co-substantively bestowed upon the other and me. (pp. 190–191)

Viewed from this angle, the Ubuntu philosophy's basic tenet is the outright positioning of the individual in relation to another individual, a group of individuals, or the community at large. This dimension of the Ubuntu concept is further echoed by many other scholars and philosophers such as Mbiti (2010) in his now classic phrase "I am because we are and since we are therefore I am" (p. 11).

Further, Eze (2011) reveals that, within the contemporary history of South Africa, there are three ways in which Ubuntu has been understood by South Africans. Therefore, before examining the bearings/impact of Ubuntu and other similar African concepts such as "Maaya" on education, it would be interesting to review how the Ubuntu concept is currently understood by the various segments of the South African people and Africans as a whole.

Eze (2011) further posits that first is the assumption that Ubuntu is an anachronistic philosophy produced by African academia. Viewed from this perspective, Ubuntu functions as an alternative narrative to replace the colonial logic. Thus, it constitutes a major paradigm shift in that it shows and highlights all the attributes of a new national philosophy which is increasingly becoming popular and is profoundly being rooted in the post-independence psyche of South Africans.

Second, Ubuntu has the character of an ideology appropriated for political ends at a time when national reconciliation ensuing the dark period of apartheid is a robust political agenda of the post-independence era in South Africa, an era characterized by the difficult interracial dialogue conducted under the leadership of President Mandela.

The third and last way is a vision of history that considers Ubuntu within the historical context in which it emerged in the post-colonial South Africa that, after gaining independence in 1994, engaged in the process of building a non-discriminatory, multiracial, and multicultural rainbow nation based, in theory and ideally, on principles of equality, solidarity, brotherhood/sisterhood, forgiveness, inclusiveness, and tolerance.

These descriptions of, or understandings about, Ubuntu do not, per se, make any specific reference to its practical bearings on the post-apartheid educational system of South Africa which has been grappling with the challenge facing the resolution of the numerous internal contradictions and shortcomings it is confronted with. The post-apartheid educational system has been, at the same time, struggling to renew itself as an efficient, effective, and non-discriminatory organization geared toward meeting its objectives and fulfilling its cardinal mission in the national period aimed at building a robust human capital base to boost the economic development of South Africa.

Relationship Between Education/Ubuntu-Inspired and Socioeconomic Development

The critique from an Ubuntu perspective of the current situation of limited and even detrimental relationship between the received education system and socioeconomic advancement, the exploration of the possibilities of more productive linkage, and impact/implications of a re-visioned education in Africa on socioeconomic and political development are clearly the major issues to be addressed as stipulated in the call to contributors to the book. Furthermore, broader social transformation and the demonstration of how the Ubuntu philosophy in practice will inspire a new type of education are legitimate issues raised in the invitation to be addressed by the chapters' contributors. Furthermore, the call stipulates that the overall analysis will attempt an examination of a credible and sustainable vision of African education, which needs to be rooted in the emerging dynamics of socioeconomic reality and the relevance to the aspirations of the youth.

The assertion that there is a limited and even detrimental relationship between the received education system or simply education and socioeconomic advancements is obviously debatable. In fact, the relationship between education in general and economic growth or development has extensively been researched and documented by scholars/academics and practitioners around the world who tend to agree that this relationship is more between educational investment and economic growth than between the received system or curriculum and socioeconomic development. In reality, it is not yet convincingly established by scholars and recognized by all that Ubuntu positively impacts economic growth and development one way or the other.

Further, the in-depth analysis that ensues attempts to discuss from different perspectives (economic, social, and philosophical) the claim that the impact of education on African socioeconomic development is quite minimal or even detrimental to this process. To better understand the situation, there is need to define concepts such as received education system, economic growth or socioeconomic advancement, re-visioned education, and social transformation to be covered in the introductory chapter of the book as they relate to Ubuntu.

First, by analyzing the three ways identified by Eze (2011) in which South Africans understand Ubuntu (an anachronistic philosophy produced by African academics, then an ideology appropriated for political ends, and finally a vision of history), one may make a case that Ubuntu at this stage of infancy of its conceptual development has little impact on the socioeconomic development of the continent. In this respect, the values that characterize Ubuntu/Maaya need to be further scrutinized and seriously tested before they are integrated into a standardized curriculum that would contribute to strengthening education and ensure that its contribution to the socioeconomic development or economic growth of the African continent is recognized beyond reasonable doubt.

Thus, despite the prospect of a promising future, Ubuntu still remains an elusive concept far from being adopted continent wide and that still has a long way to go. It may evolve from an academic buzz to a strong educational precept to be reckoned with. Viewed from this perspective and in the long run, Ubuntu/Maaya values should gain recognition, be adopted and integrated into reformed national curricula across the continent as a nexus of the entire education system.

Second, along those lines, the promotion initiative of the Ubuntu concept, its conceptual fine-tuning, and its ultimate integration into the reformed curriculum would be, among others, central to the process of re-visioning the educational systems to make them more responsive to the needs of African societies and to the imperatives of the socioeconomic development or economic growth of Africa. This initiative would be articulated around elements whose contribution is central to improving educational quality such as redefining the relevance of African education as a whole, rethinking the pre-service and in-service teacher training to ensure that no unqualified or untrained person is allowed to teach, revisiting the curriculum to ensure that it meets the international standards and to provide the right quantity and quality of instructional materials for all the types and levels of schooling in Africa. Wilson (1990) defines the received curriculum as "those things that students actually take out of classrooms; those concepts and content that are truly learned and remembered" (p. 5).

Third, in consideration of all the above, there is ample evidence that education, in general, is profitable both to the individual and to society. Further evidence shows that economic growth or socioeconomic development does not occur in a vacuum. Something must propel it and the key question is what and how? So is it the contribution of financial capital or the impact of the quality and/or quantity of human capital or the combination of both? Are there other determining factors of production such as the physical capital (the land) instrumental in boosting economic growth or socioeconomic development or is it the combination of all the above? In this scenario, what is the magnitude of the contribution of education? Is this contribution more significant in other continents than in Africa or is the variable more context- or continent-specific?

In any case, the body of evidence and literature available shows that, in general, economic growth increases as primary school enrolment increases. UNESCO posits that a country needs to achieve a threshold of 75% of primary education gross enrolment ratio (GER) to create conditions conducive for economic takeoff. Furthermore, primary education completion rates are also said to be a key factor boosting economic growth especially in Africa. The higher the rates, the more likely the probability for a country to achieve rapidly economic growth. The quality of these different rates and ratios is good and robust indicators of the quality of education whose impact on economic growth is well proven according to Cohn and Geske (1990), Psacharopoulos (1984), and Miller (1967).

Fourth, it is further established that education fosters economic growth and that there is a positive relation between education and economic growth in general. In the specific context of Africa, would Ubuntu-inspired education impact on economic growth? So how would Ubuntu-inspired education affect economic growth and what would be the magnitude of the effect? Research evidence to back up this claim is scanty for the simple reason that countries are far from embracing the Ubuntu-inspired education. However what is proven by research is that all the levels and types of education (primary, secondary, technical, and vocational, non-formal but more specifically higher education) contribute one way or the other to socioeconomic development and economic growth. For example, regarding primary education a strong case is made for the impact of higher gross enrolment ratio (GER) and grade completion rates. Regarding non-formal education, the more literate the adult population becomes, the more significant its contribution to economic development. Finally, the impact of higher education as the key contributor to the development of human capital that imparts technical and managerial skills, competences, as well as research skills and others is even more compelling (Cohn and Geske 1990 and Diarra 1997).

Fifth, what is economic growth or socioeconomic development? According to Denison (1962) "economic growth refers to the increase in the national product measured in constant dollars" (p. 3). Alternatively, other scholars, namely, Cohn and Geske (1990), reveal that "economic growth" may be defined as the rate at which per capita national product in constant dollars grows over a given period of time (p. 135). Other definitions given by economists on the concept refer to other variables, namely, social indicators such as the rate of fertility of educated women and the level of productivity of educated farmers, among others.

Finally, more evidence underscores the contribution of education to economic growth. In Africa where the traditions still weigh a lot, education makes people abandon outdated traditions and embrace new ones. Traditions then appear to be an impediment to economic growth and can even be detrimental in numerous ways to the process. This assertion is strongly put in perspective by Miller (1967) in Cohn and Geske (1990) who cautions that "not just any kind of education will promote economic growth" (p. 143). He further points out that "Education is a source of economic growth only if it is anti-traditional to the extent that it liberates and stimulates as well as informs the individual and teaches him/her how and why to make demands upon himself/herself" (p. 143). He further posits that "accordingly, a proper educational strategy would manifest itself in four growth producing strategies" (p. 143) not directly or indirectly linked to any Ubuntu-inspired education. They are as follows:

The first is the development of an environment that is conducive to economic growth and favorable to economic progress. For example, this implies an expansion of literacy among the general populace necessary for improved communication, the ability to take care of the basic paperwork including "record keeping and deposit banking" (p. 281).

The second capacity emphasizes the development of "complimentary resources for factors which are relatively plentiful and substitutes for comparatively scarce factors" (p. 281). For example, the use of natural resources is augmented by education, because it provides managerial skills that can exploit resources more effectively.

The third capacity underscores the durability of educational investment. Miller (1967) further argues that education has "greater durability than most forms of non-human reproducible capital" (p. 281).

Finally, "education is an alternative to consumption" (p. 281). Any investment in education is, in the long run, productive and growth inducing.

It is also established that education sharpens cognitive, communication, technical, and relational skills that all boost economic growth. Training on the job is also a very important factor that boosts economic growth. Furthermore, other scholars/academics/practitioners such as Psacharopoulos (1984) identified a number of factors that boost economic growth one way or the other. His findings are complemented with those of other economists and scholars who extensively researched the topic. They are as follows:

- Education, according to Griliches (1969), Psacharopoulos (1973), Fallon and Fayard (1975), may be complementary to physical capital.
- Lau (1979) reveals that education has a direct impact on farmers' productivity in a number of countries including African. Two additional years of primary education can significantly boost farmers' productivity by 5%.
- Psacharopoulos (1984) posits that education enhances the adoption and efficient use of new inputs. He further reveals that "schooling acts as a catalyst in behavioral change conducive to growth" (p. 144).
- Finally, according to Cochrane (1979) more highly educated women are more likely to have lower fertility rates.

Ubuntu-Inspired Education Benefits on Education Sub-sectors

Bold education sector reforms were undertaken by the overwhelming majority of sub-Saharan African (SSA) countries at the beginning of the millennium through the systemic or sector-wide approach. They were aimed at reinventing or revisiting the systems as a whole by designing policies and strategies through ten-year development plans whose main objectives were basically threefold: (i) improve educational access, (ii) enhance quality, and (iii) strengthen management. These reform initiatives encompassed numerous components including but not limited to curriculum reform to ensure it meets the needs of the learners.

The reform process started at a time when Ubuntu-inspired education was in its infancy, as it was not even recognized as an element to be integrated in any sub-sectors' curriculum in any country, let alone South Africa. Ubuntu-inspired education being a vector of revitalizing African values and cultures, each sub-sector could eventually benefit from it by integrating its key elements in its programs of study. This process is an enduring one and is forcibly bound to take time for its accomplishment.

The African Renaissance/Ubuntu-Inspired Education and Educational Initiatives

Initiated and developed by the Senegalese philosopher and thinker Cheikh Anta Diop, the African Renaissance is the concept calling upon African people and nations to overcome the current challenges confronting the continent and achieve cultural, scientific, and economic renewal. Education, especially the one aimed at revitalizing African values and endogenous knowledge such as Ubuntu, is an integral part of this revival movement. Interesting educational initiatives, not necessarily linked to Ubuntu/Maaya, sprung up at both the country and continental levels. These ideas concern the promotion of African values and cultures by integrating into the national curriculum, notably at the local level, elements of local history, geography, and society in countries like Mali, Burkina Faso, and Senegal. The use of some national languages as medium of instruction or subject matters in these countries is an integral part of the initiatives which constitute a giant step forward toward attaining the objectives of the African Renaissance.

At the continental level, the design and implementation of the Pan African Conference on Teacher Education and Development (PACTED) as a complement of the Second Decade of Education for Africa Plan of Action is an interesting initiative aimed at curbing the endemic teacher shortage issue. This plan of action (2006–2015) underscores "the African Union (AU) vision of an integrated, peaceful, prosperous Africa, driven by its own people, predicated on the development of Africa's human resources, education being the key vehicle for preparing its citizenry" (p. 1).

Unfortunately, none of the eight objectives of the plan or any of the six goals of the Education for All (EFA) was attained by any African country at the end of their lifespan (2015). This is why the AU launched the Continental Education Strategy for Africa (CESA 2016–2025) to overcome the considerable education deficit confronting the continent.

UBUNTU AS HUMANISTIC EDUCATION: CHALLENGES AND PERSPECTIVES

Africa entered the new millennium bewildered with a myriad of educational issues such as the poor quality of teaching and learning, the chronic shortage of teachers, the obsolescence of educational infrastructures, and the poor quality and very limited quantity of instructional materials. Of course there are other issues linked to the rigid nature of the national curricula that are far from meeting the international norms and standards. It is doubtful that an Ubuntu-inspired education could bring solutions to these complex issues that have been with the African educational systems for years.

Like many other African philosophies, ideologies, concepts, and constructs, Ubuntu, Unhu, and Maaya have not sufficiently been researched, studied, and documented by scholars/academics/practitioners in the continent or from the diaspora. In this respect, there is need to undertake more in-depth investigation to better understand their theoretical underpinnings, their epistemological foundations, as well as their constitutive essence.

It should be pointed out that their integration into the official curriculum of many African educational systems has not, so far, been a priority for the overwhelming majority of African countries.

Based on the specificities of the South African Ubuntu construct and the tenets of other similar concepts prevailing in other parts of the continent, especially the "Maaya/Hadama de ya" philosophy in Mali and Guinea, and Unhu in Zimbabwe, an attempt is made to identify, examine, and highlight some of the key functions of these various African philosophies including their educational and other aspects. For obvious reasons, the Maaya/Hadama de ya philosophy to which I have been exposed since childhood and with which I am pretty much familiar and knowledgeable about constitutes the main thread of the chapter discourse and is therefore put into more perspective than any other.

Bearing this principle in mind and in order to achieve the intended objective, five major functions that are inextricably linked to the Maaya or Hadama de ya philosophy and crucial for its understanding are identified, presented, and discussed. They shed light on the major characteristics of the concept and help better appreciate their various dimensions and interrelatedness. They are not exhaustive and are as follows:

Ubuntu/Maaya as Philosophy

Maaya is a comprehensive and life-shaping philosophy that goes back as far as the origin of the Mandingo/Bambara societies. Its major fundaments are values such as honesty, ethics, moral, compassion, rectitude, goodness, tolerance, and solidarity, among others. It is a philosophy based on the postulate that the individual is an integral part of a community which he/she must serve and whose rules, principles, regulations, and modus operandi he/she complies with. He/she must also ensure that the other members of the community especially the youth comply with them. Maaya/Hadama de ya, therefore, is a philosophy that has practical implications for the day-to-day running of the Mandingo/Bambara communities for centuries.

Ubuntu/Maaya as Social Constitution

In essence, "Maaya", being a body of principles governing and guiding the functioning of the Mandingo/Bambara society, is comparable, in many respects, to the constitution of a state defined by the Merriam-Webster Dictionary as "a body of fundamental principles or established precedents according to which a state or other organization is acknowledged to be governed". These principles concern, among others, the formal and organizational structure of the family, the tribe, the clan, and the community at large.

It is clear that this constitution is a code that regulates the relationships between the individual and the group, between parents and children in the extended African family, and other forms of social organizations. The Maaya compels the members of the community to be present in all the social events such as name-giving ceremonies, weddings, and burials, thus magnifying and glorifying the all-time Bambara adage that stipulates that "one comes in the hands of people and departs from this world in the hands of people". In essence this adage is very similar to the Ubuntu statement "I am because you are".

Ubuntu/Maaya as a Code of Conduct

Along those lines, these philosophies function based on an unwritten code of conduct, a set of rules outlining the social norms, rules, and responsibilities of, or proper practices for, an individual, an ethnic group, a clan, a community, or an organization. Furthermore, a code of conduct is a "body of principles, values, standards, or rules of behavior that guide the decisions, procedures, and systems of an organization or community in a way that contributes to the welfare of its key stakeholders" (CFA Institute 2014). The code of conduct is defined by the elders who are also its major custodians. It applies to all the members of the community.

Ubuntu/Maaya as an Initiation Guide

The third function of this prominent philosophy is its role as a guide for social initiation and orientation. In fact, Maaya plays a major role in the organization and implementation of numerous social events especially the five key African initiation rites (birth, adulthood, marriage, eldership, and ancestorship) which are fundamental to human development and social cohesion. These rites impart the individual or the group with values, principles, attitudes, and behavior consistent with the social morals and destined to facilitate his/her integration in society.

In essence, the rites of passage shape the character of the youth and help make them well-rounded members of the community who are ready to take their rightful position in the society in which they live and serve it with compassion, respect, dignity, pride, and responsibility at all levels with a view of guaranteeing the total satisfaction of all its members. A case in point is the circumcision of 18-year-old adolescents (an adulthood rite) which fundamentally marks their admission into the circle of adults. Thus they work their way up the social ladder as they come of age.

Ubuntu/Maaya as an Educational Precept

The width and breadth of the various subjects or topics covered by Ubuntu and Maaya are just impressive. They include but are not limited to social treaties and precepts such as child upbringing (care and education), moral conduct, and good behavior that make the individual a well-rounded member of the community as well as a prominent role model, a source of inspiration for the entire clan, tribe, or community.

The Ubuntu/Maaya educational precept further relates, basically, to a robust knowledge base constituted by the Bambaras/Mandingos on a wide range of disciplines such as Astrology, Philosophy, Cosmogony, Cosmology, Sociology, Anthropology, Ethnology, History, Geography, Mathematics (Geometry and Algebra), Metaphysics, Agriculture,

Husbandry, Pharmacology, Meteorology, Occult Sciences, and Economics, among others. Interestingly, among all these disciplines, more focus is placed on those related to Humanities and Social Sciences. Thus the key challenge facing African educational systems today is how to integrate all this wealth of fragmented and endogenous knowledge base into a coherent and cohesive curriculum at the national, regional, and local level that is responsive to the learning needs of students at all levels of schooling.

Ubuntu/Maaya, genuine African philosophies, comprise compassion, good moral conduct, and ethic, African values to capitalize on and that need to be promoted by further researching them. However this preliminary academic work is in its infancy, and very few national curricula have integrated Ubuntu or Maaya as intrinsic values to be internalized and taught at all levels of the system. As such their impact on socioeconomic development or economic growth still remains to be demonstrated. Therefore one may present the following key arguments to back up this claim:

1. Both concepts are new and, as such, have not extensively been researched and documented to date. This situation presents drawbacks and real limitations for their immediate integration into the educational systems' curricula around the continent.
2. The rhythm, scope, and implementation of the integration strategy will depend, to a large extent, on the ability of each individual country to recognize, adopt, and willingly promote the strategy, thus showing interest in and commitment for the renaissance of African endogenous knowledge.
3. African societies have, for centuries, predominantly been guided by orality. In this respect, many of these disciplines have insufficiently been researched, codified, and extensively tested. Nonetheless, there is potential as they are an integral part of the rich African endogenous knowledge system.
4. A strong political will needs to emerge and studies are to be undertaken to determine the feasibility of the integration with specific emphasis on the pedagogical and methodological aspects of it.

CONCLUSION

Ubuntu-inspired education still has a long way to go. There is need to rethink the mission of African educational systems and redesign their curricula so as to integrate in them a satisfactory dose of African cultures, values, and endogenous knowledge to counterbalance their content that is basically Eurocentric. Ubuntu is an African concept with values that may guide and inspire education across the continent if integrated in the curriculum. However, at this stage of its evolutionary process and before it is endorsed by the majority of Africans, there is need to further fine-tune the concept of Ubuntu in its birthplace, Africa, and test it against established norms and standards before integrating it into the educational curricula and starting to gauge its impact on socioeconomic development and economic growth.

It should be reminded that the Ubuntu perspective is entered around the outright positioning of the individual in relation to another individual, a group of individuals, or the community at large. It emphasizes values such as compassion, solidarity, ethic, tolerance, exemplary moral conduct, as well as sharing and caring. These strong and invaluable attributes make Ubuntu a humanistic philosophy and education whose objectives are somewhat convergent and underscore the transcendence of the individual as a productive member of the clan, the tribe, and the community at large. It may be concluded that education and training are major contributors to the formation of human capital that enhances the skills, competences, knowledge, and know-how of the labor force which increases their level of productivity whether on the farm, in an office, or in a plant whether in Africa, Europe, Asia, or America. For this to happen, it is vital to create all the necessary conditions conducive to boosting economic growth. Further, education if well-conceived cannot be detrimental to socioeconomic advancement for the simple reason that we all know that education exists for this purpose. It may be that in the application of the process there are loopholes that need to be bridged for educational effects or spillovers to be more sustainable.

References

African Union Second Decade for Education in Africa. (2006–2015). Plan of Action Department of Human Resources, Science and Technology, September 2016, Addis Ababa.

CFA Institute. (2014). *Code of ethics and standards of professional conduct.* www.cfainstitute.org. Website consulted on July 25, 2015.

Cochrane, S. H. (1979). *Fertility and education: What do we really know.* Baltimore: John Hopkins University Press.

Cohn, E. R., & Geske, T. (1990). *The economics of education* (3rd ed.). Oxford: Pergamon Press.

Denison, E. F. (1962). *The sources of economic growth in the United Sates.* New York: Committee for Economic Development.

Diarra, M. C. (1997). *Educational costs and cost recovery in developing countries: The case of Mali.* Unpublished dissertation, Louisiana State University, Baton Rouge.

Eze, M. O. (2011). *Ubuntu: A communitarian response to liberal individualism.* Pretoria: University of Pretoria.

Fallon, R. P., & Fayard, R. (1975). Capital skill complementarity, income distribution and growth accounting. *Journal of Political Economy, 83*(April), 279–301.

Griliches, Z. (1969). Capital skill complementarity. *Review of Economics and Statistics, 51,* 465–468.

Lau, L. J. (1979). Educational production function. In D. M. Windham (Ed.), *Economic dimensions of education* (pp. 33–69). Washington, DC: National Academy of Education.

Mbiti. (2010). *I am because you are and therefore we are because I am in Eze (2011).* Burgdorf.

Miller, W. L. (1967). Educations as a source of economic growth. *Journal of Economic Issues, 1*(December), 280–296.

Psacharopoulos, G. (1973). *Returns to education; an international comparison.* San Francisco: Jossey-Bass, Inc., Publishers.

Psacharopoulos, G. (1984). The contribution of education to economic growth. International comparison. In J. W. Kendrick (Ed.), *International comparisons of productivity and causes of the slowdown* (pp. 335–355). Cambridge, MA: Ballinger/American Enterprise Institute.

Wilson, L. O. (1990, 2004 & 2006). *Curriculum course packets.* ED 721 & 726. Unpublished at; http://thesecondprinciple.com/instructional-design/types-of-curriculum

CHAPTER 8

Putting the Cart Before the Horse? Early Childhood Care and Education (ECCE) the Quest for Ubuntu Educational Foundation in Africa

Hamidou Boukary

Introduction

Over the last three decades, early childhood care and education (ECCE) has gained much currency among policymakers in Africa and their partners. From a sub-sector usually thought to be only for the children of the rich city dwellers and in great part disowned by ministries of education, it has now become a full-fledged sub-sector of education systems deserving important policy considerations (Humphreys and Crawford 2015). Intensive evidence-based advocacy work using new knowledge on cognition/neuroscience and effective pedagogical approaches has contributed to the current change

---

This chapter relies heavily on a forthcoming publication by UNESCO and written by the author entitled, *School Readiness for Children in the West and Central African Region: A review of the policy frameworks for its implementation and case studies of three West African countries (Cote D'Ivoire, Ghana and Nigeria).*

H. Boukary (✉)
HDB Education and Training Consulting, Niamey, Niger

© The Author(s) 2018
E. J. Takyi-Amoako, N. T. Assié-Lumumba (Eds.),
Re-Visioning Education in Africa,
https://Doi.org/10.1007/978-3-319-70043-4_8

of heart in policy. However, the road to this important realization has not been a smooth one, and the destination, a culturally domesticated and fully articulated sub-sector as part of a coherent and seamless system, is still far in regard to the socioeconomic and structural challenges that bedevil the sub-sector. This situation begs the following question: Did Africa put the cart before the horse by overlooking the development of a key sub-sector that holds the key to the quality and relevance of its education systems?

To answer this question, this paper will first review the concept of ECCE as it is currently being implemented in Africa and explore the extent to which it integrates the Ubuntu philosophy that will ensure that African children are reared and educated within the humanistic values and communalist worldview that characterize African culture and society. Indeed, there is a concern that ECCE policies and programs currently implemented in Africa are underpinned by Eurocentric principles and worldview that seek to divorce the African child from his /her sociocultural roots and environments (Nsamenang 2008). Secondly, implications for Ubuntu-based/African-centered ECCE policy formulation will be discussed and contrasted with the different policy options being tried across the continent to mainstream relevant and quality preschooling and care into the formal education systems.

This chapter is a desk review and analysis of the theoretical, policy, and implementation frameworks for the development of ECCE in Africa. It provides a critical analysis of these frameworks vis-à-vis the need for the development of an ECCE that is rooted in African culture and practices which promote the Ubuntu philosophy. In so doing, the paper will explore the extent to which existing policies, relevance and quality standards, the curriculum, and monitoring tools are geared toward facilitating smooth transitions from home to school and from preschool to primary school for African children.

What Is ECCE and Why Is It Important?

Different terminologies are used to describe *the structured care and cognitive stimulation and preparation for early learning provided to infants, toddlers, and children under the age of seven or eight.* One thing that immediately becomes clear for anyone who delves into the different conceptual frameworks out there is that many terminologies are being used to frame the concept of childhood and the types of learning that can occur at particular developmental stages in a child's life.

What's ECCE?

This paper uses the concept of early childhood care and education adopted by the EFA movement and clarified in the 2007 Global Monitoring Report (GMR) as it seems to be the most comprehensive compared to all the others. The GMR team describes rather than defines ECCE. It states that "ECCE supports children's survival, growth, development and learning – including health, nutrition and hygiene, and cognitive, social, physical and emotional development – from birth to entry into primary school in formal, informal and non-formal settings (EFA GMR 2007, p. 3)". In programmatic terms, ECCE encompasses "very diverse arrangements, from parenting programs to community-based child care, center-based provision and formal pre-primary education, often in schools. Programs typically aim at two age groups: children under 3 and those from age 3 to primary school entry (usually by age 6, always by age 8) (ibid. p. 14)".

It is important to note that the ECCE concept described above is used by multilateral and bilateral development organizations such as the Global Partnership for Education (GPE), UNESCO, and a few others. Given the great influence of these organizations on education policies in Africa, most policies being formulated and implemented on the continent invariably reflect the ECCE concept described above.

Another important fact to note is that the ECCE concept adopted here has its origin in the USA. Therefore, it is not surprising to see the definitional similarity as the American concept uses early childhood education (ECE) instead of ECCE. They define ECE as any "activities and/or experiences that are intended to effect developmental changes in children prior to their entry into elementary school.... Early childhood education (ECE) programs include any type of educational program that serves children in the preschool years and is designed to improve later school performance".[1]

The United Nations Children's Fund (UNICEF), a key global player and proponent of early learning and development, uses the concept of early childhood development (ECD). It defines ECD as any "comprehensive approach to policies and programs for children from birth to eight years of age, their parents and caregivers. Its purpose is to protect the child's rights to develop his or her full cognitive, emotional, social and physical potential" (UNICEF 2002, p. 2). UNICEF emphasizes a rights-based approach to ECD in order to make it mandatory for governments to devote more resources to the sub-sector.

The World Health Organization (WHO) extends the ECD concept to encompass unborn babies in their mothers' wombs. For WHO "early childhood is defined as the period from prenatal development to eight years of age".[2]

An African ECCE Concept

A small body of literature has emerged since the 1990s to question the relevance of the above ECCE concept and its implementation in Africa. The main criticism leveled against the concept is that it ignores African ECCE concepts and practices and imposes Eurocentric/Western conceptual and cultural frameworks on African societies (Awopegba, Oduolowu, and Nsamenang 2013). Indeed, and with very few exceptions, ECCE curriculums and structure (segmentation by age groups of children aged 0–8 years) are basically carbon copies of the programs found in Europe and the USA.

The proponents of an African-centered ECCE advocate a shift from the prevailing western model to a new one that would combine the strengths of both the traditional African child-rearing practices and western practices. Among the African practices identified as strong are indigenous games, music, increased reliance on community-based provision, incorporation of pre-adolescents as mentors, use of African languages, and use of indigenous knowledge.

A brief background is necessary here to put ECCE in historical context in Africa. To a great extent, UNICEF introduced and championed ECCE on the continent. UNICEF made use of the adoption of the *Convention on the Rights of the Child* (CRC) by African governments in 1989 as a lever to push them toward developing a sub-sector essentially devoted to the developmental needs of children aged 0–8. At the initial stages, UNICEF used a human rights framework rooted in the CRC to engage the health sector. As a result, systematic and nationwide vaccination campaigns were launched and culminated into significant achievements in terms of immunization coverage, capacitation of health personnel, and improvements in healthcare practices at family and community levels.

In addition to the gains in the healthcare systems, the protection of children's rights in Africa brought about significant improvements in legislation and institution building. Many laws and bills have been passed over the years to protect children's rights along with their mothers and families. An increasing number of countries have now put in place family codes to ensure the well-being of children and their parents.

With regard to institution building, many African governments have now established or reinforced institutions (ministries and para-public agencies) solely dedicated to the promotion of children's rights and family welfare. For example, it is common to come across one or two ministries dealing with child and family welfare in most African governments. With the support of UNICEF and other bilateral and multilateral funding agencies, the capacity of the institutions thus created has been strengthened with the view to implementing CRC-inspired legislations and policies. For instance, law enforcement agencies such as the police and judicial courts have been strengthened and retooled to protect children's rights.

After the healthcare and social welfare systems for children and their families were created and institutionalized, the education dimension of the ECCE in Africa was championed by the Education for All (EFA) movement starting in the 1990s. It is important to note that the EFA movement was also led by the same influential multilateral organizations that have dominated the development agenda in Africa: UNESCO, UNICEF, World Bank, UNDP, and UNPF.

Article 5 of *the World Declaration on Education for All: Meeting Basic Learning Needs* issued in 1990 in Jomtien explicitly called for the expansion of the concept of basic education to include ECCE. It stated that "Learning begins at birth. This calls for early childhood care and initial education. These can be provided through arrangements involving families, communities, or institutional programmes, as appropriate". Ten years later, and after a very disappointing evaluation of the implementation of the Jomtien agenda, the same conveners gathered governments, civil societies, and development partners in Dakar, Senegal, in 2000 to reframe the agenda and reaffirm their commitment to supporting a set of six goals to be achieved by 2015. This constituted the Dakar Framework for Action. Topping the six goals was the need to "expand early childhood care and education".

Policy and Structural Challenges to the Development of ECCE in Africa

Between 2000 and 2015, the ECCE agenda under EFA in Africa had contributed to many notable gains but had also exposed quite a few policy as well as socioeconomic and cultural challenges. In terms of achievements, the 2016 Global Education Monitoring Report (GEMR) indicates that 70% of 3-year-olds and 80% of 4-year-olds were developmentally on track in SSA. However, when it comes to access to ECCE, the same report shows that SSA still lags behind other regions of the world. Net enroll-ment rate in pre-primary school is estimated at 41% in sub-Saharan Africa, while it is 59% in Northern Africa and 78% in South East Asia. So, what is preventing Africa from making great strides in expanding quality and relevant ECCE?

Inability to Formulate a Genuine African Education System: The Missing Ubuntu Framework

One of the criticisms leveled against African policymakers is that, with very few exceptions, they have not developed and implemented what can be called genuine African education systems underpinned by a philosophy and a vision rooted in African culture and values. Instead, at independence in the 1960s, they adopted "wholesale" the education systems inherited from the former colonial powers. One of the few earlier African education thinkers, remarked that "[T]he current educational system as it exists in almost all the African countries of former French Equatorial and West Africa is essentially identical to the French system. In the same way, it is the educational system implanted by the British colonialism which contin-ues in the main to be applied in Nigeria, Ghana and the other countries colonized by English imperialism".[3]

As a result, the structure, contents/curriculums, pedagogical, and ori-entation of the systems have by and large remained the same. Ever since the independence days, most of the reform efforts consisted of tinkering with a few elements of the systems to improve access and quality and to some extent relevance.

Following from the above, and structurally speaking, it is therefore not surprising to note that ECCE had never been in the radar of the African education policymakers as a key sub-sector of the education system. For one, the colonial powers never intended to build a first-class education system that would extend the benefit of education to all African children; the plan was rather to educate a few who would provide the necessary cadres for the needs of the colonial economy and administration. Underscored this plan by pointing out the perverse intent of French colo-nialists: "[T]o French colonialism, establishing an educational system in Black Africa similar to that in France was an ideological and political step. Such education was an effective way to 'depersonalize' the African, to spread paternalist and assimilationist propaganda, and also control and limit the number of intermediate-and top-level African cadres" (p. 145). Indeed, the French provided primary, secondary, and tertiary education to a select few and on demand but never provided ECCE as a matter of policy to promote comprehensive educational development in their colonies.

Secondly, the African policymaker, a pure product of the colonial education system, paid little heed to what pre- and post-independence African thinkers and philosophers were saying with regard to the necessity of reforming the inherited education systems in order to entrench it into African culture and values. Advocated the use of African languages as media of instruction in a linguistic transition process that would mainstream African culture and values into schooling and at the same time address the high dropout rates and failure that characterized colonial education due to non-mastery of European languages by pupils. He was among the first African educationists to express shock and concern over the fact that there were no policies and strategies for the development of pre-primary school education. He strongly recommended the integration of the systematic development of ECCE not only in urban centers but especially in the rural areas where, he argued, it could help increase women's productivity by freeing them from childcare so they could work. Pedagogically, he articulated the main argument that is currently being used to convince the new generation of African policymakers to embrace ECCE: a foundational period that would support children's cognitive development by preparing them for subsequent cycles of education, teach them the importance of learning about hygiene, and allow them access to balanced nutrition to facilitate children's psychomotor development.[4]

It is this neglect that makes this paper argue that sub-Saharan African policymakers had missed the opportunity to build a strong foundation for education by ignoring earlier calls to integrate ECCE as part of a well-balanced and culturally sensitive and relevant education system. Given that they have "put the cart before the horse", meaning ECCE *after* the other sub-sectors (primary, secondary, and tertiary), policymakers are now going through the pain of system redesign that presents major and far-reaching implications in terms of curriculum, pedagogy, teacher training, and financial resources.

Nsamenang's Theory of Social Ontogenetic[5] Development (1992): Ubuntu

Nsamenang (1992) has developed a theory of African social ontogenetic development which he defines as "a theoretical articulation phrased within an eco-cultural perspective". It unpacks African indigenous conceptions of child development and socialization practices that are relevant and deserve recognition and "modernization". He and Serpel (2014) advocate their integration into ECCE policy development and social service provision in Africa.

Nsamenang's (1992) theory is based on his observational research and his own personal experience and socialization practices of the rural Nso community in Western Cameroon and which is shared by most of the African communities across the continent. In line with the Ubuntu philosophy, Nsamenang describes the seven dimensions of *selfhood* that prepare the African child to integrate early on the values of "intense humanness, caring, sharing, respect, compassion and associated values". For instance, in the first phase of selfhood, African babies are taught the notions of generosity and the unattractiveness of greediness or selfishness through stimulation and play. The second phase consists of recognizing, cognizing, and rehearsing "social roles that pertain to four hierarchical spheres of life: self, household, network and public" (Serpell and Nsamenang 2014, p. 17). The responsibility to guide/train toddlers and older infants is delegated to pre-adolescent and adolescent who serve as mentors and caregivers in order to instill the notion of social responsibility in them.

The remaining five phases correspond each to specific echelons in achieving selfhood. One important difference to note between Western and African ECCE concepts and practices is that African children are not "taught" in structured interactions/instructions in a setting but learn essential competencies and skills through work and play and participation in cultural life and economic activities (Nsamenang 2008, p. 142).

Current Situation of ECCE in Africa

Absence of a Drive to Evolve an African Concept of ECCE

Given that ECCE as a concept has not been domesticated by Africans to reflect values, socioeconomic conditions, and cultural mores and practices of child-rearing on the continent, its institutionalization as a sub-sector and implementation is facing many hurdles. This concern was echoed by

Serpell and Nsamenang (2014) who framed the main constraints to the development of ECCE in SSA. They pointed out that as a result of the colonial legacy, high illiteracy, and insufficient use of research in policy-making, "planning and delivery of early childhood care and education (ECCE) services in the region have been constrained".[6] Moreover, *linguistic diversity, rapid social change, rural-urban contrasts in lifestyle, and widespread biculturation* have further compounded the situation.

More specifically, alluded to the following practical issues that policy-makers and practitioners would face in universalizing and delivering ECCE in SSA:

> There is no doubt that establishing a network of nursery schools and kindergartens, at first in large urban areas and then throughout the country, poses a certain number of problems: premises, equipment and qualified teachers... An attentive examination of these difficulties shows that they can be solved, providing that governments assume in this particular area of education the responsibilities. (pp. 208–209)

In a policy review commissioned by UNESCO in 2016, Boukary et al. (forthcoming) listed the issues facing ECCE expansion and quality.

Governance of ECCE

As in Europe where the concept of ECCE evolved, the main difficulty has been reconciling the two dimensions of ECCE: care and education. As a result, ECCE governance in SSA is fragmented. African policymakers are still confused by the definition of ECCE as introduced by UNICEF and other development agencies. The subdivision of the target groups of children concerned (pre-natal–3 and 3–6) has led to serious challenges in designating line ministries (health, family, and social protection or education). The pre-natal to 3 years period is problematic for education policy as it falls under the care dimension of ECCE. Care is seen as *"something additional rather than education, such as children's health and nutrition, their evolving emotional and social abilities, as well as their minds.* This dimension is very important to ECCE proponents who have introduced it 'to move policy makers and program providers away from thinking exclusively in terms of pre-schooling'".[7] However, their attempt is not always successful as most educators still believe that pre-natal to 3-year children should be placed elsewhere other than preschooling.

In addition to the conceptual challenge, formulating adequate legal and regulatory frameworks, coordinating programs across and within sectors and institutions have remained major obstacles. These issues have combined to create turf battles between sectors, preventing adequate financial resources going to ECCE.

Socioeconomic and Cultural Barriers to Transitions
A study carried out by UNESCO and UNICEF in 2010–2011 on the state of ECD in West and Central Africa[8] (WCA) revealed that these two regions of SSA are the farthest from achieving EFA goal 1 (ECCE expansion and quality). The socioeconomic barriers standing on the way of ECCE attainment are still formidable. The following findings shed light on some of these barriers:

1. Alarming levels of poverty and insecure health and social environments for meeting the needs of children and their families.
2. Only a third of children aged 3–5 years enroll in preschool and early learning activities.
3. Income and housing insecurities, lack of a stimulating literate environment and poor hygiene, and health and nutrition conditions affect negatively the child-friendly quality of the family environment.

These abovementioned social and economic barriers constrain transition from home to preschool. Children aged 0–3 require more nutritional and healthcare as well as support systems for their mothers and communities. Poverty has constrained the home environment by adversely impacting nutrition and hygiene. As a result, a large number of infants in SSA develop debilitating and deadly health conditions before transitioning from home to preschool (UNESCO & UNICEF 2014).

Moreover, poverty also affects early stimulation that is necessary for cognitive development by depriving children of their primary caregivers (parents) who have to earn a living by working in farms or doing odd jobs in cities. In urban areas, children are usually left in the care of older siblings (mostly girls who by the same token miss out on schooling), and in rural areas, it is the grandmothers who traditionally care for their grandchildren. Parental education, which is more prominent in the 0–3 ECCE programs, often targets parents in rural areas, whereas the child-rearing is actually done by grandmothers and other family members.

In rural areas where most governments are struggling to build the infrastructure and capacity for addressing basic health and nutrition needs of poor communities, ECCE programs are scarce and lack the resources to cater for children. A few NGOs and funding and technical agencies have sprung to assist the rural communities and marginalized groups, but they do not have the commensurate means to face the magnitude of the needs; nor do they have the will to invest in ECCE alone if it is not integrated into their mandates.

Inequities
Poverty and the weak capacities of most African governments have created inequitable conditions for underprivileged children. For instance, children with disabilities in both rural and urban areas are much less likely to attend ECCE programs, and income disparities negatively impact girls' attendance. Rural parents faced with the choice of schooling a limited number of their children would more often than not choose boys over girls (UNICEF 2012).

Evidence from research also shows that children of educated parents are more likely to benefit from ECCE programs as they come to school with the cultural capital needed to succeed. In most cases, children of the urban elites master the language of instruction and have been exposed to multiple stimuli such as books, TV programs, and games.

The choice of the language of instruction in ECCE programs holds the key to its expansion (Arnold, Bartlett, Gowani, and Merali 2006). Most governments are faced with the dilemma of choosing either the official language, which is never an African language except in a few countries, such as Ethiopia and Tanzania, or the child's mother tongue. This choice is further compounded by the rural exodus toward major urban centers which brings different ethnic groups together in cities and makes the choice of an African language as the language of instruction a very complex undertaking (Sooter 2013). Indeed, one of the major paradoxes in SSA is the use of foreign languages inherited from the former colonial powers in the modern spheres of governance and education. This situation has created a major organic chasm in the transmission of developmental messages between the elites and the vast majority of the unschooled and illiterate masses.

New Developments and Models of ECCE Programming
With respect to the transition from preschool to primary schools (3–6-year-old children), great strides have been made in enrolling children. As indicated above, the average net enrollment rate for SSA was estimated at 41% in 2016 from 20% in 2012. Heavy investment from SSA governments and multilateral development agencies such as the Global Partnership for Education (GPE), UNICEF, and other bilateral agencies has contributed to the infrastructure development and training of teachers. This support has also been translated into an increasing number of countries in SSA formulating and implementing ECCE policies even if the ECCE models being tried do not appear to engage parents beyond contributions to the functioning of the centers (food and construction of buildings).

UNESCO and the Association for the Development of Education (ADEA) have greatly contributed to the formulation of an expanded vision of basic education that takes into account preschooling as part of a 9–10-year compulsory basic education system. Most sub-Saharan African countries have now adopted policies that make basic education compulsory until the age of 16. For instance, the Basic Education in Africa Program (BEAP) spearheaded by UNESCO calls for the articulation of the three sub-sectors (preschool, primary, and lower secondary) in order to form a coherent and seamless system. More specifically, it aims at:

(i) extending basic education to a minimum of 9 years with emphasis on one or 2 years of early childhood education (i.e. preschool or kindergarten);

(ii) ensuring an appropriate balance in learning outcomes covering knowledge, skills, values, and attitudes in the curricula of basic education;

(iii) integrating curriculum development and curriculum-related initiatives, such as entrepreneurial education, quality learning, life skills, mathematics, science and technology, pre-vocationalization, and guidance;

(iv) supporting and coordinating existing resources and initiatives in countries so that the priorities and needs identified by the pilot countries can be considered;

(v) strengthening country capacities in curriculum design, development and implementation, teacher training, and assessment and certification systems;

(vi) support country teams in assessing the financial implications of implementing reforms in basic education; and

(vii) encouraging South-South cooperation and sharing expertise (UNESCO 2009, p. 17).

BEAP has inspired an increasing number of strategies in SSA to integrate ECCE in the current basic education system. One of these strategies that is gaining currency consists of annexing a preschool classroom for children aged 5–6 years in every primary school nationwide. Cote d'Ivoire, Ghana, and Nigeria have already implemented this strategy (Boukary, Amanze, Ventimiglia, forthcoming). The 2008 Education Act in Ghana has now institutionalized ECCE as part of the basic education sub-sector.

In other countries, the implementation of embedded-ECCE/school readiness system is in the pipeline. Policymakers and practitioners are still debating the duration of the transition between ECCE and primary education: should it be 1 or 2 years? Another major hurdle facing governments in the countries that have adopted the embedded-ECCE model is curriculum development. This is a crucial phase for the integration and articulation of the system with the primary sub-sector. Its success also hinges on how well it is developed and integrated into teacher training programs and development of learning and teaching materials (Koffi, Brousset-Kassi 2001). Countries are in need of assistance, and a south-south collaboration as advocated by BEAP should be the way forward.

For ECCE covering children aged 0–3, African governments have yet to take responsibility for its development. Somehow, they have absconded the care and education of this age group to NGOs, faith-based organizations, and multilateral organizations such as UNICEF (Sowe 2012, The World Bank 2014). The argument goes that children aged 0–3 years do not really require cognitive development, and therefore all they need is care and support.

With respect to models being used to cater for this age group, two models stand out: the *Baby-Friendly Community Initiative* (BFCI)[9] introduced in 1995 in the Gambia by WHO and UNICEF and the "cases des tout-petits" (CTP) in Senegal, a homegrown and government-led ECCE model that caters for children aged 0–6 (Soudee 2009).

The BFCI model focuses on the importance of maternal, infant, and toddlers' health and nutrition. It consists of promoting breastfeeding as an effective method of ensuring child health and survival. Breastfeeding has always been a major feature of nutrition of babies and infants in African society and recent research has demonstrated the importance of this ancestral practice in allowing the strong bonding between mother and child. So, this is a welcomed development toward the recognition of African contributions to modern ECCE.

The CTP on the other hand was launched in 2002 as a presidential initiative. It was managed and coordinated at the highest echelons of power through a parastatal, the *Agence Nationale de la Case des Tout-Petits* (ANCTP). The aim of the CTP is to ensure that all Senegalese children aged 0–6 have access to adequate and integrated health, nutritional, educational, and psychosocial services. It is based on the active role of children's grandmothers which is in line with African traditional practices whereby intergenerational transmission of knowledge and wisdom is usually entrusted to grandparents (Awopegba, Oduolowu, and Nsamenang 2013).

In SSA, there are many other ECCE models, but all in all these models are run by the private sector (the main provider ahead of the government), and their cumulative effect is negligible in terms of the enrollments and quality of the programs (Sooter 2013). They have contributed very little to ECCE coverage in the countries. For instance, in Cote d'Ivoire, the gross enrollment rate (GER) in ECCE rose from 2.8% in 2000/2001 to 6.9% only in 2013/2014.[10] Also, in most countries the urban and rural divide in terms of access to ECCE programs is still extremely wide as urban areas get the lion's share of the provision (République de Côte d'Ivoire 2011).

Conclusion: What's the Way Forward?

Making ECCE Locally Relevant for Quality Improvement

In line with the Ubuntu philosophy,[11] and in contrast with the economic/human capital arguments put forth to justify investment in ECCE, Pence and Nsamenang (2008) and Serpel and Nsamenang (2014) have been arguing for a change in the way ECCE is approached programmatically by multilateral agencies such as UNICEF, UNESCO, and the World Bank in SSA. In a publication commissioned by UNESCO in 2014, Serpel and Nsamenang further expounded their argument:

We further contend that the indigenous cultures of rural African families contain many elaborate and effective, informal socialization practices for nurturing such competencies. ECCE initiatives in rural areas should therefore build on the strengths of indigenous cultures by respecting their meaning-systems and adapting their demonstrably beneficial practices. For instance, in an era of falling academic standards and the promotion of consumerism, school curricula would benefit from promoting values of reciprocal accountability and cooperation evident in African family traditions. (p. 8, underlining added)

This drive to "Africanize" ECCE in SSA is crucial in this day and age when we are witnessing a very frightening trend: a generation of African children who are being reared and educated without any anchorage in their own cultural and ancestral value systems. In many urban settings, children only speak the official language (a European language in most cases), and when they meet their illiterate grandparents, their parents have to become interpreters between the two generations. This is a recipe for disaster for the future leadership of Africa as warned that:

[I]t is Africans whose cultural tap roots, implying individual and collective identities, have been withering for centuries who are the citizens being called upon and expected to lead and develop Africa... In fact, a good number of institutions can be seen actively advertising training programmes for Euro-Western employment agencies and labor markets. School leavers and graduates are thus alienated from their cultural roots by dint of education and are mostly ignorant of their status quo because they have been "educated" not to reflect the factors that create and sustain their sorry state. How can such an educated elite class be expected to understand and effectively govern and develop communities and countries their education has qualified them to ignore, much less present their interests skillfully in the competitiveness of global geopolitics?[12]

This warning from Nsamenang and Tchombe should be a wake-up call for African leaders, intellectuals, and education practitioners to ensure that the African Renaissance[13] promised by the African Union through its Agenda 2063[14] will not be another deferred dream come 2063. Therefore, ECCE should be a key sub-sector, not an afterthought, for preventing the "depersonalization" of the African in this era of globalization reckoned that:

the forces of globalization are moving the global economy toward a single unified economy and, by extension, the world's education systems toward a universal model. Such a trend, he said, "is not in the interests of Sub-Saharan Africa, its economy, and certainly not its education systems – at least not without some strong and significant caveat.[15]

There is just too much at stake.

NOTES

1. Encyclopedia of Children's Health (http://www.healthofchildren.com/E-F/Early-Childhood-Education.html#ixzz3rh90zXA0)
2. World Health Organization (WHO). 2007. ECD- A Powerful Equalizer. A final report for the WHO's Commission on the Social Determinants of Health.
3. Moumouni. A. (ed.1968). *Education in Africa*. Andre Deutsch, London. (p. 144).
4. Abdou Moumouni articulated a whole vision of general education for Africa and proposed what he called a "unitary education system" of 11 years preceded by a pre-primary education consisting of nursery and kindergartens education.
5. Ontogeny is defined as "the origination and development of an organism, usually from the time of fertilization of the egg to the organism's mature form – although the term can be used to refer to the study of the entirety of an organism's lifespan" (Wikipedia).
6. Serpell, John & Nsamenang, A. Bame (2014). Locally relevant and quality ECCE programmes: Implications of research on indigenous African child development and socialization.
7. http://wikieducator.org/Early_childhood_care_and_development
8. UNESCO & UNICEF. 2014. State of Early Childhood Development in West and Central Africa in 2010–11, Analysis based on MICS4 Surveys, UNESCO-IIEP Pole de Dakar.
9. Wikipedia defines BFCI as "a worldwide program of the World Health Organization and UNICEF, launched in 1991 following the adoption of the *Innocenti Declaration* on breastfeeding promotion in 1990. The initiative is a global effort for improving the role of maternity services to enable mothers to breastfeed babies for the best start in life. It aims at improving the care of pregnant women, mothers and newborns at health facilities that provide maternity services for protecting, promoting and supporting breastfeeding, in accordance with the International Code of Marketing of Breastmilk Substitutes".

10. *Examen national 2015 de l'Éducation pour tous: Côte d'Ivoire.*
11. "I am, because we are, and since we are, therefore I am". It is "a comprehensive ancient African worldview based on the values of intense humanness, caring, sharing, respect, compassion and associated values".
12. *Introduction: Generative pedagogy in the context of all cultures can contribute scientific knowledge of universal Value.* In *Handbook of African Educational Theories and Practices: A Generative Teacher Education Curriculum* (Nsamenang & Tchombe; eds. (2011). Human Development Resource Centre (HDRC), Bamenda, Cameroon.
13. The concept of African Renaissance was revisited by former President Mbeki of South Africa. Among other things, he proposed that one way of rekindling African intellectual and socioeconomic vibrancy is *encouraging education and the reversal of the "brain drain" of African intellectuals.* He also urges Africans (led by African intellectuals) to take pride in their heritage and to take charge of their lives.
14. Agenda 2063 is a bold strategic trajectory spanning the next 50 years to transform the continent into a prosperous, integrated, secure and peaceful, democratic, and dynamic force in the world.
15. A book Review of African Education and Globalization: Critical Perspectives (Ali A. Abdi, Korbla P. Puplampu, and George J. Sefa Dei. Lanham), MD: Lexington Books, 2006. 214 pp.

References

Arnold, C., Bartlett, K., Gowani, S., & Merali, R. (2006). *Is everybody ready? Readiness, transition and continuity: Lessons, reflections and moving forward.* Background paper prepared for the Education for all global monitoring report 2007: Strong foundations: Early childhood care and education. UNESCO. http://unesdoc.unesco.org/images/0014/001474/147441e.pdf

Awopegba, P., Oduolowu, E., & Nsamenang, A. B. (2013). *Indigenous early childhood care and education curriculum framework for Africa: A focus on context and contents.* UNESCO-International Institute for Capacity Building in Africa (ICCBA).

Bassama, S. T. (2010). La case des tout-petits au Sénégal. *Revue internationale d'éducation de Sèvres,* No. 53, avril 2010. URL: http://ries.revues.org/903

Boukary, H., Amanze, N. O., & Ventimiglia, L. (2017, forthcoming). *School readiness for children in the West and Central African region: A review of the policy frameworks for its implementation and case studies of three West African countries (Cote D'Ivoire, Ghana and Nigeria).* UNESCO.

Humphreys, S., & Crawford, L. (2015). *Issues of educational access, quality, equity and impact in Nigeria: The Education Data, Research and Evaluation* in *Nigeria (EDOREN) review of the literature on basic education.* Abuja: EDOREN initiative.

Koffi, Dje Bi Tchan, Brousset-Kassi.C.A.C.E. (2001). Opérationnalisation d'une politique sociale et outil de Formation des éducateurs préscolaires en Côte d'Ivoire. http://www.aifris.org/IMG/pdf/KOFFI-ABOUA-Joseph-2.12.pdf

Nsamenang, A. B. (1992). *Human development in cultural context: A third world perspective.* Newbury Park: Sage.

Nsamenang, A. B. (2008). (Mis)Understanding ECD in Africa: The Force of Local and Global Motives. In M. Garcia, A. Pence, & J. L. Evans. (Eds.), *Africa's Future, Africa's Challenge: Early Childhood Care and Development in Sub-Saharan Africa.* The International Bank for Reconstruction and Development/The World Bank.

Pence, A., & Nsamenang, B. (2008). *A case for early childhood development in sub-Saharan Africa.* Working Paper No. 51. The Hague: Bernard van Leer Foundation.

République de Côte d'Ivoire. (2011). *Plan d'Action à Moyen Terme (PAMT) du secteur de l'éducation/formation: 2012–2014.* Abidjan: Gouvernement de Cote D'Ivoire.

Serpell, R., & Nsamenang, A. B. (2014). *Locally relevant and quality ECCE programs: Implications of research on indigenous African development and socialization.* UNESCO.

Sooter, T. (2013). Early Childhood in Nigeria: Issues and problems. *Journal of Educational and Social Research, 3*(5), 173–179.

Soudee, A. R. (2009). *Incorporating indigenous knowledge and practice into ECCE: A comparison of programs in the Gambia, Senegal and Mali.* New York: Columbia University.

Sowe, M. (2012). *School Readiness and Transition in the Gambia.* A contribution to ADEA's 2012 Triennale on *Promoting Critical Knowledge, Skills and Qualifications for Sustainable Development in Africa: How to design and implement an effective response by education and training systems.* Unpublished document.

The World Bank. (2014). SABER country report 2013. *The Gambia: Early Childhood Development.* The World Bank.

UNESCO (United Nations Educational, Scientific and Cultural Organization). (2007). *EFA global monitoring report 2007. Strong foundations. Early Childhood Care and Education.* Paris: UNESCO.

UNESCO. (2009). *The Basic Education in Africa Programme (BEAP) A policy paper – Responding to demands for access, quality, relevance and equity.* UNESCO-GIZ.

UNESCO, & UNICEF. (2014). State of Early Childhood Development in West and Central Africa in 2010–11, Analysis based on MICS4 Surveys, UNESCO-IIEP Pole de Dakar.

UNICEF. (2002). *Early childhood development: A key to a full and productive life.* UNICEF.

UNICEF. (2012). *School readiness and transition. A companion to the child friendly schools manual.* New York: UNICEF.

World Health Organization (WHO). (2007). *ECD-A powerful equalizer.* A final report for the WHO's Commission on the Social Determinants of Health. WHO.

CHAPTER 9

Re-visioning Technical Vocational Education and Training (TVET) for the Youth in Sub-Saharan Africa (SSA) and the Sustainable Development Goals (Sdgs): Prospects and Promises Within the Framework of the Ubuntu Paradigm

Benjamin A. Ogwo

INTRODUCTION

It has been established that Africa is one of the earliest locales of human civilization. The trailblazing activities/feats of Africans of that and subsequent epochs obviously required highly disciplined workforce and resilient social order that were encapsulated in a people-oriented philosophy. Various artefacts validating the authenticity of African civilization adorn museums across the world. These ingenious African artefacts provoke serious thoughts on the yawning lag between the philosophical foundations that enabled these artefacts and the developmental chaos prevalent among African countries, today. Accounting for the yawning developmental lag is colonial disorientation and neo-colonial servitude that have dissipated the

B. A. Ogwo (✉)
State University of New York (SUNY), Oswego, NY, USA

© The Author(s) 2018   155
E. J. Takyi-Amoako, N. T. Assié-Lumumba (Eds.),
Re-Visioning Education in Africa,
https://doi.org/10.1007/978-3-319-70043-4_9

philosophical foundations of these sub-Saharan African (SSA) countries. The greatest casualties in these interactions are trust and social capital. Africans seem to have lost trust in among themselves as creative individuals and in their shared values of social capital. These factors have eroded their collective strive for a better life through technological development. Fukuyama (1995) affirmed the link among the general level of social capital, trust and economic development of a society. He explained that social capital is reflected by the stock of values like honesty, loyalty, integrity, and trust. The colonial and the preceded disruption of about three centuries created by the transatlantic slavery and neo-colonial experiences of SSA leadership have crystallized into malignant viral variants of these cherished human constructs that have impeded economic growth in the region. Fukuyama (1999) further buttressed the contributions of culture to modern economics and also expressed optimism in human nature as well as the ability of humans to re-engineer social order for good.

Apparently, the SSA countries are in dare socio-cultural quagmire that is impeding their sustainable development. The associated struggle is the product of the ideological arm twisting that leaders of SSA countries have experienced through colonial and neo-colonial interactions with the Western leaders. This struggle should transcend the acknowledgement of the historic facts of how Europe underdeveloped Africa (the asymmetrical relationship created and needed for colonial policies for the systemic resource exploitation) and emphasize the fact that perceptual reorientation and mental emancipation are the missing links that explains the unsung reasons for the underdevelopment of SSA countries. Invariably, there is an epistemological lag between the time-tested socio-cultural African philosophy (Ubuntu) and the Western belief system. The adoption of the Western belief system by sub-Saharan leaders in designing their developmental initiatives accounts for the prevalent socio-cultural and economic challenges, confusing/inconsistent development policies (youth unemployment, poor infrastructure, food insecurity, etc.), debilitating corruption among the leaders (primitive accumulation of wealth, inordinate overvalue of material wealth), religious conflicts (traditional/western), value crises—mental slavery and neglect of brotherly/sisterly love (traditional/western), and technological underdevelopment (loss of pride in our craftsmanship) of the sub-continent. This explains why economic prosperity or otherwise cannot be adequately explained by the abundance of natural resources (wildlife, solid minerals, crude oil, etc.), the brilliance of intelligentsia, and good policies/laws and institutions (Fukuyama, 1995). Indeed, sustainable development of SSA countries can only be rekindled by reverting back to the Ubuntu world view that promises to rebuild the culture of trust within the individual/community and reknitting the social fabric.

Fortunately, the sustainable development goals (SDGs) developed by the United Nations Organization hold lots of promise for the SSA leaders in retracing their steps back to the Ubuntu roots wherein every individual's value imperatives for the pursuit of happiness are reconciled on their benefits for all. However, it is pertinent to remind the SSA leaders that the SDGs cannot be adopted hook, line, and sinker in evolving their development initiatives. There are apparent limitations and challenges inherent in any wholesale approach towards implementing the SDGs in SSA without sufficient local input/ownership. One of such limitations is the perpetuation of the feeling of helplessness and imposition by the citizenry. Furthermore, it will amount to intellectual indolence and dereliction of duty for the SSA leaders to use the SDGs as if they are written in stone. This is particularly important when considering the receipt of grants and development ideas from donor agencies. Based on the forgone, the objective of this chapter is to explain the concept of Ubuntu and analyse how its precepts could be adopted in conceiving the design/implementation of technical vocational education programmes that could enhance the attainment of the sustainable development goals in sub-Saharan African countries. The methodology/conceptual approach adopted in this discourse is to use the Ubuntu lens to re-vision technical, vocational education, and training (TVET), which is the fundamental means for technically acculturating the youth who will steer the sustainable development goals (SDGs) programmes towards eradicating poverty, enhancing food security, encouraging gender empowerment, improving quality of life, and sustainable progress of sub-Saharan Africa. It also proposes an Ubuntu-based template for evolving the soft skills, affective competencies, and ethical re-engineering of TVET programmes for environmentally friendly, justice-driven, people oriented, and communally derived sustainable development of sub-Saharan Africa.

Re-visioning TVET entails adopting the Ubuntu philosophy to develop its objectives, contents, instructional materials, learning experiences, and evaluation of the programmes. All these elements of the TVET curriculum (Ogwo and Oranu, 2006) will have to be passed through the sieve of the Ubuntu paradigm as part of the re-visioning. The Ubuntu-based TVET will involve permeating the design and implementation processes of TVET programmes with the Ubuntu philosophy. The Ubuntu world view will be the invisible thread that will be used to tie all aspects of the design and implementation processes of the TVET programmes. It will be the unseen and indispensable spirit of the curriculum that will also be reflected in the wordings of the content. This will highlight the humane and communal factors influencing the TVET programme as well as emphasizing the worth of every individual enrolled in the programme. Re-visioning TVET is important because of the years of neglect and financial underinvestment in its programmes which have led to high rate of programme failure. The chapter is organized under the following subheading: Contextualizing TVET Principles Within the Ubuntu Paradigm, Re-visioning TVET for the Youth of Sub-Saharan African Countries, The Sustainable Development Goals (SDGs) in Sub-Saharan Africa and the Ubuntu Development Paradigm, and Conclusion. In contextualizing TVET principles within the Ubuntu paradigm, the chapter uses the epistemology of Ubuntu to explain how TVET programmes can be designed and implemented. Re-visioning TVET for the youth of sub-Saharan Africa discusses novel ways of prospecting TVET in order to ameliorate the challenges facing the SSA youth, while the subheading on SDGs in SSA and the Ubuntu development paradigm explores how the SSA leaders should pursue the SDGs by electing to implement their Ubuntu-based TVET programmes.

CONTEXTUALIZING TVET PRINCIPLES WITHIN THE UBUNTU PARADIGM

Every civilization has relied on material artefacts for the sustenance of its values and ways of life. Thus, the design, development, and utilization of these artefacts are intricately interwoven into the people's world view and socio-economic development model, at any given time. Hence, societies educate and encourage their youths to produce those artefacts that are consistent with their belief systems, religions, and world views. In traditional African societies, the programmes that educate the youths in occupations that enable them to produce these artefacts are referred to generically as vocational training. However, with the advent of the European types of formal education in SSA countries, the programmes that prepare the youths for working in these occupations are referred to as vocational education. According to UNESCO and ILO (2002, p. 7), technical and vocational education and training (TVET) is used as a comprehensive term referring to those aspects of the educational process involving, in addition to general education, the study of technologies and related sciences, and the acquisition of practical skills, attitudes, understanding, and knowledge relating to occupations in various sectors of economic and social life. Presently, in most SSA countries, TVET is conducted in informal (out-of-school and outside the formal economy), formal (in-school), and non-formal (out-of-school and within the formal economy) structures (Ogwo, 2015). Invariably, the many years of inter-cultural interactions, such as have been orchestrated by globalization, resulted in intense artifactitious contests as well as value struggles between the SSA and Western countries. These interactions abound in the developmental and cultural exchanges, aids/grant activities, educational exchange programmes, and technical training between the developed nations and sub-Saharan Africa. The interactions tended to overshadow and sometimes compromise SSA core values. The essentially temporal focus of development models suggested by the developed nations' TVET models for sub-Saharan Africa neglects the live-and-let-live and common-good philosophy encapsulated in the Ubuntu paradigm which is the capstone of the subregion's world view.

Furthermore, the goals of TVET as defined by UNESCO and ILO (2002) are to integrate occupational skills training into general education, prepare for occupational fields and participate in the world of work, be an aspect of lifelong learning and prepare for responsible citizenship, and promote environmentally sound sustainable development. These goals are derived from the sociological and philosophical bases of TVET. Among other things, TVET provides equal opportunity education for all people in the community, provides each individual with a balanced education, improves the community by providing different skill sets for gainful employment, and reduces societal problems by providing the individual with dignity and the confidence concomitant with skilfulness. Universally, these goals and philosophy are infused into various TVET programmes across the world, but each country implements its programmes based on the prevailing world view. The same could be said of the sustainable development goals (SDGs). This explains why the ideological crises and existential challenges caused by conflicting Western and African developmental/world views in the course of implementing TVET and SDGs in SSA can best be solved at its ideological roots.

The African world view is rooted in the communal character of life as expressed by the Ubuntu paradigm (Brock-Utne, 2016). In this paradigm, the individual and community are intricately linked, and the individual's

dignity/reputation reflects on the community (Gyekye, 1998). The striking difference between the western and Ubuntu world views is the emphasis of individualism in Western world view as against communalism by the
Ubuntu paradigm. It is portrayed in Ubuntu philosophy that the best of
the individual is best manifest in the shared values/resources (joy, advancement, peace, mutual coexistence) that promotes the welfare of all. The
epistemology of Ubuntu holds that knowledge is experiential and society-
based rather than being propositionally obtained, although abstract thinking also has value. Across different societies in SSA, the Ubuntu paradigm
is expressed in various forms. For example, the Igbo people of Nigeria
expresses its Ubuntu philosophy as "onye aghala nwanneya" literally translated as no one should abandon/neglect the concerns/interests of one's
people in whatever pursuits. The Igbos are republicans by nature and exalt
individual achievements, yet they examine all these achievements from the
prism of "onye aghala nwanneya." An individual's achievement that com-
promises communality is deemed useless and counterproductive. The paradox is that any society is as rich as its poorest citizens, as much as the
strength of the chain is determined by its weakest link. Thus, in order to
properly apply the Ubuntu paradigm in TVET programmes, it is necessary
to reconcile the centrality of the individual's perception of his/her role in
ensuring the survival of the society in which he/she lives. The reconciliation will entail people deciding anew on their own systems of knowledge,
content, and delivery that correspond to their particular conditions of life,
social, and cultural structures (Melber, 1997).

RE-VISIONING TVET FOR THE YOUTH OF SUB-SAHARAN AFRICAN COUNTRIES

The youths in SSA countries are the worse hit in the cultural lag and politico-economic crises in the sub-continent. They face serious cultural and
ideological dilemma of really knowing who they are in the global scheme
of things. It is increasingly becoming impossible to find suited mentors for
them, who will inspire hope and mentally empower them. The prevailing
individualism, corrupt leadership, and debilitating unemployment/under-
employment in the sub-continent make the gospel of the Ubuntu paradigm a bit of some fresh air. The Ubuntu paradigm will redirect the
sub-continent to the path of sustainable growth. Many Ubuntu-less
Africans hardly appreciate the direct relationship between high ethical standards and economic development. A low-trust society that deemphasizes

communal welfare and allows a privileged few to indulge in massive corruption that is manifested in primitive accumulation of public wealth cannot develop economically. Re-visioning TVET based on the Ubuntu raison d'être would ameliorate the disadvantages associated with many years of colonialism, neo-colonialism, and kleptocracy, in order to ensure economic growth as well as high-quality education for all in SSA countries (Piper, 2016). A sustainable re-visioning of TVET in SSA has to be based on the Ubuntu paradigm in a way that accommodates the ever-evolving socio-economic realities and relating them to the aspirations of the youths in the context of a globalized world.

The statistics on educational and circumstances of the youths in SSA are depressing. According to Keiko et al. (2015), it is estimated that 89 million youths, ages 12–24 years, are out of school in sub-Saharan Africa, and in the next decade, an estimated 40 million more youths will drop out and face an uncertain future without adequate work and life skills. They stated that most out-of-school youths drop out before secondary school and many never set foot in a school. Furthermore, in sub-Saharan Africa, three in five young workers (61.4 per cent) do not have the level of education expected to make them productive on the job, and the incidence of long-term unemployment among youths in sub-Saharan Africa reached 48.1 per cent in 2014; consequently, few youths are able to match their aspirations to reality, with limited job opportunities quickly slipping away (ILO, 2015). The employment challenge in sub-Saharan Africa is therefore not just to create jobs in the formal sector, important as that may be, but to increase the productivity of the almost 80 per cent of the workforce who will be in the informal sector—thereby addressing the underemployment associated with work in this sector (Filmer et al., 2014). Successfully re-visioning of TVET will entail incorporating Ubuntu-based philosophy into all elements of the TVET programme, namely, objectives, contents, instructional materials, learning experiences, and evaluation. Such effort will reduce youth poverty, improve national and individual productivity, and improve the youths' confidence in themselves. An Ubuntu-oriented TVET would find a role for all (formal and informal sectors of the economy), using unique individual skills and comparative advantages to support the development efforts of the entire community (Piper, 2016). The envisaged TVET programmes will be demand-driven based on community and industry needs rather than being supply-driven. The supply-driven approach that has orchestrated the obvious development disconnect between TVET institution and industry's needs is a manifest of the top-to-bottom method of TVET policy formulation.

Evidently, re-visioning the TVET programme objectives will entail applying the Ubuntu paradigm in selecting the objectives that are people/community oriented and empowering to the learners so as to assume the role of communal well-being protector. In this vein, TVET programme objectives have to be related to community (individual/industry) needs and not to those of the donor agencies. This will result in improved community/student ownership of TVET programmes and reduce the level of programme failures associated with unemployment among the youths who graduated from existing TVET programmes. On the other hand, ubuntu-based TVET content means deriving it from the needs and occupations relevant to the community in addition to accommodating the religious beliefs, world views, and material state of the society. A community that believes in the sanctity of the human life has no reason teaching how to manufacture weapons of mass destruction in its TVET programmes. The re-visioned TVET content will also provide for soft skills as much as hard skills, be justice-driven, integrating general education content (science, and arts), and environmentally friendly themes. For these contents to afford a balanced education to the youths, they have to emphasize morals and good work ethics, affective competencies, critical thinking and reconnecting technical content, and civics (the study of rights and duties of citizens to the community).

Furthermore, re-visioning the TVET instructional materials and learning experiences will necessitate the use of appropriate technology which the community can afford, local resources/craft, and challenge the youths to study/cherish the physical objects found in their community. There should be provisions for the planned use of open-source resources like the Ubuntu computer operating system and the massive open online courses (MOOCs) in instructional delivery. Finally, re-visioning the TVET evaluation should adopt the process rather than the product technique of evaluation. This will reduce students' urge to cheat and the winner-takes-it-all approach to teaching/learning and involve parents/guardians in educating and evaluation of TVET students.

THE SUSTAINABLE DEVELOPMENT GOALS (SDGs) IN SUB-SAHARAN AFRICA AND THE UBUNTU DEVELOPMENT PARADIGM

The Millennium Development Goals (MDGs) that were pursued globally ended in 2015, and the SSA countries participated actively and fared well in some goals better than others. According to the United Nations'

(2015b) report on MDGs, the poverty rate in SSA has fallen only by 28 per cent since 1990, from 57 per cent to 41 per cent of the population living on less than $1.25 a day between 1990 and 2015. SSA has shown limited progress in hunger reduction in recent years. SSA remains the region with the highest prevalence of undernourishment, but the sub-continent has achieved a large increase in youth literacy, and of 57 million of global out-of-school children of primary school age in 2015, 33 million are in sub-Saharan Africa (UN, 2015b). Even with these modest achievements in different areas of the MDGs, the MDG initiative was a wake-up call for SSA leaders. It helped guide governments and policymakers to properly focus their national development programmes in order to sync them with the citizens' aspirations.

At the end of the MDGs, the sustainable development goals (SDGs) were negotiated over several years based on a simple yet powerful idea: everyone of the 193 United Nations member countries can benefit from a globalization that combines economic, social, and environmental objectives (Sachs, 2016). The central principle of the 17 sustainable development goals is "Leave No One Behind," which apparently is similar to the earlier cited Igbo people of Nigeria's Ubuntu philosophy of "onye aghala nwanneya." Table 9.1 shows the 17 SDGs, while Fig. 9.1 shows the six essential elements of the SDGs. This principle is akin to the Ubuntu paradigm of community-oriented development if only the UN nations are considerate of one another in their global implementation of the SDGs. The United Nations frames the 17 goals with six essential elements: *dignity*, to end poverty and fight inequalities; *people*, to ensure healthy lives, knowledge, and the inclusion of women and children; *prosperity*, to grow a strong, inclusive, and transformative economy; *planet*, to protect our ecosystems for all societies and our children; *justice*, to promote safe and peaceful societies, and strong institutions; and *partnership*, to catalyse global solidarity for sustainable development (UNDP, 2015). Regarding implementation, each member country is advised to use the 230 indicators in the global indicator framework to guide its policies and programmes designed to attain the objectives of SDGs.

Ostensibly, there is congruity between the six elements of the SDGs and the Ubuntu paradigm. For example, people, human dignity, and justice are common to the SDGs and the Ubuntu paradigm. It follows that SSA leaders should leverage on the Ubuntu world view in designing and implementing the SDG projects. In the same vein, the SSA leaders should explain the Ubuntu paradigm to donor agencies willing to fund the SDG projects in order to promote ownership of the project by the community.

Table 9.1   Sustainable development goals (SDGs) and their descriptions

Goal	Goal caption	Description of the sustainable goal
Goal 1	No poverty	End poverty in all its forms everywhere
Goal 2	No hunger	End hunger, achieve food security, and improved nutrition and promote sustainable agriculture
Goal 3	Good health and well-being	Ensure healthy lives and promote well-being for all at all ages
Goal 4	Quality education	Ensure inclusive and equitable quality education and promote lifelong learning opportunities for all
Goal 5	Gender equality	Achieve gender equality and empower all women and girls
Goal 6	Clean water and sanitation	Ensure availability and sustainable management of water and sanitation for all
Goal 7	Affordable and clean energy	Ensure access to affordable, reliable, sustainable, and modern energy for all
Goal 8	Decent work and economic growth	Promote sustained, inclusive and sustainable economic growth, full and productive employment, and decent work for all
Goal 9	Industry, innovation, and infrastructure	Build resilient infrastructure, promote inclusive and sustainable industrialization, and foster innovation
Goal 10	Reduce inequalities	Reduce inequality within and among countries
Goal 11	Sustainable cities and communities	Make cities and human settlements inclusive, safe, resilient, and sustainable
Goal 12	Responsible consumption and production	Ensure sustainable consumption and production patterns
Goal 13	Climate action	Take urgent action to combat climate change and its impacts
Goal 14	Life below water	Conserve and sustainably use the oceans, seas, and marine resources for sustainable development
Goal 15	Life on land	Protect, restore, and promote sustainable use of terrestrial ecosystems, sustainably manage forests, combat desertification, and halt and reverse land degradation and halt biodiversity loss
Goal 16	Peace, justice, and strong institutions	Promote peaceful and inclusive societies for sustainable development, provide access to justice for all, and build effective, accountable, and inclusive institutions at all levels
Goal 17	Partnership for the goals	Strengthen the means of implementation and revitalize the Global partnership for sustainable development

Source: United Nations (2015a)

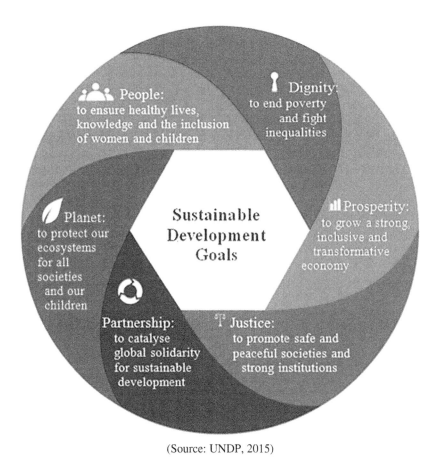

(Source: UNDP, 2015)

Fig. 9.1   Six essential elements of the sustainable development goals. Source: UNDP 2015

The elements of the TVET programmes should incorporate the Ubuntu paradigm at all phases of design and implementation as well as relate them to SDG projects. Indeed, the SDG projects should include the proviso that youths enrolled in TVET programmes should be engaged in SDGs project execution as part of their training. Notably, the MDGs achieved a reasonable level of youth literacy which the sustainable development project could advantageously utilize in implementing the re-visioned TVET programmes and the SDGs. The role of the youths in achieving the SDGs can never be overrated being that they represent a high percentage of the population and possess the agility as well as the audacity of hope needed to accomplish tasks. Training should be provided in information communication technology and other emerging occupations. Given the number of out-of-school youths, it is important to provide for more out-of-school TVET programmes while designing the SDG projects. These youths should be placed in more decision-making positions when determining SDG projects and TVET programmes.

The United Nations and many other non-governmental agencies should be commended for their painstaking approach in guiding UN member countries towards designing and implementing the SDGs. One of such painstaking effort is the development of the SDG index (2015 as the starting point) as a monitoring and evaluation mechanism that allows a country to compare itself with countries in its region and other countries outside its region that are at the same level of economic development. According to Sachs et al. (2016), the SDG index will help the world to determine the best and worst performers and assist every country to identify priorities for early action, understand the key implementation challenges, and identify the gaps that must be closed in order to achieve the SDGs by 2030. The various index measures for each SDG are such that they immediately indicate a country's position on a 0-to-100 spectrum from the "worst" (score 0) to the "best" (score 100). With the SDG index in place, the world is set for a fierce global developmental contest such that is unknown in human history. By indicating and measuring the progress made by individual countries at the start of 2015, it eases data collection for the impact assessment of SDG projects and indirectly provides the scorecard on how these countries fared on the just concluded MDGs. Tables 9.2 and 9.3, which the author derived/collated from the SDSN website, depict the dashboard progress of the top- and bottom-ranked SSA countries on the overall 17 SDGs' index score (0–100) and the SDGs that directly relate to TVET and the aggregate of seven SDG indices with implications for quality skills development, namely, poverty, hunger, quality education, decent work, industry, sustainable cities and peace, justice, and strong institutions.

Table 9.2 shows that there is a lot of work to be done in the region since the overall ranking of the worst country, Central African Republic (26.1), is less than the half of the best country, Mauritius (60.7). There is apparently a yawning gap between the top and bottom countries within

Table 9.2 SDGs' index and dashboard progress/starting point (as at 2015) of the top- and bottom-ranked sub-Saharan African countries

S/n	Country Top in the region	Population in million	Ranking in SSA of 38 countries	Global ranking of 149 UN member countries	Overall 17 SDGs' index score (0–100)
1	Mauritius	1.3	1	69	60.7
2	Botswana	2.3	2	80	58.4
3	Gabon	1.7	3	93	56.2
4	Cabo Verde	0.5	4	96	55.5
5	South Africa	55	5	99	53.8
6	Ghana	27.4	6	104	51.4
7	Namibia	2.5	7	108	49.9
8	Zimbabwe	15.6	8	109	48.6
9	Congo	4.6	9	111	47.2
10	Cameron	23.3	10	112	46.3
11	Lesotho	2.1	11	113	45.9
12	Senegal	15.1	12	114	45.8
	Bottom in the region				
13	Mali	17.6	27	135	38.2
14	Gambia	2.0	28	136	37.8
15	Sierra Leone	6.5	29	138	36.9
16	Madagascar	24.2	30	140	36.2
17	Nigeria	182.2	31	141	36.1
18	Guinea	12.6	32	142	35.9
19	Burkina Faso	18.1	33	143	35.6
20	Chad	14.0	34	145	31.8
21	Niger	19.9	35	146	31.4
22	Congo, Dem. Rep.	77.3	36	147	31.3
23	Liberia	4.5	37	148	30.5
24	Central African Rep.	4.9	38	149	26.1

Source: Sachs et al. (2016)

the region. Worse still the first country in SSA, Mauritius is ranked 69 out of the 149 countries that participated in the global ranking. The challenge for the SSA countries is to apply the Ubuntu principles in cooperating among themselves in order to bridge the gap they have with the rest of the world. There is no other age group better placed than the youth to embark on this herculean task.

Table 9.3 Dashboard progress/starting point (as at 2015) of the top- and bottom-ranked sub-Saharan African (SSA) countries on selected SDGs directly related to TVET

S/n	Country	Goal 1 Poverty SSA score (42.26)	Goal 2 Hunger SSA score (37.53)	Goal 4 Quality education SSA score (41.78)	Goal 8 Decent work SSA score (35.50)	Goal 9 Industry SSA score (12.63)	Goal 11 Sustainable cities SSA score (49.53)	Goal 16 Peace, justice SSA score (46.67)
	Country	Country-level score						
	Ranked top in the region's overall index							
1	Botswana	73.47	35.13	68.93	49.22	29.84	88.10	48.23
2	Gabon	88.41	51.37	66.68	41.17	9.45	73.71	44.02
3	South Africa	75.91	60.74	72.65	29.01	42.48	80.76	41.76
4	Ghana	63.41	52.94	58.94	47.64	21.63	36.47	57.80
5	Namibia	67.12	24.36	57.97	35.80	25.05	75.03	49.56
6	Zimbabwe	0.00	31.69	65.30	40.90	16.64	76.56	34.65
7	Congo	58.23	34.05	50.57	42.83	0.10	52.04	58.46
8	Cameron	57.42	44.15	59.40	31.72	6.31	39.43	43.78
9	Lesotho	13.22	48.69	46.69	25.25	12.73	72.97	33.32
10	Senegal	44.75	47.32	21.66	39.62	17.96	46.98	54.65
Bottom in the region's overall SDGs' index ranking								
11	Mali	28.35	33.96	7.64	34.10	10.99	29.13	55.14
12	Gambia	34.11	40.57	20.84	17.35	11.40	38.65	50.20
13	Sierra Leone	23.87	33.63	24.91	29.75	5.37	28.14	49.12
14	Madagascar	0.10	36.07	31.72	35.38	4.74	48.81	41.22
15	Nigeria	22.21	43.52	19.78	42.08	16.45	19.49	37.30
16	Guinea	48.69	36.91	10.94	31.36	1.68	38.47	38.81
17	Burkina Faso	19.57	31.99	2.22	30.70	9.65	30.70	62.51
18	Chad	44.09	15.43	24.11	37.09	3.57	28.23	32.08
19	Niger	26.77	21.40	0.10	35.31	2.69	29.36	67.98
20	Congo, Dem. Rep.	0.10	23.35	32.38	32.18	1.65	37.11	33.22
21	Liberia	0.15	34.01	11.72	38.46	10.37	26.51	43.56

(continued)

Table 9.3 (continued)

S/n	Country	Goal 1 Poverty SSA score (42.26)	Goal 2 Hunger SSA score (37.53)	Goal 4 Quality education SSA score (41.78)	Goal 8 Decent work SSA score (35.50)	Goal 9 Industry SSA score (12.63)	Goal 11 Sustainable cities SSA score (49.53)	Goal 16 Peace, justice SSA score (46.67)
	Country	Country-level score						
	Ranked top in the region's overall index							
22	Central African Rep.	3.59	23.06	0.00	26.03	7.80	30.01	55.07

Source: Sachs et al. (2016)

Table 9.3 shows very interesting statistics on the state of various SSA countries on goal 1 (no poverty), goal 2 (no hunger), goal 4 (quality education), goal 8 (decent work and economic growth), goal 9 (industry, innovation, and infrastructure), goal 11 (sustainable cities and communities), and goal 16 (peace, justice, and strong institutions). Furthermore, Table 9.3 indicates that on all the seven goals, the regional indices are all less than 50.00 on a 100-unit scale. The least index for the region is Goal 9 on industry, innovation, and infrastructure (12.63).

These SDG indices indicate that there is a lot to be done in SSA if the region is to attain any reasonable gains on its dashboard progress report before the year 2030. It is certain that these developmental challenges cannot be solved by applying the same western developmental paradigm that caused them; hence, there is the need for an African-derived Ubuntu developmental paradigm to tackling the challenges. Applying the principles of Ubuntu in re-visioning TVET and designing SDG projects will entail more emphasis on shared economy, a higher level of community ownership of the projects and a fairer world order. For example, history remembers kindly the application of shared economy in precolonial and postcolonial African economy. There were cases of farmers (cooperative societies) and builders collectively farming and building houses for their members as well as disadvantaged members of the community. Even in contemporary times, citizens' use of privately owned vehicles to commute people at a cost lower than public transportation ("kabu kabu") which is akin to what Uber/Lyft is globally deploying in many countries of the world. There is a place for crowdsourcing, open-source software development (Ubuntu—Linux operating system), and the technical service to the community from rainmakers, town criers, chief priests, and so on in attaining the 17 SDGs.

Among the seven goals identified in Table 9.3, four of them relate directly to the re-visioning of TVET programmes, namely, quality education, hunger, decent work and economic development, and industry, innovation and infrastructure deserve urgent attention. SSA countries need to synergize their five-year SDG initiatives to focus aggressively on attaining these goals since they will yield the ripple effects that will enhance the attainment of the other SDGs. Another very important SDGs is goal 16 that is emphasizing peace, justice, and stronger institution. The SSA countries are having a disproportionate share of global conflicts against the background of unjust societies. Injustice against one individual, tribe, and race amounts to injustice to all of our humanity, according to the Ubuntu principles. Every unjust act corrodes the collective trust of any society, and as trust continues to deplete so also the prospects of development. Similarly, the SSA countries need to build stronger institutions in which no individual, no matter how highly placed, is deemed to be wiser and stronger than established institutions. This breeds and nurtures the culture of impunity that is commonplace in the region.

CONCLUSION

This chapter made systemic efforts at articulating how re-visioned TVET for the youth could be used to enhance the prospects of attaining the SDGs' objectives in Africa before 2030. The most of what is required is a mental and perceptual re-engineering of SSA leaders and the youths' world view. The SDGs engender competition among the regions of the world. Once the leaders/youths of SSA countries are emancipated from their mental slavery and diffident disposition, by embracing the Ubuntu principles, then the region would be ready to lead the rest of the world in the next epoch of human civilization. The Africans that built the Egyptian pyramids, commenced the human civilization, supplied the slave labour that developed the United States/Europe still have living descendants in sub-Saharan Africa who can achieve even greater feats if only they go back to their Ubuntu roots. Mental emancipation is needed for establishing the African moral compass and reknitting the moral fabrics of African societies, where "monkey work and monkey 'chop' (gets rewarded) and not monkey work while baboon 'chop' without working." The primitive accumulation of wealth by SSA leaders should stop so that the common resources would be more purposefully used to develop the region. The citizenry should desist from glorifying corrupt leaders and evolve ways of recognizing selfless leadership at all levels. These sets of philosophical realignment will crystallize into the high-trust landscape that will enhance the technological development of the region as well as reignite the people's ingenuity.

At the global level, a new world order is overdue, where there should be proportionate valuing of natural resources obtained from SSA countries compared to the developed products sold by the developed countries. The cycle of poverty debilitating the region requires a global application of the Ubuntu philosophy to understand that SSA countries will remain poor so far as the natural resources obtained from the region are made to be increasingly worthless. However, a re-visioned TVET promises to supply the competent human capital that would transform the natural resources to either semi-finished or finished products. Re-visioning TVET in line with Ubuntu philosophy will guarantee the success of the SDGs' initiatives implemented by SSA countries. This will meet the needs of a diversified and heterogeneous youth that needs to be globally connected and ICT savvy. The audacity of hope on the Ubuntu philosophy has the validity of historical evidence regarding its workability and the epistemological reliability consistent with theories of sustainable development, which when properly blended with a re-visioned TVET will guarantee a secure future for the youth of sub-Saharan Africa.

REFERENCES

Brock-Utne, B. (2016). The Ubuntu paradigm in curriculum work, language of instruction and assessment. *International Review of Education, 62*(1), 29–44. https://doi.org/10.1007/s11159-016-9540-2.
Filmer, D. & Fox, L. with Brooks, K., Goyal, A., Mengistae, T., Premand, P., Ringold, D., Sharma, S. & Zorya, S. (2014). *Youth employment in Sub-Saharan*

Africa. Washington, DC: International Bank for Reconstruction and Development/The World Bank.

Fukuyama, F. (1995). *Trust: The social virtues and the creation of prosperity.* New York: The Free Press.

Fukuyama, F. (1999). *The great disruption: Human nature and reconstitution of social order.* New York: The Free Press.

Gyekye, K. (1998). Person and community in African thought. In P. H. Coetzee & A. P. J. Roux (Eds.), *The African philosophy reader* (1st ed., pp. 317–336). New York: Routledge.

International Labour Organization. (2015). *Still no recovery for Africa's youth unemployment crisis.* Press Release. Retrieved July 15, 2016, from http://www.ilo.org/addisababa/media-centre/pr/WCMS_413566/lang--en/index.htm

Keiko, I., Emanuela di, G., Sayin, Y. T., & James, G. (2015). Out-of-school youth in Sub-Saharan Africa: A policy perspective. Directions in development-human development. Washington, DC: World Bank. Retrieved July 20, 2015, from https://openknowledge.worldbank.org/bitstream/handle/10986/21554/9 47410PUB0978100Box385416B00PUBLIC0.pdf?sequence=1

Melber, H. (1997). Centralisation/decentralisation in the context of educational globalisation. In R. Avenstrup (Ed.), *Shaping Africa's future through innovative curricula* (pp. 63–69). Windhoek: Gamsberg Macmillan.

Ogwo, B. A. (2015). Nigeria: Technical, vocational education and training. In E. J. Takyi-Amoako (Ed.), *Education in West Africa* (pp. 377–392). London: Bloomsbury Academic – An imprint of Bloomsbury Publishing Plc.

Ogwo, B. A., & Oranu, R. N. (2006). *Methodology for formal and non-formal technical/vocational education programmes.* Nsukka: University of Nigeria press.

Piper, B. (2016). International education is a broken field: Can Ubuntu education bring solutions? *International Review of Education, 62*(1), 101–111. https://doi.org/10.1007/s11159-016-9544-y.

Sachs, J. (2016). Sustainable development: A new kind of globalization. *The Boston Globe.* Retrieved July 21, 2016, from https://www.bostonglobe.com/opinion/2016/07/18/sustainable-development-new-kind-globalization/8n33gJ UKfUVDymMUD3J5iJK/story.html

Sachs, J., Schmidt-Traub, G., Kroll, C., Durand-Delacre, D., & Teksoz, K. (2016). *An SDG index and dashboards.* New York: Bertelsmann Stiftung and Sustainable Development Solutions Network (SDSN). http://sdgindex.org/data/dashboards/. Accessed 20 July 2016.

UNESCO & ILO. (2002). *Technical and vocational education and training for the twenty-first century.* Paris\Geneva: Authors.

United Nations. (2015a). *Transforming our world: The 2030 agenda for sustainable development.* New York: Author. Retrieved July 15, 2016, from https://documents-dds-ny.un.org/doc/UNDOC/GEN/N15/291/89/PDF/N1529189.pdf?OpenElement

United Nations. (2015b). *The millennium development goals report.* New York: Author. Retrieved July 20, 2016, from http://www.un.org/millenniumgoals/2015_ MDG_Report/pdf/backgrounders/MDG%202015%20PR%20Bg%20SSA.pdf
United Nations Development Programme [UNDP]. (2015). *Building the post-2015 development agenda.* New York: Author.

CHAPTER 10

Ubuntu as a Framework for the Adoption and Use of E-Learning in Ghanaian Public Universities

Eric Kemeh

INTRODUCTION

The advent of the Internet and advances in information and communication technology (ICT) have revolutionized teaching and learning in higher education as well as promoted organizational growth and survival (Afari-Kumah and Tanye 2009). While technology has enabled online education in various regions of the world, the same cannot be said for African public universities. African public universities, by not using e-learning extensively, lack the ability to better manage their large faculties and effectively engage the large student population. In Africa, in general, regardless of the improved investment in e-learning systems in public universities, actual usage of these technologies for teaching and learning is quite low due to countless factors such as lack of training for faculty members, inadequate infrastructure, limited computer literacy among staff and students, retaining ICT human resource, brain drain in public universities, and resistance to change toward e-learning issues (Lwoga 2012; Loing 2005).

E. Kemeh (✉)
University of Ghana, Accra, Ghana

© The Author(s) 2018
E. J. Takyi-Amoako, N. T. Assié-Lumumba (eds.),
Re-Visioning Education in Africa,
https://doi.org/10.1007/978-3-319-70043-4_10

Leaders of public universities in Ghana are now thinking through and negotiating the potential contribution of e-learning to their organizational future. At a nascent stage, most of these universities are moving away gradually from depending on lecture notes and textbooks only to online courses and e-resources. Universities in Ghana have made some progress in building network infrastructure and acquiring computers, but integrating technology into the teaching and learning processes has been a challenge (Awidi 2008). Likewise, instructional delivery remains largely instructor-led, with limited or no electronic collaboration between students and lecturers. Implementing e-learning is not an easy task for faculty and staff members as decision makers, and academics are sometimes reluctant to change curriculum and pedagogical approaches. The concerns of pundits, among many issues, have been to look into ways and extents to which governments can convert or are converting the fast technological and economic advancement in the international sphere into tangible transformation and enhanced higher educational opportunities for Africa's youth. There are also concerns on how e-learning systems can be harnessed to achieve the sustainable development goal (SDG) 4 which aims to "ensure inclusive and quality education for all and promote lifelong learning" (www.un.org/sustainabledevelopment/education). Part of the solution, as articulated in this chapter, lies in the proper application of the Ubuntu philosophy to e-learning systems in higher education. This chapter therefore concerns itself with explanations of how Ubuntu as philosophical persuasion can be harnessed to help in the adoption and use of e-learning systems in Ghanaian public universities. In the process, it also shows that e-learning systems can ensure inclusive and quality education for the African youth, and promote lifelong learning for students who get the opportunity to complete higher education. The main contribution of this chapter is in identifying a pathway in which values espoused in Ubuntu can be harnessed to accelerate the extensive use of e-learning technologies for teaching and learning in Ghanaian public universities. Although there are 16 public universities and 74 private universities in Ghana, the present research focused on the former. This is because they are more established and have a much longer history of academic experience. Consequently, they were an interesting case for research given that they admit more students and face greater challenges in implementing e-learning systems due to bureaucratic difficulties (Awidi 2008).

To achieve the aims of this paper, the author uses a combination of an empirical quantitative research conducted on e-learning in Ghanaian public universities and literature analysis of the concept of Ubuntu. Following this introduction, the second section of this chapter discusses briefly the status of e-learning in Africa and Ghana, as well as the concept of Ubuntu and its relationship with e-learning systems. The third section includes a concise description of the methodology, the research questions, and the findings of the study on the status of the adoption and use of e-learning systems in public universities in Ghana. The final section, which is followed by the conclusion, is a forward-looking discussion of the connection between Ubuntu, the state of e-learning in Ghana, and the sustainable development goal 4.

General Issues of the Status of E-Learning in Africa and Ghana and the Concept of Ubuntu and E-Learning Systems

Many of the e-learning systems in Africa pay attention primarily to the use of the web to gather information and to e-mail for communicating with students. Little real use seems to be made of integrated learning management systems (LMS) (Unwin et al. 2010). For e-learning to be effective, it is crucial that integrated systems are introduced that can maximize the access that students and learners can have to organized packages of learning resources. This is particularly so in the context of the development of shared educational resources as well as the provision of distance-based learning.

Although technology has enabled online education in many countries, the situation is virtually not the same in Ghana (Addah et al. 2012). Universities in Ghana have made some progress in building networking infrastructure with acquisition of computers, but the integration of the technology into the teaching and learning process has been a challenge. This has made instructional delivery mainly instructor-led with a limited electronic collaboration or absence of it among students and lecturers. All the country's major public universities have their own separate ICT policies, which include an ICT levy for students. The policy and levying could enable students to have access to 24-h computer labs with a broadband connection. Not all tertiary institutions in the country are equally endowed, and there are instances where the computer facilities are run purely by the private sector as cyber cafes on campus (Omoda-Onyait 2011). Universities in Ghana find it very difficult to maintain their ICT infrastructure due to the quantum of resources (human and financial) required for the maintenance of the facilities.

Theorizing about Ubuntu is usually concerned with the identification of a value system that accepts people as social and co-dependent beings. It expresses the need for a basic respect and compassion for others (Louw 2003). It encourages "communalism and interdependence" (Mapadimeng 2007: 258) and approves that "all human beings are connected not only by ties of kinship but also by the bond of reciprocity rooted in the inter-weaving and interdependence of all humanity" (Goduka 2000: 70). Ubuntu espouses values that tend to be associated with societal well-being, including consensus, agreement and reconciliation, compassion, human dignity, forgiveness, transcendence, and healing (Battle 1995; Mokgoro 1999). Equally understood as a value system, it should be extended to incorporate notions of nation building, transformation, reconstruction, and transition into democracy (Mbigi 1995; Skelton 2002; Swanson 2007). Such extensions can also be integrated into the vision of the potential role of the benefits of e-learning in African universities. The values espoused by Ubuntu challenge the use of traditional methods of teaching and learning in public universities, which predominantly target individual student progress. On the contrary, they (Ubuntu values) offer an alternative that seeks to build and enhance relationships, collaboration, and coordination among students: "I am because we are; we are because I am" (Masolo 2010; Menkiti 2004; Gyekye 1998).

The concept of Ubuntu can offer a unique lens for understanding how universities in Africa can organize and implement successful e-learning programs to harness the untapped talents and capabilities of its youthful populations. This chapter seeks to determine the extent to which the notion of Ubuntu can challenge and address the issues of e-learning adoption and use in Ghanaian public universities. In short, aspects of the concept of Ubuntu that are relevant for this chapter are encapsulated in the humanitarian values of communalism, interdependence, caring, sharing, and openness.

In view of the Ubuntu framework, this chapter responds to two questions. First, in what ways can Ghanaian public universities harness the values espoused by Ubuntu to accelerate the extensive use of e-learning technologies for teaching and learning? As articulated further, embracing the values of communalism, interdependence, caring and sharing, and openness in knowledge production and IT/ICT use in higher education institutions is a pathway toward Ubuntu-inspired education. Second, how can the use and adoption of the e-learning systems of Ubuntu contribute to the achievement of SDG 4? The chapter reveals that the increasing and inescapable role of IT/ICT in teaching and learning inspired by the principles of Ubuntu has the potential to teach knowledge and skills needed to promote sustainable development for employment, as well as to develop useful and active citizens for development.

Methodological Approach and Findings of the Study on the Status of the Adoption and Use of E-Learning Systems in Public Universities in Ghana

This chapter uses data and findings from a study undertaken by the author in 2011 on "Adopting e-learning in Ghanaian public universities: Analysis of the phenomenon of Resistance to change" as primary data source, coupled with a conceptual articulation of Ubuntu as a framework for analysis. The population of the study is composed of students, faculty members, and management staffs of all public universities in Ghana. A combination of quota and simple random sampling techniques were employed to select a sample of 850 students and 200 faculty members in six public universities in Ghana. In addition to the quantitative data, qualitative interviews were undertaken for 12 management staffs within the ICT departments of the universities. The study revealed that the six public universities[1] in Ghana have e-learning platforms situated in a department and were being used by champions at the department. With the current stage of adoption and use of e-learning systems, this section of the chapter briefly discusses the teaching and learning culture of the universities, the faculty culture within the universities, factors that influence resistance to the adoption of e-learning, and the extent of usage of e-learning in the universities.

The Teaching and Learning Culture of Ghanaian Public Universities

The study revealed that university faculties use ICT tools as well as e-learning in the teaching and learning process. Table 10.1, for instance, shows the tools lecturers prefer to use for teaching.

Specifically, a high proportion (61.5%) of lecturers indicated their use of laptops and overhead projectors for teaching as against using whiteboard and markers. Reasons given for the use of ICT tools by the lecturers are

Table 10.1   Distribution of tools lecturers prefer to use for teaching

Usage	Frequency	Percentage
Overhead lamp and projectors	123	61.5
Whiteboard and markers	6	3
None of the above	71	35.5
Total	200	100

Source: Author's field work

Table 10.2   Reasons for lectures preference of ICT tools for teaching

Reasons	Frequency	Percentage
Making teaching easier	43	21.5
It is more convenient	14	7.0
Able to deliver much content within a short period of time	40	20.0
Saves time	102	51.0
No response	1	0.5
Total	200	100.0

Source: Author's field work

that it makes teaching easier and more convenient, enables the delivery of more content within a given period of time, and is ultimately more productive. Lecturers from the public universities used ICT tools to send e-mails (communication), conduct research, administer assignments, and teach, in addition to using other non-ICT tools when the need arose. Table 10.2 presents reasons for the use of ICT tools by lecturers.

The next body of data from our sampling, as seen in Table 10.3 below, provides insights into how students actually apply ICT tools to their academic effort.

According to the study, 97.3% of the students used ICT tools for the following academic activities: to read notes, download assignments, post assignments to lecturers, conduct forum discussions, e-mail, and visit the e-library. Smeets (2005) largely corroborates the trend discovered by the study by indicating that open applications of ICT tools for learning included Word applications, drawing, simulations, e-mail, web surfing, use of dictionary, and encyclopedias. Another body of data from the field work

Table 10.3 Students' use of e-learning

Use of e-learning	Responses frequency	Percentage
To read your lecture notes	271	19.4
To download your assignment	291	20.8
To post your assignment to your lecturers	229	16.4
To have forum discussions	130	9.3
E-mail	295	21.1
E-library	145	10.4
None	38	2.7
Total	1399	100.0

Source: Author's field work

concerns the existence of e-learning policies at the universities. According to Directors of ICT at public universities in Ghana interviewed for this study, e-learning policies did not exist in the schools, but this study discovered otherwise. For instance, 66% of the respondents said that e-learning was in use while 33.3% denied its use. The figures above point to the existence of e-learning platforms at public universities in Ghana. The e-learning platforms used in the universities were KEWL, MOODLE, Web-CT, SAKAI, and Blackboard.[2]

As discussed in the previous sessions, teaching and learning culture of Ghanaian public universities encourages the adoption and usage of ICT tools as well as e-learning programs. Measures taken by these public institutions include the purchase of computers, the acquiring of e-learning management software, and the building of infrastructure. Nonetheless, instruction delivery still remains significantly face-to-face between student and lecturers. As discovered in this study, this is due to reasons such as complex e-learning interfaces, lack of sufficient training for faculty members and students, lack of reliable Internet connectivity, absence of policies that enforce the use of e-learning, lack of adequate support from the corresponding ICT/IT departments of the institutions investigated, and computer illiteracy (Kemeh 2012). Indeed, authors such as Awidi (2008) have confirmed that in spite of successes chalked in acquiring computers and building network infrastructure, integration of technology into teaching and learning processes has remained largely rudimentary in public universities in Ghana.

Faculty Culture as a Phenomenon of Resistance to Change in Ghanaian Public Universities

From the research, it is evident that e-learning platforms exist in the public universities, but their usage is carried out on only voluntary basis. A culture of interest in the universities regards provision of lecture notes to students. Table 10.4 below shows the proportions of the various ways lecture notes are delivered to students.

From Table 10.4, though 54% of lecturers indicated lecture notes were delivered online, a significant 46% preferred face-to-face delivery of notes because it allowed for personal interaction, helped with the retention of lecture notes by students, allowed for further explanation of topics, and increased concentration. The phenomenon of face-to-face note delivery represents one of the indicators of resistance to change. The phenomenon occurs because the execution of e-learning tools is not mandatory, and therefore not enforced, allowing faculty to choose whether or not to use them. Faculty culture on submitting assignments online revealed that, though more respondents (37%) preferred online submission, 28% representing quite a good number preferred physical submission because of unreliability of electrical power supply for online delivery, system failures, slow network systems, and the complicated nature of dealing with transfers online. About 34.2% were indifferent on the issue, and this tells us that not everyone embraces the idea of submitting assignments online.

Responses of lecturers on advocating for online discussion forums also made it evident that a majority of lecturers representing 80% were interested in posting forums online for discussion with students since this helped to bring out the best in students, enabled them to express their views with less intimidation, and provided convenient means of interaction with students. Table 10.5 below shows the data regarding the response given by lecturers on whether they will put their lecture notes online.

Table 10.4 The ways of delivery of lecture notes to students

Usage	Frequency	Percentage
Hard copy	369	46
Online	436	54
Total	805	100

Source: Author's field work

Table 10.5 Preference
to delivering lecture
notes online

Response	Frequency	Percentage
Yes	101	50
No	28	14
Undecided	71	36
Total	200	100

Source: Author's field work

Next, the study examined the reasons for the use or disuse of e-learning platforms by faculty and student. The following reasons were provided as accounting for the use of the platforms: computer literacy among lecturers and students, ease of platform usage, encouragement for usage, access to e-lecture notes, discussion forums, and access to notes before meeting lecturer. Reasons given for not using e-learning include difficulty of usage, inadequate training, lack of connectivity, low enforcement of usage by faculty, inadequate support from ICT/IT department, and personal dislike of the system. From the above analysis, it can be inferred that since lecturers have voluntarily accepted the move from the traditional face-to-face teaching and learning methodology to online practices, they are ready to embrace new technologies for academic purposes.

The acceptance will translate into better engagement with students through the use of tools such as the chat tool, forum tool, lesson tools, resource tools, and pool tool. There will be adequate interaction between students, between lecturers and students, and between institutions. This will fit into Ubuntu philosophy of collaboration and coordination and finally will fit in the SDG target 4 goal on education, which is to ensure inclusive and quality education for all as well as to promote lifelong learning and access to education.

Factors That Influence Resistance to the Adoption of E-Learning

In general, the attitude toward the adoption of e-learning by lecturers and students had a mixed level of reaction with proportionate sections of the sample showing different levels of acceptance. For instance, 33.3% of the sampled respondents showed that the introduction of e-learning was not well accepted by the entire student and lecturer body. Also, 33.3% of the sample thought that e-learning was very well accepted by students and lecturers, while another 33.3% were indifferent as to whether students and lecturers had embraced the concept of e-learning in their academic activities. There is therefore a fair distribution in terms of the level of acceptance of e-learning in the Ghanaian public universities.

To further understand the level of acceptance that e-learning would have if introduced into public universities, several attitudinal questions were answered and analyzed. The sampled students involved were asked about their preference for having notes delivered to them online before they met their lecturers. A greater proportion of the students, 520 students, representing 64% of the sample were in support of the idea of having their lecture notes delivered to them online before they met their lecturer. Reasons given by these students largely rested on the fact that receiving their notes online before a scheduled meeting with their lecturers ensured advanced preparations which promoted effective learning.

However, 28 students, representing only 3.5% of the sample, were against the idea, while 225 of the sample were indifferent. This finding disagrees with Omollo (2011) who stated that technology adoption among instructors for teaching and research is low. Resistance to change occurs when an organization struggles with changing practices and process that people perceive as hostile (Eke 2011). From this working definition of resistance to change, the research concludes that the attitude of students and lecturers toward e-learning does not constitute resistance to change in the adoption and use of e-learning system in Ghanaian public universities.

The Extent of Use of E-Learning in Ghanaian Public Universities

From Table 10.1, 64% of lecturers indicated that they used e-learning as a teaching platform. The lecturers who used the e-learning did so on a pilot or voluntary basis in addition to the traditional methods of teaching. Specifically, they used e-learning platforms as an aspect of blended learning to read lecture notes, post assignments to students, organize forum discussions, send e-mails, and use e-library. Directors of ICT in all the public universities indicated that e-learning existed in a few faculties and the level of implementation of e-learning in the schools was very low. The research found that though e-learning was an acceptable platform, it could complement but not replace the traditional system of teaching and learning since the interactive touch, body language observations, and prompt understanding that came with the traditional methods are very essential to education and could not be ignored.

Reasons given for the non-usage of e-learning by the faculties included cost of implementation, low level of IT skills among students and lecturers, inadequate training for its use, lack of connectivity to the service, lack of e-learning technology, inadequate awareness, and support from the ICT centers in the various public universities. As a result of the plethora of issues and challenges, e-learning was practiced on a pilot or voluntary basis in Ghanaian public universities. E-learning only persisted as an option at the university. The systematic use of e-learning across universities in Africa in general is limited (Sife et al. 2007), and only a few and selected course offerings benefit from e-learning. Because no broad e-learning system is in place to serve as a benchmark for expansion, e-learning will continue at a slow pace of growth (Addah et al. 2012; Unwin et al. 2010; Arenas-Gaitán et al. 2011). Sheikha Moza (2015) has observed that training workshops on how to use e-learning and develop e-learning materials have been offered, and software packages are made available to those wishing to engage in e-learning. Yet, within the African context, the author could not identify any broad and practical strategies that exist to guide deployment of e-learning in most universities.

In the case of Ghana, several feasibility studies have been undertaken on the applicability of e-learning at public universities to propel action. However, e-learning is not extensively used in Ghanaian public universities. This will not only negatively influence teaching and learning; it will also influence the attainment of the sustainable development goals on education at the higher level. The ICT Directors from the public universities suggested the following ways the technological gap can be bridged by the universities. The proposed paths include (a) committing more resources and infrastructure to the program, (b) providing reliable Internet connectivity, and (c) promoting awareness of e-learning among students and staff while advocating for e-learning policies to be in place and to be implemented by the heads of the Ghanaian public institutions.

Ubuntu, the State of E-Learning in Ghana and Sustainable Development Goal 4

As indicated earlier, this chapter advocates embracing values espoused in Ubuntu as another pathway to accelerate the extensive use of e-learning technologies for teaching and learning in Ghanaian public universities. In pushing forth this ideal, Ghanaian public universities need to first find the appropriate medium to strengthen and embrace the Ubuntu principles. Students and faculty as well as school authorities must relate the Ubuntu principles to their own specific contexts as well as community values. Public universities could start by adopting Ubuntu as a way of life, that is, as a community where everyone is affirmed and supported to be the best they can be.

Ubuntu as a cultural approach to improving social relations and enhancing the spirit of communalism is not new to the Ghanaian society. Communalism as a family value has been part of the Ghanaian society since time immemorial. Nukunya (2003) posits that European type of formal education, given its philosophy and practice, has influenced the Ghanaian society to take on Western world view where the individual is valued, rather than an African world view where value is placed on being a part of the community. It can be said that the Western world view has permeated many facets of the African society and explains the state of e-learning in Africa and Ghana. It must be noted that many Western societies are however ahead in the use of ICTs. This shows that it is not actually the technology per se but the cultural foundation for using it that can benefit from an Ubuntu advantage.

E-learning in Ghanaian public universities is to complement the traditional face-to-face approach to teaching and learning. Ghanaian public universities stand to gain immensely if e-learning technologies are adopted extensively for academic work. Much of the reasons for the slow adoption and use of e-learning as a critical complement to the face-to-face approach to teaching and learning is the lack of emphasis on the importance of humanity and societal well-being for the African youth.

First, the value of communalism as espoused in Ubuntu would propose that the provision of ICT infrastructure as isolated investment by the university be abolished and such investment be seen as a social good and placed in the custody of the community. The investments, installations, and use of e-learning facilities should be seen as a social good with communal ownership. Policymakers, university authorities, faculty and student, and other stakeholders in public universities must begin strong advocacy on the provision of ICT infrastructure such as electricity, Internet connectivity, and building of the ICT system. This should be done based on the enormous benefits that e-learning approaches to teaching and learning bring to the African youth. The medium of e-learning, applied properly, can save human power hours and costs, enhance content quality, expand audiences, and bring the very best content to more students. Higher education through e-learning approaches can also enhance the development of critical minds to be bold to speak their mind, being creative, and innovative through the use of the various tools on the e-learning platform, for example, the forum, chat, and pool tools. This should encourage investors, such as Internet service providers (ISP), educational investors, and entrepreneurs to support the building of e-learning infrastructure, so the universities can produce top-class employees. Communalism will also espouse that students will be better equipped to solve industry needs and problems if the infrastructure for e-learning is constituted without any breaches. In the spirit of communalism, students enrolled onto e-learning platforms when admitted should not end there, but efforts must be made by faculty to encourage students to adopt and use the ICT system beyond the classroom.

Ubuntu, as Murithi (2006) and Mapadimeng (2007) argues, gives insights into how the principles of empathy, sharing, and cooperation can be utilized in efforts to resolve problems in human relations. E-learning adoption and use in Ghana public universities have operated in an environment with no faculty support and no university-wide policy. It had been run by champions of e-learning, that is, faculty members with some experience in the use of e-learning with the desire to adopt it in teaching their respective courses. In the spirit of Ubuntu, these champions must be supported by their respective universities by putting in place e-learning policies that are enabling enough to empower both faculty and students. Also, faculty champions must cooperate with other faculty champions to accelerate the slow pace of adoption and usage on university campuses. Since cost-sharing became a policy for access into public universities in Ghana, the cost of university education has been soaring higher and becoming burdensome for parents. In the spirit of empathy, university managers and faculty must quickly embrace e-learning approaches to make learning a rewarding experience for parents and students. By this, students can afford high-quality education and will gain greater accessibility to the Internet as they pursue their educational goals.

The Ubuntu values of sharing and cooperation practiced on the campuses of public universities in Ghana will help take away the apprehensions of students and lecturers concerning the adoption and use of e-learning platforms. Lecturers feel students will consistently absent themselves from their class because lecture notes and other reading materials will be sent online to students. Lecturers are also not comfortable with the sharing of copyrighted materials and will prefer that students buy their academic materials. Embracing Ubuntu as an academic culture by lecturers should help them easily share these academic materials. Copyrighted materials should be built into user fees of public universities. Also, lecturers should not worry too much about absenteeism because students will like to meet lecturers face-to-face in most instances. The policy on student absenteeism at Ghanaian public universities, though not monitored, serves as a check on most students. E-learning platforms could help university managers and faculty to properly monitor students' academic activities for each course on which a student enrolls.

Ubuntu also espouses the value of interdependence; it encourages members of the university community to be mutually reliant on each other. In other words, e-learning platforms will enable faculty and students to learn from each other. At the level of university faculty, it helps to always engage with the students. Students can also engage among themselves. There can also be efficient interfaculty interdependence. For instance, the faculty of Agricultural Science and that of Engineering Science can depend on each other to facilitate teaching and learning in areas where they converge. E-learning platforms can ensure the interdependence among public and private universities. For instance, to enhance teaching and learning in Development Studies, faculty and students from the four public universities in Ghana that teach and take this course, respectively, can collaborate on research, teaching materials, and resources. This will make the course less costly and improve its quality. More importantly, to achieve target 3 of the SDG goal 4, public universities in Ghana can follow the SAKAI LMS model, where in 2004, four leading US universities began a collaboration to combine and synchronize their assorted learning software into a collection of integrated, open-source tools. E-learning policies that are being designed must also begin to look at collaboration so as to combine and synchronize assorted learning software from various public campuses into a collection of integrated, open-source tools. This will have an enormous benefit for both registered and non-registered students.

Finally, Ubuntu also espouses the value of openness, that is, it promotes accessibility. The openness of the Internet makes public debates more possible. E-learning platforms within public universities can foster the sharing of information and ideas among students, faculty, and the higher education community in general. The main goal of an e-learning platform should be to improve teaching, learning, and research by providing a compelling alternative to patented learning systems, an innovative platform for learning and collaboration that is produced by and for the higher education community.

In theory, the UN sustainable development goal framework resonates with the Ubuntu framework in that what underpins both frameworks is making equal opportunities seamlessly available to all. The overarching SDG goal on education is to ensure inclusive and quality education for all as well as to promote lifelong learning. In terms of higher education, targets 3, 4, and 5[3] of the SDG 4 become very important. Ghana's new policy directions for secondary education are to provide free access. This will mean that more young people would gain access, and there may be the need to provide access to affordable and quality tertiary education for more youth, more women, and the disabled. E-learning platforms will provide a big opportunity to facilitate this process. Based on the Ubuntu philosophy, public universities should work hard for a speedy adoption and integration of e-learning systems into teaching and learning, so that more youth will gain access to affordable and quality higher education. Again, in terms of providing lifelong learning beyond secondary education or tertiary education for the majority of younger people in Ghana, target 7[4] of SDG goal 4 is significant. The adoption and use of e-learning platforms to teach knowledge and skills needed to promote sustainable development will not only be useful for employment but also the nation will develop useful and active citizens for development.

CONCLUSION

Based on the empirical findings that emerged from the above study of e-learning in public universities in Ghana, this chapter has looked at an alternate way policymakers, academics, and university authorities can harness values espoused by Ubuntu to accelerate the extensive use of e-learning technologies for teaching and learning in public universities in Ghana. It is evident that the various public universities in Ghana do not have e-learning policies. However, they have e-learning platforms in their faculties. E-learning platforms are based in a few faculties where lecturers use them to enhance their teaching and learning practices on voluntary basis. Among the proposed change paths, this chapter advocates embracing values espoused in Ubuntu as another pathway to accelerate the extensive use of e-learning technologies for teaching and learning in Ghanaian public universities. The strengths of the values of communalism, interdependence, caring and sharing, and openness as espoused within Ubuntu all point to the facts that the adoption, use, and integration of e-learning systems will create access to affordable and quality higher educational opportunities for the majority of youth in Ghana.

I shall relate the account of the Ubuntu culture in Africa to end the chapter. An anthropologist proposed a game to the South African tribal children. He placed a basket of sweets near a tree and made the children stand about 100 meters away from the tree. He then announced that whoever reached the sweets first would get all the sweets in the basket. When he flagged for the race to start, the children devised a strategy of cooperation. They held each other's hands and run together toward the tree. They then shared the sweets equally among themselves. When the anthropologist asked why they did so, they all answered: "Ubuntu," which meant "how can one be happy when the others are sad?" This is a powerful message for all generations and has useful lessons for the developmental challenges that confront Africa (www.m.timesofindia.com).

NOTES

1. University of Ghana, University of Professional Studies, Kwame Nkrumah University of Science and Technology, University of Cape Coast, University of Winneba, and University of Development Studies.
2. KEWL, MOODLE, Web-CT, and Blackboard.
3. Targets 3
   By 2030, ensure equal access for all women and men to affordable and quality technical, vocational and tertiary education, including university.

   Target 4
   By 2030, substantially increase the number of youth and adults who have relevant skills, including technical and vocational skills, for employment, decent jobs, and entrepreneurship.

   Target 5
   By 2030, eliminate gender disparities in education and ensure equal access to all levels of education and vocational training for the vulnerable, including persons with disabilities, indigenous peoples, and children in vulnerable situations.
4. Target 4.7
   By 2030, ensure that all learners acquire the knowledge and skills needed to promote sustainable development, including, among others, through education for sustainable development and sustainable lifestyles, human rights, gender equality, promotion of a culture of peace and non-violence, global citizenship, and appreciation of cultural diversity and of culture's contribution to sustainable development.

REFERENCES

Addah, K., Kpebu, D., & Kwapong, O. A. F. (2012). Promoting E-learning in distance education programs in an African country. In *E-Learning-Long-Distance and Lifelong Perspectives*. InTech. Online library.

Afari-Kumah & Tanye. (2009). Tertiary student's view on information and communication technology usage in Ghana. *Journal of Information Technology Impact*, Africa, Campus-Wide Information Systems, *29*(2), 90–107.

Arenas-Gaitán, J., Ramírez-Correa, P. E., & Rondán-Cataluña, F. J. (2011). Cross cultural analysis of the use and perceptions of web based learning systems. *Computers & Education, 57*(2), 1762–1774.

Awidi, T. I. (2008). Developing an e-learning strategy for public universities in Ghana. *Educause Quarterly, 31*, 2.

Battle, M. (1995). *The Ubuntu theology of Desmond Tutu: How Desmond Tutu's theological model of community facilitates reconciliation among races in a system of apartheid* (Doctoral dissertation, Duke University).

Eke, H. N. (2011). Modeling LIS students' intention to adopt E-learning: A case from university of Nigeria, Nsukka. *Europe, 348*, 26–24.

Goduka, I. N. (2000). African/indigenous philosophies: Legitimizing spiritually centered wisdoms within the academy. In P. Higgs, N. C. G. Vakalisa, T. V. Mda, & N. T. Assie-Lumumba (Eds.), *African voices in education* (pp. 63–83). Lansdowne: Juta.

Gyekye, K. (1998). Person and community in African thought. *The African philosophy reader, 317*–335. Routledge London.

Kemeh, E. (2012). *Adopting e-learning in Ghanaian Public Universities: Analysis of the phenomenon of resistance to change*. Unpublished Master's thesis. Open University of Malaysia (OUM)/Accra Institute of Technology(AIT).

Loing, B. (2005). ICT and higher education: 9th UNESCO/NGO higher education collective consultation on higher education. [Online]. Retrieved on January 22, 2017.

Louw, D. J. (2003). Philosophy in Africa. *Ubuntu: An African assessment of the religious other*. University of the North.

Lwoga, E. (2012). Making learning and Web 2.0 technologies work for higher learning institutions.

Mapadimeng, M. S. (2007). Ubuntu/botho, the workplace and 'two economies': Part two: Policy and political choices. *Africa, 37*(2), 257–271.

Masolo, D. A. (2010). *Self and community in a changing world*. Bloomington: Indiana University Press.

Mbigi, L. (1995). *Ubuntu: A rainbow celebration of cultural diversity*. Pretoria: Ubuntu School of Philosophy.

Menkiti, I. A. (2004). On the normative conception of a person. In *A companion to African philosophy* (Vol. 1, pp. 324–331). Oxford: Blackwell.

Mokgoro, Y. (1999). The protection of cultural identity in the constitution and the creation of national unity in South Africa: A contradiction in terms. *SMUL Review, 52,* 1549.

Nukunya, G. K. (2003). *Tradition and change in Ghana: An introduction to sociology.* Accra: Ghana Universities Press.

Omoda-Onyait, G. (2011). E-learning readiness assessment model: A case study of higher institutions of learning in Uganda, *Lecture Notes in Computer Science.*

Omollo, K. L. (2011). Growing an institutional health OER initiative: A case study of the University of Ghana. Online library, University of Michigan.

Sheikha Moza, H. H. (2015, November 4). Inaugurates 7th WISE conference. (Conference news). *Qatar News Agency (QNA).*

Sife, A., Lwoga, E., & Sanga, C. (2007). New technologies for teaching and learning: Challenges for higher learning institutions in developing countries. *International Journal of Education and Development using ICT, 3*(2), 57–67.

Skelton, A. (2002). Restorative justice as a framework for juvenile justice reform: A South African perspective. *British Journal of Criminology, 42*(3), 496–513.

Smeets, E. (2005). Does ICT contribute to powerful learning environments in primary education? *Computers & Education, 44*(3), 343–355.

Swanson, D. M. (2007). Ubuntu: An African contribution to (re)search for/with a 'humble togetherness'. *Journal of Contemporary Issues in Education, 2*(2), 53–67.

Unwin, T., Kleessen, B., Hollow, D., Williams, J. B., Oloo, L. M., Alwala, J., et al. (2010). Digital learning management systems in Africa: Myths and realities. *Open Learning, 25*(1), 5–23.

INTERNET SOURCES

http://www.un.org/sustainabledevelopment/education/. Accessed 10 Mar 2017.

http://m.timesofindia.com/city/bengaluru/Protest-in-karnataka-against-SC-direction-to-release-water/amp_articleshow/54024749.cms

http://www.nab.gov.gh/

http://thebftonline.com/business/education/23815/private-varsity-costly-tag-a-myth-prof-yankah.html

Addressing the Challenge of Coloniality in the Promises of Modernity and Cosmopolitanism to Higher Education: De-bordering, De-centering/ De-peripherizing, and De-colonilizing

José Cossa

It has been long argued, by theoreticians and practitioners alike, that education and social or human development are intrinsically connected through a linear logic in which education leads to development. The Social Development Department of the World Bank (2008) claims that

> Social development focuses on the need to 'put people first' in development processes. Poor people's own voices tell us that poverty is more than low income—it is also about vulnerability, exclusion and isolation, unaccountable institutions, powerlessness, and exposure to violence. As such, efforts to overcome poverty must not just get economic policies right. They must also promote social development, which empowers people by creating more inclusive, cohesive, accountable and resilient institutions and societies.

J. Cossa (✉)
Department of Leadership, Policy, and Organization,
Peabody College, Vanderbilt University, Nashville, TN, USA

© The Author(s) 2018   193
E. J. Takyi-Amoako, N. T. Assié-Lumumba (eds.),
Re-Visioning Education in Africa,
https://doi.org/10.1007/978-3-319-70043-4_11

Within this framework of attending to human needs, we often wrestle with the understanding of such needs and with our journey toward reaching accurate empathy in order to best respond to this overwhelming human predicament. Immediately after independence, African countries attempted to address the needs of their citizenry by re-shaping the educational agenda within their borders. Unfortunately, this re-shaping of educational agendas was seen as both necessary and sufficient conditions to address the people's needs. In other words, political leaders (some of whom were part of the intelligentsia) were victims of their own lack of sophistication in understanding the complex system that they were convinced to be eradicating and the tinted glass cubicle in which they were building what they thought to be a new system. At the core of what was lacking is the sophistication to self-critique and to ask questions about one's condition in a way that nothing stays unturned.

In order to illustrate the importance of asking questions about our own reality, especially from the perspective of the so-called poverty standpoint, I will start by telling a story about a young boy who came to grips with this reality at a very early age.

It was a beautiful afternoon. A 9-year-old boy got up early in the morning to walk about two to three miles to school, on his own. He was among the most fortunate who had had the privilege of living in a metropolitan area of a recently independent, yet in conflict, Southern African country. The civil war (or the war of destabilization, as some prefer to call it) had affected the country in such a way that the supply chain between the city and countryside, where agricultural production took place, were mostly interrupted and so was the regional international supply chain, in part because of the country's adoption of a new ideological stance. In essence, the country was caught between a Cold War that its citizenry did not understand at all and a civil war that was nurtured, partly, by such Cold War. In addition to suffering inflicted by humans, natural calamities such as droughts and floods had their share in intensifying the suffering of its people—poverty was inevitable!

Albeit the fortune of not being in harm's way by enjoying state protection from the direct ills of the civil war such as kidnappings and all the evils that accompany them, the inability to attend school because schools were recruitment centers for the parties involved in the conflict, and not having to live in high alert and in hiding for fear of being killed, the effect of the inevitable poverty found its way to him perhaps because his parents, who had been able to provide him with a relatively good life, had undergone a harsh separation and his mother was now raising him and his four siblings as a single mother. That day, as the boy walked to school, all seemed usual—drinking a cup of tea without bread for breakfast, walking to school with the excitement to learn and to meet and play with his friends, and returning home to his family and friends. Nonetheless, when he got home that afternoon, he asked his mother a question that was to change his life by opening his eyes to a reality he had taken for granted perhaps because of his innocence. He asked his mother: "mom is there anything to eat?" At first the question seemed reasonable until he noticed that his mother was overwhelmed by the weight of the question that she was in tears—silent, but in tears. At that very moment, for a 9-year-old boy in standard 5 (i.e., middle school) with a heart for God, a boy who fasted and prayed and went to church every day to attend whatever meeting or activity there was, this was a moment that would mark him forever as he grew up to confront the place of his faith amidst the context of such dire human needs. He understood, immediately, how there was something wrong about that question as he realized that the normal question is to ask 'what's for lunch' rather than whether there is 'anything' to eat, or not. The former is based on the knowledge (or at least the assumption founded on the experience) that having lunch is not in question; the latter is based on the knowledge (or at least the assumption founded on the experience) that having something to eat is in question. The boy's understanding of the difference in these questions laid a foundation for his journey toward wrestling with questions pertaining to human suffering in the light of a faith that promises that 'God will supply all our needs!' and toward his commitment to a struggle for global justice that reconcile his faith, a multitude of human efforts to attain justice, and the reality of an unjust world around him.

The example of the little boy illustrates the fact that asking the adequate questions about our experiences in the world is crucial to our understanding our condition and purpose. Dr. Martin Luther King, Jr. (1968), in his life application of the parable of the Good Samaritan, argued that what distinguished the priest and the Levite from the Samaritan was the question they each asked when confronted with the situation of the man that had fallen prey of robbers: both the priest and the Levite asked 'if I stop to help this man, what will happen to me?'; the Samaritan, on the contrary, asked 'if I do not stop to help this man, what will happen to him'. Like the boy who found enlightenment in the question 'is there anything to eat?' by becoming aware of his own state of helplessness, the Samaritan found enlightenment in the question 'if I do not stop to help this man, what will happen to him' by understanding that as soon as he encountered the man undergoing pain and suffering, the man's life became his business—his calling! So it is with us, as we encounter the little boy—in the millions of impoverished peoples of the world—that asks if 'there is anything to eat', their need translates into our calling and our question becomes 'if we do not stop to help those in need, what will happen to them?'

In the same token, our educational visions, our research, our action, must all find meaning in our calling to participate in the livelihood of our fellow humans, especially those who (for whatever reason) are less fortunate than us in terms of fulfilling everyday basic health and nutritional needs. However, this calling, if interpreted as a calling to help our fellow humans, can be misleading to ourselves as it can be to those we deem to be recipients of our help—it is not surprising that academic research has fueled and sustained social (and environmental) evils such as colonialism, imperialism, and their respective posts and neos. This calling ought to be fundamentally conceived and perceived as an extension of our own humanity—Ubuntu. One may then ask if asking the adequate question about our responsibility toward the human conditions of poverty, suffering, and injustice is only an aspect of our inquiry, thus requiring further reflection to avoid committing the same mistakes and errors of the past, what else is there for us to pursue? In order to answer that question, let us revisit the framework of the Universal Declaration of Human Rights (United Nations 1948), a document developed with the aim of guiding our humane actions. The key framework of the Declaration states the following:

> Whereas recognition of the inherent dignity and of the equal and inalienable rights of all members of the human family is the foundation of freedom, justice and peace in the world... disregard and contempt for human rights have resulted in barbarous acts which have outraged the conscience of mankind, and the advent of a world in which human beings shall enjoy freedom of speech and belief and freedom from fear and want has been proclaimed as the highest aspiration of the common people.

Taking this framework into consideration, one must assume that human beings are born worthy of respect—that is, inherent dignity—and that such worth cannot be given away by the subject born with it nor taken away by someone else, that is, inalienable rights. The Declaration claims a strong relationship between this conceptualization of humankind, as a creature born with a worth that cannot be given away nor taken away, and how humans behave toward one another. However, the shortcoming in this framework is the centrality of conscience as the part with which we ought to be concerned (e.g., the disregard and contempt of human rights have resulted in barbarous acts which have outraged the conscience of mankind...). In other words, if our consciences are not fazed by the circumstances we witness, we are permitted to escape this ethical conundrum. This centrality of conscience can easily bring us back to our question, 'if I stop to help this man, what will happen to me?' Framed with a concern for conscience, one would ask, 'if I do not stop to help this person, what will happen to my conscience?' In this sort of framework, it makes sense then to find creative ways to alleviate our conscience and reduce our sense of guilt. Consequently, we create institutions and programs that make us feel good because we help others; we educate our children to be social entrepreneurs, corporate executives, and employees carrying a pseudo social responsibility shield with the goal of developing pseudo social equity framed in terms of helping others; and we can continue to claim a commitment to transformational education notwithstanding our commitment to counterintuitive philosophical foundations and perceptions of the other based on neocolonial assumptions. Asking the adequate question will require engaging in deeper introspection, a willingness to accept radical change in our perception of what it means to be human, a willingness to accept the call that emerges from such perception, and striving toward fulfilling our responsibility as human beings.

At this point, allow me to turn this exposé toward an alternative vision for global transformation and development by pointing you to an old African proverb (perhaps mostly common in Guiné-Bissau), 'When your house is burning, it is no use beating the tom-toms', and also to Western idealists like St. Augustine, Descartes, Kant, and Hegel who advocated for an education interested in the search for truth through ideas because with truth comes responsibility to enlighten others. The African proverb presupposes action on our part, when we are faced by an issue that affects our well-being; the Western idealism presupposes that education is transformation because this search for truth through ideas can (and ought to) change lives—Beating the tom-toms when your house is burning will not quench the fire; an education that is not transformational is, in essence, no education! So, the question—or this search for transformative truth—then becomes 'How do we quench the fire?' In order to embark in such a quest, one has to inspect the underlying reality cast by this proverb. It should be noteworthy that I am not arguing that perceptions of transformative truth are universal, as would Western idealists due to their project of modernity and consequent limited view of the world and cosmopolitan coloniality. In addressing cosmopolitanism as a project that carried both a secular nature

(Immanuel Kant's conception of modernity) and religious nature (Francisco de Vitoria's conception of modernity), Mignolo (2000) argues that coloniality is the hidden face of modernity and requires a nuanced critical examination; thus, in this article, I take such coloniality seriously even when making claims of transformative truth that seem to give positive credit to Western idealists who participated in such coloniality.

Returning to the proverb, one of the aspects we can draw from it is that it is an irrefutable proverb based on centuries of experience and verification that were passed on from generation to generation, perhaps mainly through oral means.[1] Amílcar Cabral (1966), one of the most impressive African intellectuals who led the liberation struggle in Guiné-Bissau and Cabo Verde, used this proverb to reiterate the importance of theory in understanding social dynamics—such dynamics required for cultural permanence, historical contingencies, and purposeful fusion for Africa's progress. My interest herein is to apply this proverb to education and to global transformation, which by nature encompass theory; thus, in this line of argumentation, African education and transformation are like a house set on fire by modernity, classical cosmopolitanism, imperialism, colonialism, slavery, and their respective manifestations in 'neo' forms. Therefore, knowing the source and their complexity—and the complexity of their effect (both covert and overt)—is a critical step in quenching the fire. Since arriving at an educational agenda and transformation requires some sort of inquiry, our inquiries about education and transformation ought to rest on the spirit and wisdom of this proverb, perhaps as a philosophical foundation, in order to challenge us toward a search for 'a truth' (note the use of quotation marks here) that will enlighten our attempts to build relevant educational systems and engage in meaningful transformation, which will propel us toward an active and equitable role in global dynamics with consequent global transformational effects. It goes without saying that global transformation, to be legitimate and just, presupposes global participation, which in turn presupposes a rooting on transformational educations and radical mind-sets, original and contextual national and continent-wide visions, and a shared confidence in the possibility of fusion of key tenets inherent in these multiple visions. We need to understand, once and for all, that the root of the problem is not in the kinds of tom-toms we are beating (e.g., Southern, Western, Eastern, etc.), but in the fact that the fire is still lit and that we are beating tom-toms to quench it. What is needed is not merely a paradigm shift, albeit its potential radicalness; rather, what is needed are **risk-taking contextual-cognitive**

soulful enterprises toward (re)building alternative paradigms to address the quenching of the fire. For some this calls for a distancing of ourselves from modernity and its sneaky homogenizing process of convergence or Westernization, as argued favorably by Schmidt (2010), and a moving toward a series of reflections on the possibility of multiple modernities, as Eisenstadt (1977) might have wished, or of a critical cosmopolitanism and border thinking, as Mignolo (2000) might have wished; however, framing the argument in these two latter critical lenses might also present the dilemma of indirectly promoting a modernistic agenda perhaps best categorized as neo-modernistic and neo-cosmopolitan under the guise of 'multi' and 'critical'. This is not to say that these frameworks are per se promoters of some form of coloniality or imperiality, but to self-caution (and caution the reader and critic) against falling under the same epistemological entrapments that have held captive the so-called[2] African intelligentsia.

Like beating the tom-toms, for decades, there have been continuous attempts to quench Africa's fires (e.g., of subjugation, dependency, poverty, unending conflicts and wars, education, etc.) through political processes of independencies and transitions, fashioned after colonial structures and ontological predispositions transferred through colonial educational systems; consequently we have fallen victims of blind trust in such, thus unable to reconcile the odd reality that the fire we once believe to have extinguished has remained alive while we were asleep. This dilemma has been haunting some of us for a very long time! Assié-Lumumba (2016) argues that

> Safeguarding the mind and soul of Africans through education became a pivotal motivation in the battle against colonialism, as this embodied the present and future existence of Africans as a people with their own culture and civilization. Indeed, the first generation of Africans who fought against colonialism had a clear sense of direction in their struggle against the colonial forces. Their resolve to claim their humanity, their rights to be free and to govern themselves was defined by the education they had received from their respective communities before the Berlin Conference and process of military conquest.

Perhaps noteworthy is the fact that, in my reading, Assié-Lumumba is by no means claiming that such generation was flawless—even my great-grand-father Maguiguane was a man of great fault who might have left an army of children wherever his military assignments led him (had it not been the case, my grandfather would have been raised by his father)—but that their sense of direction was clear, at least to a large extent and albeit divergent strategic plans for liberation from the yoke of colonialism. It is also important to note that their clarity of intention was in constant battle with the undeniable and daunting force of coloniality inherent in modernity (as a design) and cosmopolitanism (as a project) that shaped their own experiences as students in Western institutions or Africans who had some level of encounter with the descendants of Immanuel Kant and Francisco de Vitoria. Whether subsequent generations of anti-colonial fighters held steadfastly to such clarity of intent in the long run is a matter that calls for an evaluation of personalities and the myriad manifestations of the forces at work in the histories of individual countries—in other words, context also plays a part in understanding individual African countries' experiences and responses; after all, there are many ways of beating the tom-toms. Also, we now know that such flaws in individual and group characters as well as the power of the forces at work obliged the proliferation of myths around revolutionary leaders and movements, which are being challenged today more than ever before as a newer generation of scholars, who are inspired by the disenchanted older generation of scholars and by the most recent unwelcome socio-political and economic changes in numerous African countries, engage in questioning legitimacy and coherence.[3]

Assié-Lumumba's argument resonates with my argument herein that beating the tom-toms is not enough to quench the fire; nonetheless, there came a time when we (Africans) forgot the advice deriving from the wisdom of our ancestors and opted to embrace a counterproductive paradigm of modernity perhaps in the hopes that we, too, would be modernized or that we could fool coloniality by decolonizing through a Western-modeled education replete with decolonial jargon framed within coloniality (from either side of the Cold War).[4] This argument of decolonial jargon framed within coloniality can be also be understood, from Mignolo's articulation of arguments of beginnings of cosmopolitanism through the lenses of the imperial difference and the colonial difference, by employing lenses of 'the neo-imperial difference'[5] characteristic from the Cold War, if we understand the attempt of newly independent nations having to pledge allegiance to the Eastern or Western block. Assié-Lumumba further argues that this loss, which is in large part due to the transatlantic slave trade, of connection and continuity between the ancestral wisdom and our current educational systems characterized by 'European-inherited formal education, especially higher education' has led to inconsistencies and the impossibility of fostering the envisioned social transformation we so much hope for. Unfortunately, due to the intricate nature of such a conundrum, my own experience has proven that engaging Africans in a serious consideration of this inconsistency and its crucial place in discourses about Africa's future is likely to be the hardest undertake. So, one asks 'how can there be a consensus about the adequate mechanism to quench the fire, if most people in our community have stubbornly embraced the fantasy that beating the tom-toms is the only way to quench a fire?' We (Africans) of diverse sub-communities, which include education as a field of study and specialization, have a serious ongoing commitment to mechanisms that are contrary to our ancestral wisdom; in fact, we have detached from such wisdom to the point of renouncing it altogether. It is not uncommon for Africans (this designation includes Africans in the distant and near past diaspora) to claim that a discourse on neocolonialism, neo-imperialism, neo-slavery, or anything in that regard is outdated and a means to justify African corruption. What is lost in such counter-discourses is the fact that discourses on neocolonialism and such are not only in reference to the colonial past but to the current form of colonialism perpetrated by the very governments, political parties, and leaders we once trusted—we would not need to go too far in time to remember that most, if not all, post-independence wars and political conflicts in Africa (e.g., Zaire, DRC, Rwanda, Burundi, Nigeria, Mozambique, South Africa, Zimbabwe, etc.) have been triggered and nurtured by forces of both neocolonial nature and Afro-coloniality.[6] Therefore, to negate our criticism of colonial and neocolonialism simply because it uses the same rhetoric once adopted (and often misused) by the corrupt and bully governments of present-day Africa does not preclude its necessity, utility, and adequacy.

Achebe (2013) presents an argument that might shed some additional light into our position of both being caught in a conundrum brought by coloniality and a place of transformative agency when stating that

Clearly there is no moral obligation to write in any particular way. But there is a moral obligation, I think, not to ally oneself with power against the powerless. An artist, in my definition of the word, would not be someone who takes sides with the emperor against his powerless subjects. If one didn't realize that the world was complex, vast, and diverse, one would write as if the world were one little country, and this would make us poor, and we would have impoverished the novel and our stories. (p. 53)

In Achebe's perception perhaps beating the tom-toms would be equated to a writer's detachment from the realities and complexities of such reality, particularly that of the 'powerless', while in Wa Thiong'o's (2004) perception, it would be equated to our allegiance to international NGOs and by default to the foreign finance capital that fuels their anti-corruption operations in Africa. Wa Thiong'o argues that 'The irony is... that the generous NGOs and the local state—rivals for the gratitude and allegiance of the people—are armed by the same Western sources. The state is armed with weapons, and the NGO with coupons' (p. 25). Ultimately, just as there is no good colonialism or imperialism, there is no good neocolonialism or neo-imperialism. So, what is needed is a more critical look at our own condition as well as the complex context of a rapidly changing world characterized by an atmosphere of pressure for quick solutions and little reflection. Such pressure amputates us from engaging in soulful introspections that could lead to genuine and organic transformation of our own mechanisms to quench the fire. For that, we need to revisit our adopted conceptions and adopted models of education, since the ones we adopted following our so-called independencies have not served us any good; instead, we have tried so vehemently and so constantly to quench a fire by beating such overrated tom-toms. Our adoption of such conceptions and models has confined the questioning of our own condition to the tinted glass cubical structures in which we were locked up by the colonizers—we have managed to take off the curtain to see what lies outside our structure and managed to engage dreams of grandeur inspired by such views we bestow from within, but our condition remains that of caged beings who can emulate behaviors of the inhabitants of the outside world we see through the almost clear glass.

The complexity of our process toward an education that is not fashioned after modernity (let us lay aside Eisenstadt's multiple modernities at least for now) and a global transformation that is not fashioned after coloniality can be spotted in the conundrum faced by both Achebe and Wa Thiong'o as their outcry is confined by the frameworks of modernity (despite the inherent decoloniality in intention). This dilemma is not unique to Achebe and Wa Thiong'o; other celebrated figures of Africa and the diaspora have suffered the same framing limitations. For instance, Appiah's cosmopolitanism (Appiah 2006) could not escape the frames of modernity when arguing in favor of (Western) literature and writers as vehicles for exchanging ideas in the current cosmopolitan world; DuBois (DuBois 1917) was confined by an understanding of civilization and modernization informed by modernity and cosmopolitanism (both secular and religious), and thus the logic of making an appeal to 'the great powers of the civilized world'.

We must remind ourselves that shifting centers is not enough to undo coloniality hidden in modernity and inherent in the promise of modernity. For instance, when the shift from Orbis Christianus to Orbis Universalis occurred in the sixteenth century, it seemed to offer a promise to human-ity. However, we should not be fooled by the coloniality inherent in the emancipatory simulation of such a shift. Shifting centers from Christians vs Gentiles (as in Vitoria's conceptualization of the others as Gentes) to Citizens vs Foreigner (as in Kantian conceptualization of the Western European as citizen) did very little to change the condition of the others, that is, those labeled as 'gentes or gentiles' and those labeled as 'foreigners'. Fast-forward five centuries and we are still imprisoned by both religious and secular classifications of citizens versus aliens—it is not surprising that our very African governments adopted the concept 'aliens' to describe Africans originating from outside their borders, who dwell in those colonial spaces called nation-states, republics, countries, and so on. What will distinguish us from previous generations, as we wrestle with conceptualizations of higher education, scholarship, and development, is the extent to which we are willing to challenge our own coloniality hidden in modernity, as a set of designs to manage the world and, in cosmopoli-tanism, as a set of projects dictating planetary conviviality. **I call for an engagement toward a de-bordering, de-centering/de-peripherizing, and de-colonilizing.**

NOTES

1. We need to read this with the understanding that Western dominance in the knowledge sphere has influenced our perceptions and understandings, or place, of qualifies such as experience and verification in non-Western contexts.

2. The use of 'so-called' is intended here as an outright expression of activ-ism and protest against the promotion of some knowledges and cognitive systems (e.g., Western) over others.

3. See Cossa, J. (2011). Al di là del "mito": un ritrato di Eduardo Chivambo Mondlane negli Stati Uniti d'America. In Luca Bussotti & Severino Ngoenha (Eds), Le Grandi Figure dell'Africa Lusofona. Fra storia e attual-ità, Aviani Editore, Udine.

4. During my school years as a student at Escola Secundária Estrela Vermelha in 1981–1982, in Mozambique, I took a subject called Educacao Politica (Political Education) which attempted to advance the government's agenda to create um Homem Novo, that is, a New Man.
5. This is my own addition to capture a historical and structural inception of a new form of cosmopolitanism.
6. My term to refer to coloniality perpetrated by African governments on their people.

REFERENCES

Achebe, C. (2013). *There was a country*. New York: Penguin Group.
Appiah, K. A. (2006). *Cosmopolitanism: Ethics in a world of strangers*. New York: W. W. Norton.
Assié-Lumumba, N. T. (2016, February). Evolving African attitudes to European education: Resistance, perverted effects of the single system paradox, and Ubuntu framework for renewal. *International Review of Education, 62*, 11–27.
Cabral, A. (1966, January). *Amilcar Cabral*. Retrieved from Marxists Internet Archive. https://www.marxists.org/subject/africa/cabral/1966/weapon-theory.htm
Cossa, J. (2011). Al di là del "mito": un ritrato di Eduardo Chivambo Mondlane negli Stati Uniti d'America. In L. Bussotti & S. Ngoenha (Eds.), *Le Grandi Figure dell'Africa Lusofona. Fra storia e attualità*. Udine: Aviani Editore.
DuBois, W. (1917). To the nations of the world. In A. Walters (Ed.), *My life and work* (pp. 257–260). New York: Fleming.
Eisenstadt, S. N. (1977). Convergence and divergence of modern and modernizing societies: Indications from the analysis of the structuring of social hierarchies in middle eastern societies. *International Journal of Middle East Studies, 8*(1), 1–27. Retrieved from http://www.jstor.org/stable/162451
King, M. L., Jr. (1968). I see the promised land. In J.M. Washington (ed. 1991) *A testament of hope: The essential writings and speeches of Martin Luther King Jr.* New York: HarperCollins Publishers, pp. 279–286.
Mignolo, W. (2000, Fall). The many faces of cosmo-polis: Border thinking and critical cosmopolitanism. *Public Culture, 12*(3), 721–748. Retrieved January 5, 2017, from https://muse.jhu.edu/article/26217
Schmidt, V. H. (2010). Modernity and diversity: Reflections on the controversy between modernization theory and multiple modernists. *Social Science Information, 49*(4), 511–538.
Thiong'o, N. w. (2004). African identities: Pan-Africanism in the era of globalization and capitalist fundamentalism. *Macalister International, 14*(1). Retrieved from http://digitalcommons.macalester.edu/macintl/vol14/iss1/9
World Bank. (2008). *IDA at work: Social development – Putting people first*. Washington, DC: The World Bank.

CHAPTER 12

Towards an Alternative Approach to Education Partnerships in Africa: Ubuntu, the Confluence and the Post-2015 Agenda

Emefa J. Takyi-Amoako

INTRODUCTION

Background

The national, regional and continental autonomy of Africa's formal educational systems has been virtually non-existent, particularly, during colonialism, and after the postcolonial project of those who fought for Africa's independence from colonial rule, and strived for its progress was undermined (BBC News 2016; Quist-Adade 2016; Mahoney and Name not declassified 1965). Thus, formal education policy and practice in Africa have over the years been driven by globalization and external western frameworks, bolstered by neoliberal, capitalist and neo-colonial macro-economic policy paradigms and consolidated by foreign aid donor-recipient interactions, which are ridden with power inequalities (Abdi et al. 2006; Amoako 2009; Takyi-Amoako 2012; Böröcz 2016; Klees 2017).

E. J. Takyi-Amoako (✉)
Oxford ATP International Education, Oxford, UK

© The Author(s) 2018   205
E. J. Takyi-Amoako, N. T. Assié-Lumumba (eds.),
Re-Visioning Education in Africa,
https://doi.org/10.1007/978-3-319-70043-4_12

While succinctly assessing the Education for All (EFA) goals and Millennium Development Goals (MDGs) as it interacted with education and partnership in Africa, this chapter explores the sustainable development goals (SDGs) of the post-2015 agenda, with specific spotlight on SDG4 ("Ensure inclusive and equitable quality education and promote lifelong learning opportunities for all") and SDG17 ("Strengthen the means of implementation and revitalize the Global Partnership for Sustainable Development") within Africa. The chapter concentrates on the SDGs but also makes reference to some of the Education for All Global Monitoring Reports (EFA/GMRs) and the Global Education Monitoring Reports (GEMR) relating to pre-2015 and post-2015 agendas, respectively. Also, cited are Africa's own education strategies such as the African Union Commission (AUC) Agenda 2063's ten-year Continental Education Strategy for Africa 2016–2025 (CESA 2016–2025) where relevant.

The pre-2015 MDGs agenda was the grounds for definite neoliberal, capitalist, neo-colonial development and poverty reduction plans, which determined donor-recipient interactions and shaped education policies (ibid.; Klees 2016). It encompassed a global development cooperation strategy and a logic as well as policy dialogue about means to foster national progress and alleviate poverty (Gore 2010; Takyi-Amoako 2017). Both represented the new global development agreement. The MDGs as global integration with a human face comprised a comprehensive form of the Washington Consensus often claimed redundant but stayed in force—a consensus—which is yet to promote Africa's development (ibid.). An overview of the economic history of Africa shows how the neoliberal approach purveyed by the consensus and its advocates in macro-economic policies for Africa undermined socioeconomic development and social responsibilities of states and governments, while decimating social protective structures, thereby deepening inequalities, particularly, within Africa and between it and the rest of the world (Olamosu and Wynne 2015).

The present SDGs, despite their comprehensiveness, are still being seen in the same light (Sengupta and Muchhala 2016; Klees 2017). While the SDGs seem to have overcome the often criticized parochialism of the MDGs, the SDG text and praxis are still being indicted of lacking the essence of global partnership for development, and usurping the policy space for developing countries (Gore 2015; Muchhala and Sengupta 2014).

As the introductory chapter of this book and other studies before it reiterate and enumerate, in spite of tremendous investment in the education systems in Africa over the years, the current statistics on education outcomes are discouraging. From early childhood education through primary and secondary to higher education, educational outcomes paint a depressing picture in the region despite the acknowledgment of slight progress (UNESCO 2014, 2015, 2016; Takyi-Amoako 2015, 2017; Takyi-Amoako and Assie-Lumumba 2018). In particular, sub-Saharan Africa has been trailing all the other regions globally as far as educational outcomes are concerned. Despite some progress, by 2015 none of the Education for All (EFA) and MDGs, especially those related to education, were attained in Africa. Poor quality education, poor access, high dropout rates, the problem of out-of-school children, gender inequality, and funding gaps abound (ibid.).

Meanwhile, studies have expressed the inadequacy of the existing global development paradigm to address the above educational challenges. It is argued that poor development outcomes in SSA are the result of the repudiation of the enduring concept of promoting growth in national economies (Gore 2010, 2015; Takyi-Amoako 2015, 2017). According to Gore (2010) the MDGs engendered a new world development accord, but this consensus largely failed to reduce poverty as it was grounded on a "Faustian bargain" (70). In other words, the benefits of this agreement were gained at the cost of a tremendous deficit. Global responsibility to supporting economic progress and tackling income variations worldwide has vanished, while state and global policies have clustered to advance global integration rather than production and employment in SSA countries, an indication of the power differential in global partnership, particularly, North-South partnerships (ibid). This epitomizes a major cause why efforts to tackle poor educational outcomes and partnership disparities even at the basic level of education and the MDGs failed to produce the required result in Africa (ibid.).

In response, this chapter proposes an alternative approach derived from the fusion of the philosophy of Ubuntu and the notion of the Confluence (Amoako 2009; Takyi-Amoako 2012). Employing a reflective, interpretive approach and documentary analysis, I argue that: a thoughtful consciousness of and sensitivity to "our communal inter-connected-ness, our common humanity, our interdependence and our common membership to a community", which nurtures the shared benefit of society and holds humanness as an essential prerequisite of human development, blended with a deep understanding of the Confluence (meeting point) by African national governments, decision makers, education stakeholders and other agents of change in Africa, and how countries are positioned within this space on the cusp or in the nexus of the global and local, is crucial for the effectiveness and relevance of Africa's current and future development and educational processes and systems (ibid., Venter 2004; Letseka 2013, p. 339; Takyi-Amoako 2015, 2017). Not only will this amalgamation enable these drivers of change to identify, formulate and implement relevant and effective education policies for Africa but also equip them to strategically negotiate and navigate the power dynamics at the core of local/global networks and partnerships and, subsequently, drive education and training processes towards the advantage of their beneficiaries, in particular, and Africa and its progress in general.

The chapter is divided into four sections. The first provides the introduction, by delineating the background to the problem; the second outlines the theoretical and methodological framework by examining the notion of the Confluence and the framework of Ubuntu; the third discusses the interactions and partnership processes around policy issues engendered by the education and partnership SDGs in regard to the educational systems and partnerships in Africa and how the continent is educationally and socioeconomically positioned globally in its navigation and negotiation of the power dynamics. The section recommends the extent to which the notion of the Confluence and an Ubuntu-inspired education for humanity could mitigate or even address these power inequalities to enable the continent to lead in the harnessing of the potential of and for its very youthful populations in order to forestall the danger presented by unexploited aptitudes and abilities of the youth.

The Problem

According to Sachs, the comprehensive Global Education Monitoring Report (GEMR) 2016 is very clear on how remote we are from attaining the SDGs and, therefore, "should set off alarm bells around the world and lead to a historic scale-up of actions to achieve SDG 4", particularly, in SSA (UNESCO 2016, p. ii). Why does Africa continue to lag behind all the other regions of the world socioeconomically and educationally? The capitalist, neoliberal and neo-colonial make-up of the globalization nexus is represented by the intersection of the global and local. That is, when African countries, regional and continental organizations in the Global South interact with countries, bi/multilateral, international organizations and financial institutions from the Global North during education policy processes power inequalities are generated (Klees 2017; Amoako 2009; Abdi et al. 2006).

Moreover, the Paris Declaration of aid effectiveness agenda that underpins global partnerships, and drives development goals in Africa, remains at the level of rhetoric. Aid effectiveness, described essentially as aid that effectively culminates in a developing country's economic growth and assuages poverty, has had its standard reemphasized by aid architects and recipients as donor harmonization, alignment with recipient governments' national strategies, recipient ownership, managing results and mutual accountability, all of which, among other things, are aimed at equalizing donor-recipient power differential. Its real test lies in its developmental impact in terms of real change in the lives and rights of those affected by deprivation and inequality (Tujan and Tomlinson 2008; Takyi-Amoako 2009). The agenda emphasizes that it is not only the amount of aid released but also how it is released that secures its success in attaining its objectives (HLF 2005; Takyi-Amoako 2010). Thirteen goals were set to be achieved in 2010. Conversely, the monitoring survey findings suggested that only one had been attained. Overall, there is a vast gap between theory/objectives and practice/outcomes (Addison and Scott 2011; Killen 2011; Kharas 2014; Takyi-Amoako 2017). The Results Report by the Global Partnership on Education (GPE), which is connected to their strategic plan, GPE 2020, also lamented missing a number of milestones in three years, one of which is alignment of GPE grants with national systems, a crucial aid effectiveness principle (GPE 2016).

It is, however, unfortunate that the current global partnership for sustainable development and all its predecessors have been parochially structured by traditional foreign aid (e.g. North-South) relations and instruments replete with power inequalities, which render development partnerships, especially, in Africa asymmetrical. The post-2015 agenda for development attempts to redress this imbalance through its SDG17, which aims to reinforce the process of execution and invigorate the global partnership for sustainable development by widening the process to embrace other segments and actors including South-South (which are already occurring in Africa anyway), triangular and public-private partnerships, civil society and others. Yet, the power inequalities durably persist because the partnership process is fundamentally flawed. Thus, for the education and partnership SDGs as well as the goals of the African Union Commission's Agenda 2063 to be achieved, this basic error has to be rectified. Indeed, the bleak state of affairs reflected in the current poor educational outcomes and incongruent and inadequate education systems, on one hand, and the fundamentally flawed global partnership process within which African countries participate, on the other, call for an urgent search for new directions in education in Africa—paths that will ensure that education policy systems/processes and educational partnerships in Africa are culturally revamped and made more relevant and beneficial on the continent educationally, socioeconomically and environmentally.

Defining the Question

Consequently, the chapter proposes a framework shaped from the notion of the Confluence interwoven with the principles of Ubuntu, which espouse African traditional values of humanness. It examines the post-2015 agenda for sustainable development, focusing on the partnership SDG in relation to the education SDGs as well as Agenda 2063 education strategy (CESA 2016–2025) within the context of Africa, what the pitfalls are, and how the principles of Ubuntu performed at the Confluence can help avoid these pitfalls for a successful global partnership enactment, a prerequisite for the attainment of the education and partnership SDGs in Africa. In this chapter, I examine the following question:

- How can global/international agents and local/national/regional/ continental actors undo the effects of external and internal domination at the Ubuntu-inspired Confluence of global educational policy partnership in a manner that would reduce economic, income and power inequities between and within nations/regions/continent for the benefit of the youth in Africa?

THE CONFLUENCE AND UBUNTU CONCEPTS AND METHODOLOGY

Analytical Method

In tackling the above question, the chapter assumes an introspective interpretive stance based on documentary analysis and theoretical articulation with some credible instances to explore how global education partnerships in and for Africa require a re-visioning within the framework of Ubuntu intertwined with the notion of the Confluence. Employing existing scholarship, this chapter offers an analysis of re-visioning education in African countries from the perspective of redressing the power imbalance of education partnerships at the Confluence through the lens of the philosophy of Ubuntu—an education partnership process within a development agenda entrenched with global integration that repudiates economic growth and creation of productive capacities in Africa and fails to address global income inequalities. This stance not only involves tackling power and educational inequalities between groups but also between education policy agents that inhabit global (e.g. North-South, etc.) partnerships within development paradigm under examination, while strengthening the education constituent of global partnerships in Africa (Takyi-Amoako 2015, 2017; Gore 2010; Amoako 2009).

Africa's Regional Variation

First, it is important to note that the weight of the analysis falls more on sub-Saharan Africa than on North Africa since the educational challenges of the latter are not as dire as those of the former. Regarding regional variation in Africa, North Africa represents the highest proportion of high human development countries, while Southern and Central Africa exhibit a combination of low and medium, and East and West Africa display a low human development category (AfDB-OECD-UNDP 2016). Thus, the analysis argues the need to consider crucial philosophical and practical partnership questions that have ramifications for human development and critical education policy issues in Africa in general, and in sub-Saharan Africa in particular, which national/regional/continental governments, development partners and other stakeholders must address at the point where the global/international and local/national/regional/continental meet, referred to as the Confluence. It further explores the extent to which an Ubuntu-inspired partnership for education for humanity could obviate the neo-colonial, neoliberal and hegemonic bent of the global development partnership for sustainable development and create education policy spaces, processes and resources to develop and harness the intellectual and entrepreneurial potential of Africa's teeming youthful populations in order to avert the threat posed by unexploited talents and abilities of the youth (Kazeem 2017; AfDB, OECD and UNDP 2016, 2017). What, then, is Ubuntu?

Ubuntu Defined

Ubuntu is the mutual reliance of people for the enactment, advancement and realization of their capabilities to be simultaneously individuals and community. This emphasizes the significance of the extended family to African societies. By means of this type of family, an individual assumes a broader existence, not merely a consequence of lineage, relatedness and matrimony but also through humanity, regarded as a family of which a person assumes membership when born and from which nobody is excluded (Battle 2009). In other words, one's humanity is entwined with the other person's. She/he affirms the other and vice versa and does not feel threatened by the success of the other for she/he has a real self-confidence that stems from the awareness that she/he forms part of the communal whole and is lessened when others are dishonoured or subjugated (Broodryk 2006). Ubuntu is the affirmation of one's own humanity by acknowledging the humanity of others and creating dignified human connections with them. It is being confronted with a decisive choice between wealth and preserving the life of another and choosing the latter. It is a ruler/leader keenly aware that leadership with its overall status and authority stems from the dictates of the governed and thus valuing and expressing this indebtedness in her/his role and service to them. (Samkange 1980). Relevant to this analysis are the above notion and following features of Ubuntu: togetherness, brother/sisterhood, equality, sharing, sympathy, empathy, compassion, respect, tolerance, humanness, harmony and redistribution (Broodryk 2002, p. 13). These virtues emphasized in the traditional way of existence in Africa promote peace and harmony. Respect is meant not only for other human beings but also for the community, natural environment, fauna and flora as well as the supernatural (ibid.). Eze (2010, pp. 190–191) summarizes the crux of Ubuntu:

'A person is a person through other people' strikes an affirmation of one's humanity through recognition of an 'other' in his or her uniqueness and difference. It is a demand for a creative intersubjective formation in which the 'other' becomes a mirror (but only a mirror) for my subjectivity. This idealism suggests to us that humanity is not embedded in my person solely as an individual; my humanity is co-substantively bestowed upon the other and me. Humanity is a quality we owe to each other. We create each other and need to sustain this otherness creation. And if we belong to each other, we participate in our creations: we are because you are, and since you are, definitely I am. The 'I am' is not a rigid subject, but a dynamic self-constitution dependent on this otherness creation of relation and distance.

Consequently, I argue that conscious deployments of these Ubuntu principles at the Confluence where global partnership for educational development is being enacted with Africa as a lead participant in regard to its education processes will help address the power inequalities, and result in indigenously led and relevant educational policy, practice and outcomes for sustainable development in Africa. The Confluence is defined next.

THE CONFLUENCE

The concept of education policy options, procedures and practices at the point where partners meet is referred to as the Confluence. This Confluence signifies the meeting point of rivers of various agents and ideas (national/ regional/continental and international) within the context of the MDGs and SDGs development framework, whose objective is not to nurture but to assimilate the national/regional/continental economies of Africa glob-ally while abolishing their productive capacities (Gore 2010, 2015). It is situated on the cusp of the global and local, the international/transnational and national/regional/continental where North-South/South-South or triangular partnerships occur (Amoako 2009; Takyi-Amoako 2015, 2017). While the depiction of policy and its procedures as representing state-cen-tred/control and diverse contexts and stages of a cycle are abundant (Ball 1994; Bowe et al. 1992; Ozga 1990; Apple 1989; Dale 1989; Vidovich 2001; Taylor 1997; Ranson 1995; Troyna 1994; Lingard 1993), what is largely unknown is describing policy processes at the Confluence of inter-actions between global/international and local/national/ regional/ conti-nental actors (e.g. foreign aid donors [bi/multilateral], recipients, non-governmental organizations, both public and private sector entities, etc.), whose deeds and choices are shaped by the powers of globalization, partnership, funding/foreign aid, policy and power processes. In other words, policy is comprehended as stages and contexts in a cycle. However, we have inadequate grasp of the concept of policy processes in a space/ field, which this study and others (by this author) before it identify as the Confluence (Amoako 2009; Takyi-Amoako 2010, 2015, 2017).

Local/national/regional/continental education policy procedures do not comprise one-way flows of ideas. They are devised in a setting influ-enced by both outside and domestic circumstances, which ensconce a complex tangle of connections between globalization, partnership, fund-ing/foreign aid, policy and power processes within and between nations, on the one hand, and between nations/regions/continents and interna-tional/global entities on the other. This intricate node is conceptualized as the Confluence, the space which cultivates the education goals that must be attained. The global partnership for sustainable development and its processes is located within this space.

Pertinent to this Confluence is Bourdieu's surmising of social organizations as constituting several social fields, each with its distinctive theories of praxis utterly enclosed in a field of power (Hilgers and Mangez 2015). His idea of field is an ordered system of specific and wide-ranging social connections, intrinsically prearranged in terms of power dealings that control access to the specific resources or capital at stake (Thompson 1991; Jenkins 1992; Calhoun 1993). This field symbolizes "the analytical space defined by the interdependence of the entities that compose a structure of positions among which there are power relations" (Hilgers and Mangez 2015, p. 5). By this I mean that the configuring of education policy processes in various national/regional/continental spaces in general and those in SSA in particular is clad within an intricate maze of both endogenous (local/national/regional) and exogenous (global/international) forces and power inequalities at this Confluence (Amoako 2009; Takyi-Amoako 2012). This social actuality is deemed fundamentally relational (Hilgers and Mangez 2015).

The increasing convergence between the global and local, international/transnational and national/regional/continental in education policy processes in Africa is resulting in new forms of association and polycentric control. Simply put, policy processes occurring on the cusp of the local and global, namely, the Confluence, are engendering spaces, fields or systems with copious hubs of executive and intensified pressures (Thompson et al. 2015). This Confluence could also be conceptualized as global policy union of national/regional/ continental and international/transnatio nal, as well as policy assemblages and networks determining relationships of exchange and interaction (Ball and Exley 2010; Thompson and Cook 2014). A deep understanding of this Confluence by African governments, policy actors and their partners can engender sensitivity to culture and context, which then can empower education policy actors and agents who/which operate at this meeting point to partner effectively to tackle the educational and partnership policy problems, disparities and inequalities (see Amoako 2009; Takyi-Amoako 2010, 2015, 2017).

Ubuntu, the Confluence and the Post-2015 Agenda for Sustainable Development in Sub-Saharan Africa

In this section, I explore the question: How can global/international agents and local/national/regional/continental actors undo the effects of external and internal domination at the Ubuntu-inspired Confluence of global educational policy partnership in a manner that would reduce economic, income and power inequities between and within nations/regions/continent for the benefit of the youth in Africa? While some of the manifestations of the power inequalities and issues that characterize the global partnership for development in Africa are highlighted, how the Ubuntu values could be employed to upset the neoliberal predilection of the global development strategy is examined.

Post-2015 Agenda

The post-2015 sustainable development agenda presents a far more comprehensive framework than the pre-2015 millennium development agenda. The education SDG, for instance, which aims to ensure inclusive and equitable quality education and promote lifelong learning opportunities for all, has seven targets whose objective by 2030 is, not only, to guarantee for all children completion of free, equitable and quality basic and secondary education that results in pertinent and successful learning outcomes but also facilitate their access to quality early childhood development, care and pre-primary education. Equitable access to affordable and quality technical, vocational and tertiary education including university must be granted to all adults of both sexes. The proportion of young people who possess required skills comprising technical and vocational competences for the job market and entrepreneurship must increase, just to mention a few. This education SDG and others and their targets as well as their means of implementation project a comprehensive agenda. The partnership SDG whose targets and means of implementation form the backbone of all the other goals displays a similar sophistication. However, the challenge here is how to transcend the rhetoric and translate all the comprehensiveness into reality when the record of such a partnership is discouraging.

At the Confluence of Power Inequalities

Educational ideologies are transferred into the policy universes of African countries, notionally, through economic or cultural globalization, and more materially through foreign aid by donors from the Global North. They are not, for ostensive purposes, termed ideologies, but the standpoints presumed in association with educational development are ingrained in the subtlety of aid agreements. Indubitably, to conceal any inference of an ideology, the idea of "partnership" is engaged to acquire a unanimity of

plans. This design is impugned, and examiners of the idea of aid partnerships repeatedly point up the lopsided make-up of donor-recipient relations
and summon the conception of unbalanced power (see Amoako 2009).
    First, educational aid policy interactions, for instance, between interna-
tional development partners and African national/regional/continental
governments, have been plagued with power inequalities which undermine the attainment of development goals historically (Addison and Scott
2011; Killen 2011; Kharas 2014). Hence, the establishment of the aid
effectiveness paradigm to forestall the failure of developmental partnership
processes, which encapsulates donor-recipient interactions around policy
processes. For instance, most global/international/financial/bi/multilat-
eral/foreign aid institutions and their allies that interact with African
national/regional/continental bodies under the global partnership for
development at the Confluence fail to uphold their own designed aid
effectiveness principles. For example, the GPE, which works in partnership with developing nations predominantly in Africa, in their recent
report, admitted that fewer than a third of their performance awards were
sufficiently aligned to countries' systems. Thus, only 39 per cent of GPE
grants utilized mutual financing or joint award mechanisms. According to
the report, it is critical to enhance this alignment as it is basic to reinforcing
countries' capacity and supports prospective endurance of GPE initiatives
(GPE 2016).
    Second, another example of power inequities at the expense of Africa
has been the World Bank spreading a capitalist neoliberal, neo-colonial
education reform agenda manifested as structural adjustment programmes
(SAPs); economic recovery programmes (ERPs); and poverty reduction
strategy papers (PRSPs) in conjunction with the Education for All (EFA),
MDGs and SDGs in SSA countries, all of which constitute liberalization
policies that undermine the national/regional economies of Africa (Mundy
2002; Abdi et al. 2006; Jones 2007; Olamosu and Wynne 2015; Böröcz
2016; Klees 2017). Indeed, low development outcomes including poor
education outcomes in Africa are the result of the rejection of the enduring
concept of promoting growth in national economies, employment and
productive capacities (Gore 2010, 2015).
    Additionally, funding limitation and gap are at the core of the educa-
tion problem in Africa (Sachs 2016). Thus, capital flight from the continent is a serious issue. For instance, Ndikumana and Boyce (2011)
demonstrated that between 1970 and 2008, Africa was a net exporter of
capital worldwide. Overall, capital flight during this era was $735 billion

(in 2008 dollars) compared to an external debt of only $117 billion (OECD/AfDB 2011). An UNCTAD study discovered that Africa obtained US$540 billion in loans between 1970 and 2002 and paid back US$550 billion. However, the continent was still indebted to the tune of US$295 billion due to mandatory arrears, penalties and interests (Loong 2007; Shivji 2009, p. 65). Yet, annually, Africa loses more than $50 billion through illicit financial outflows (AU/ECA n.d.). This resulted in the decision to concentrate on the issue of illicit financial outflows from Africa and exclusively on the choices that must be made to drastically decrease these outflows to guarantee that this development capital stays within the continent (ibid.).

An econometric study reveals that for every new dollar borrowed by African nations externally, as much as 60 cents leave Africa as capital flight in the same year (Ndikumana and Boyce 2012; Ndikumana et al. 2015). Illicit financial flows, tax avoidance and evasion by multinational corporations have deleterious effect on African countries by intensifying poverty, economic inequalities, corruption and biased competition (Mohammed 2015).

Also, a substantial portion of the development aid transferred to Africa is instantly returned to western countries through fees to overseas consultants whose daily charge is mostly equal to the monthly wage of local personnel. In 1995 it was approximated that 100,000 overseas experts were working in Africa at a cost of $4 billion. In 2005 the World Bank confessed that $20 billion of the $50 billion international aid funds were expended on consultants (Olamosu and Wynne 2015).

Furthermore, global taxation, which the Education Commission, which provides financial support to African countries, excludes in its report despite recommendations, has been proposed as a solution to stem these illicit outflows haemorrhaging Africa (Klees 2016). A suitably financed and complete representative intergovernmental UN-based tax entity was an essential request by the G77 group of developing nations during the Addis Financing for Development summit in July 2015. Regrettably, this initiative was thwarted by some Organization for Economic Cooperation and Development (OECD) governments (ibid.).

In the fray, understanding the Confluence engenders sensitivity to the pervading power inequalities and a deliberate consciousness to evoke Ubuntu values during the exercising of educational aid or development partnerships to promote human decency, prevent social exclusion and environmental degradation. This chapter, therefore, proposes that the Ubuntu framework must become the bedrock of the global partnership process that occurs at the

Confluence within which African governments, international development partners and other stakeholders interact for educational development in Africa. Ubuntu, which has at its core, human interdependence, may address the power differentials that permeate the meeting point or the Confluence where education policy formulation and implementation occur during the enactment of the global partnership for development. Both (the Confluence and Ubuntu) team up to espouse ideals that have the potential to secure a present and future where economic development avoids worsening inequities and rather brings wealth to all, where urban localities and employment are structured to empower all, and economic decisions, public and private are environmentally sound. Sustainable development perceives healthy planet as central to human progress, and education and well-educated citizenry both have a significant role to play in its realization (UNESCO 2016). To achieve the above, the following Ubuntu principles characterized by Broodryk (2006) are useful in upsetting the neo-colonial, neoliberal capitalist leanings of the global partnership for sustainable development in practice.

Ubuntu Principles as a Power Redressor

When those international/national/regional/continental actors and agents responsible for the implementation of the global partnership for sustainable development deliberately express **togetherness** as a people irrespective of differences and therefore see themselves as a **single entity** and **unchanging equals**, who **share** and **redistribute** (if necessary) resources and **complement** one another and the people for whom they bear responsibility, while expressing **sympathy** and sharing **joy**, which enable **empathy** that ensures **mutual survival**, **respect** and **tolerance** of one another for **peaceful** and **harmonious** existence even as they uphold distinct **indigenous wisdom, culture, identity** and **knowledge** for humanity, then they can declare with conviction that "we belong to each other, we participate in our creations: we are because you are, and since you are, definitely I am" (Eze 2010, pp. 190–191).

Improving the bleak educational landscape in Africa requires such interdependence between Africa and its global partners. However, this global partnership has to occur under the leadership of Africa because the continent and its people are more indigenously and experientially placed to understand its own educational problems. For instance, the Education Commission estimates that to attain its educational financing goals by 2030 on behalf of low- and middle-income countries, the latter will have to commit 8.5 per cent of GDP, an increase from 6.0 per cent in 2015. In low-income nations, this figure is 11.8 per cent by 2030 up from 6.5 per cent in 2015. It is projected that 97 per cent of this extra financing must come from the countries themselves and only 3 per cent from external sources (ECR n.d.; Klees 2017). If this is the scenario, why should Africa not assume the leadership position at the Confluence? Why should it relinquish its leadership to the international community, whose leadership for years has not yielded the desired educational/developmental results for Africa? The Education Commission's assertion that, "[w]here countries commit to invest and reform, the international community would stand ready to offer the increased finance and leadership necessary to support countries working to transform education", is moot in the case of Africa (Education Commission Report n.d., p. 15). In fact, what Africa currently needs is not global or external leadership but the ability to assume its own leadership at the Confluence of providing the much-needed solutions to its educational woes albeit in collaboration with the world especially if 97 per cent of the funding must come from African countries.

Additionally, mobilizing alternative financing from myriad sources for Africa's educational challenges is valid. However, the Education Commission's support for new education investment instrument to help scale financing from Multilateral Development Banks may not necessarily be the best option for Africa considering the neoliberal, neo-colonial and ideological record of such banks in the history of Africa's educational/development (ibid; Klees 2017; Klees et al. 2012).

Moreover, the neoliberal capitalist environment has also given prominence to the private sector in education in Africa and has become a partner in education and development initiatives. However, for the global partnership for development to benefit Africa's education efforts, it must not promote privatization of education in Africa as the way forward, since it cannot mitigate the social cost of the harsh globally led development policies that negatively affected Africa's educational and socioeconomic progress. Instead, within the Ubuntu paradigm, the Education Commission, for instance, must work with Africa within this global partnership to redistribute resources, stem illicit flows, capital flight and address the inequalities permeating global trade policies to the detriment of Africa. Financing accrued from these sources and other viable ones will significantly complement overseas development assistance (ODA), which never meets its target of 0.7 per cent of GDP, anyway, and enable Africa to withdraw strategically from aid dependency (Moyo 2009; Takyi-Amoako

2009). Promoting privatization in Africa creates opportunities for globally and locally accessible entities whose main aim is for profit to exploit Africa's poor and poverty. Rather, an Ubuntu-inspired global partnership for education/development should exercise equality, redistribution, mutual survival, respect and empathy to remedy the dismantled sovereignty and cooperative machinery of African national/regional/continental governments, strengthen their economic authority not through ODA, but through trade and other means, and help relinquish market and hegemonic control of education. This will enable governments to play their social roles by mitigating social costs and protecting their marginalized and vulnerable masses.

While policy prioritization is a valid process to enable efficient utilization of inadequate resources, ruthless prioritization being championed by the Education Commission in African countries is suspect, particularly, when the Commission seems to be reiterating the tired old argument made by the World Bank and allies in the past specifically for developing countries that "returns are highest for investments in pre-primary and primary education" (ECR n.d., p. 87; Dzeagu 2017). In fact, in the past, this stance within the global partnership for development ensured the neglect of other sub-sectors of education and near decimation of Africa's higher education till the 1990s when the World Bank under pressure had a change of heart (Jegede 2012; Sawyerr 2004; Samoff and Carrol 2004; World Bank 1988; Mihyo 2008; Lindow 2011; Bregman and Bryner 2003; Takyi-Amoako 2015). As I argued elsewhere, this creates a negative yoyo effect on policy trajectory, and for Africa and its people to avoid this, they must become the drivers/leaders and funders of their own educational systems in collaboration with external actors (Takyi-Amoako 2015). In this case, the AU, by means of its education strategy, a component of its Agenda 2063 must assume the leadership position at the Confluence. It could be argued that forming more global entities led by the North to seek financial support in the name of Africa's poor educational outcomes may not necessarily be the way forward as these continue to weaken Africa's own institutional capacities and usurp the policy space for Africa while continually undermining and squeezing out Africa's own solutions to or opportunities to devise its own educational problems.

Therefore, Ubuntu in this context would represent a power redresser at the Confluence where educational stakeholders meet to formulate and implement education policy. This will then mean that because economic, income and power inequalities are addressed in global educational and development partnerships, the SDG17 will be attained. Thus, means of implementing the global partnership will be strengthened and the process revitalized for sustainable development. This will culminate in the realization of SDG4, resulting in inclusive and equitable quality education and lifelong learning for all in Africa and for humanity—"we create each other and need to sustain this otherness creation".

CONCLUSION

Irina Bokova, the Director-General of UNESCO, summarizes the three messages that the GEM Report conveys. The first being the pressing call for novel strategies since existing trends suggest that only 70 per cent of children in low-income countries will complete primary school by 2030, a goal that should have been attained in 2015. She calls for the political resolve, the policies, the innovation and the capital to oppose this trend. The second advocates a lasting dedication to SDG4 with actions of sharp sensitivity to exigency, because anything otherwise portends catastrophe not only for education but also the attainment of every SDG or goal towards poverty eradication, hunger prevention, better health, gender balance, female empowerment, sustainable production and consumption, robust societies thriving on increased equality and inclusiveness. The final sounds the call to basically transform our understanding of education and its benefit to people's welfare and world progress. The growing need for education to cultivate the appropriate competencies, mind-sets and practices that will result in sustainable and inclusive progress has never been so intense. Thus, the responsibility to contrive comprehensive, sophisticated and incorporated remedies to the existing numerous economic, social and environmental ills is huge. This requires transcending conventional borders and engineering efficient, multi-sector partnerships and networks (UNESCO 2016; Bokova 2016). In these partnerships, often occurring within the overarching global partnership for sustainable development, significant provisions must be made not to crowd out but to support Africa's attempts to formulate its own education philosophies, theories and practices and seek its own advancement Nsamenang and Tchombe (2011). The CESA 2016–2025 re-echoes this in its strategy document:

> The lessons learned from both the African Union-led developmental efforts and those supported by the international community clearly indicate that educational development is first and foremost a national and regional

responsibility. And that meaningful educational development cannot be achieved outside of a clearly defined vision and strategic framework, owned and articulated around the socioeconomic and cultural aspirations of the people. Clearly, educational programs designed and financed from the outside unavoidably lack coherence and their impact remains limited. (AUC 2016, p. 10)

In this light, the chapter reiterates its argument that to attain these pressing goals in Africa, it is important to re-vision education in the region by considering the notion of the Confluence examined within the philosophical framework of Ubuntu. Indeed, both the Confluence notion and Ubuntu framework have significant reverberations for the 2030 Agenda appeal to devise holistic and integrated responses to development challenges, on one hand, and the global/partnerships for sustainable development and future on the other. The global partnership must promote Africa's economic growth distributed fairly, employment and productive capacities.

At the Confluence (both conceptual and material), where all actors from the various global/international, local/national/continental spaces meet, every participant must acknowledge and operate with the principle that, "…my humanity is co-substantively bestowed upon the other and me. Humanity is a quality we owe to each other. We create each other and need to sustain this otherness creation. And if we belong to each other, we participate in our creations: we are because you are, and since you are, definitely I am". Indeed, the presence of this sense of humanity is a choice we can't afford not to make!

References

Abdi, A., Puplampu, K. P., & Dei, G. J. S. (2006). *African education and globalization: Critical perspectives*. Lanham: Lexington Books.
Addison, T. & Scott, L. (2011). Linking aid effectiveness to development outcomes: A priority for Busan. *Briefing paper*. Helsinki: UN-Wider.
AfDB-OECD-UNDP. (2016). *African economic outlook 2016 sustainable cities and structural transformation*. Abidjan/Paris/New York: AfDB, OECD, UNDP.
AfDB-OECD-UNDP. (2017). *African economic outlook 2017 entrepreneurship and industrialisation*. Abidjan/Paris/New York: AfDB, OECD, UNDP.
African Union Commission. (2016). *Continental education strategy for Africa 2016–2025*. Addis-Ababa: AUC.
Amoako, E. J. A. (2009). *Shaping policy at the confluence of the global and national: Ghana's Education Strategic Plan*. DPhil thesis, University of Oxford.

Apple, M. (1989). Critical introduction: Ideology and the state in educational policy. In R. Dale (Ed.), *The state and education policy* (pp. 1–20). Milton Keynes: Open University Press.

AU/ECA. (n.d.). *Illicit financial flows: Report of the high level panel on illicit financial flows from Africa.* Commissioned by the Joint African Union Commission/United Nations Economic Commission for Africa (AU/ECA) Conference of Ministers of Finance, Planning and Economic Development.

Ball, S. J. (1994). *Education reform: A critical and post-structural approach.* Buckingham: Open University Press.

Ball, S. J., & Exley, S. (2010). Making policy with 'good ideas': Policy networks and the 'intellectuals' of new labour. *Journal of Education Policy, 25*(2), 151–169.

Battle, M. (2009). *Ubuntu: I in you and you in me.* New York: Church Publishing, Inc.

BBC News. (2016). *Four more ways the CIA has meddled in Africa.* http://www.bbc.co.uk/news/world-africa-36303327. Accessed 24 July 2017.

Bokova, I. (2016). Foreword. In *Global education monitoring report. Education for people and planet: Creating sustainable futures for all* (p. i). Paris: UNESCO Publishing.

Böröcz, J. (2016). Global inequality in redistribution: For a world historical-sociology of (not) caring. *Intersections: East European Journal of Society and Politics, 2*(2), 57–83.

Bowe, R., Ball, S. J., & Gold, A. (1992). *Reforming education and changing schools.* London: Routledge.

Bregman, J., & Bryner, K. (2003). *Quality of secondary education in Africa (SEIA).* Paris: Association for the Development of Education in Africa (ADEA).

Broodryk, J. (2002). *Ubuntu: Life lessons from Africa.* Tshwane: Ubuntu School of Philosophy.

Broodryk, J. (2006, October 12–17). *Ubuntu: African life coping skills- theory and practice-paper delivered at CCEAM conference.* Conference theme: Recreating linkages between Theory and Praxis in Educational Leadership. Lefkosia (Nicosia): Cyprus.

Calhoun, C. (1993). Habitus, field, and capital: The question of historical specificity. In C. Calhoun, E. Lipuma, & M. Postone (Eds.), *Bourdieu: Critical perspectives* (pp. 61–88). Cambridge: Polity Press.

Dale, R. (1989). *The state and education policy.* Milton Keynes: Open University Press.

Dzeagu, V. (2017, July 18). Towards a learning generation in Africa: From the Nairobi workshop, a Newfound Value for 'Ruthless Prioritization'. *NORRAG Blog.*

Eze, M. O. (2010). *Intellectual history in contemporary South Africa.* New York: Palgrave Macmillan.

Gore, C. (2010). The MDG paradigm, productive capacities and the future of poverty reduction. *IDS Bulletin, 41*(1), 70–79.

Gore, C. (2015). The post-2015 moment: Towards sustainable development goals and a new global development paradigm. *Journal of International Development, 27*, 717–732.

High Level Forum. (2005). *Paris declaration on aid effectiveness*. Paris: HLF.

Hilgers, M., & Mangez, E. (2015). *Bourdieu's theory of social fields: Concepts and applications*. Abingdon: Routledge.

Jegede, O. (2012). Higher Education in Africa: Weaving Success. An Invited Contribution to the Panel Discussion on the Launch of *Weaving Success: Voices of Change in Higher Education* – A Project of the Partnership for Higher education in Africa (PHEA) Held at the Institute of International Education, 809 United Nations Plaza, New York, NY 10017, on Wednesday, 1 February, 2012.

Jenkins, R. (1992). *Pierre Bourdieu*. London: Routledge.

Jones, P. (2007). *World Bank financing of education: Lending, learning, and development* (2nd ed.). New York: Routledge.

Kazeem, Y. (2017, June 29). More than half of the world's population growth will be in Africa by 2050. *Quartz Africa*. https://qz.com/1016790/more-than-half-of-the-worlds-population-growth-will-be-in-africa-by-2050/. Accessed 25 July 2017.

Kharas, H. (2014). *Improve aid effectiveness*. Brookings Institution. http://effectivecooperation.org/2014/04/improve-aid-effectiveness/. Accessed 06 Aug 2017.

Killen, B. (2011). How much does aid effectiveness improve development outcomes? Lessons from recent practice. *Busan Background Papers*. 29 November–1 December, Busan Korea. www.oecd.org/development/effectiveness/48458806.pdf. Accessed 1 July 2016.

Klees, S. (2016). Human capital and rates of return: Brilliant ideas or ideological dead ends? *Comparative Education Review, 60*(4), 644–672.

Klees, S. J. (2017). Beyond neoliberalism: Reflections on capitalism and education. *Policy Futures in Education*. Prepublished June 29, 2017. https://doi.org/10.1177/1478210317715814.

Klees, S., Samoff, J., & Stromquist, N. (Eds.). (2012). *World Bank and education: Critiques and alternatives*. Rotterdam: Sense.

Letseka, M. (2013). Educating for *Ubuntu/Botho*: Lessons from Basotho indigenous education. *Open Journal of Philosophy, 3*(2), 337–344. Published online may 2013 in SciRes. http://www.scirp.org/journal/ojpp. Accessed 10 Apr 2015.

Lindow, M. (2011). *Weaving success: Voices of change in higher education*. New York: Institute of International Education.

Lingard, B. (1993). The changing state of policy production in education: Some Australian reflections on the state of policy sociology. *International Studies in Sociology of Education, 3*(1), 25–47.

Loong, Y. S. (2007). *Debt: The repudiation option.* Third World Network. http://finance.thirdworldnetwork.net/article.php?aid=47

Mahoney, P. W., & Name not Declassified. (1965). 251. Memorandum of Conversation, Washington, March 11, 1965, 3–3:30 p.m. Subject: Ghana/Participants: The Director of Central Intelligence/ Ambassador to Ghana, William P. Mahoney/ Deputy Chief, Africa Division, [name not declassified]. *Foreign Relations of the United States, 1964–1968, Volume XXIV, Africa.* https://history.state.gov/historicaldocuments/frus1964-68v24/d251. Accessed 24 July 2017.

Mihyo, P. B. (2008). *Staff retention in African universities and links with the diaspora.* Accra: AAU.

Mohammed, A. (2015). *Illicit outflows: No end without global cooperation.* http://cap.africa-platform.org/news/illicit-outflows-no-end-without-global-cooperation. Accessed 20 July 17.

Moyo, D. (2009). *Dead aid.* London: Penguin Books Ltd.

Muchhala, B., & Sengupta, M. (2014). A déjà vu agenda or a development agenda? A critique of the post-2015 development agenda from the perspective of developing countries. *Economic and Political Weekly, XLIX*(46), 28–30.

Mundy, K. (2002). Retrospect and prospect: Education in a reforming World Bank. *International Journal of Educational Development, 22*, 483–508.

Ndikumana, L., & Boyce, J. (2011). *Africa's odious debts—How foreign loans and capital flight bled a continent.* London/New York: Zed Books.

Ndikumana, L., & Boyce, J. (2012). *Capital flight from Sub-Saharan African countries: Updated estimates 1970–2010.* Political Economy Research Institute. www.peri.umass.edu/236/hash/d76a3192e770678316c1ab39712994be/publication/532/

Ndikumana, L., Boyce, J. K., & Ndiaye, A. S. (2015). Capital flight from Africa: Measurement and drivers. In I. Ajayi & L. Ndikumana (Eds.), *Capital flight from Africa: Causes, effects and policy issues* (pp. 15–54). Oxford: Oxford University Press.

Nsamenang, B. A., & Tchombe, T. M. S. (2011). *Handbook of African educational theories and practices: A generative teacher education curriculum.* Human Development Resource Centre (HDRC): Cameroon.

OECD/AfDB. (2011). *African economic outlook 2011: Africa and its emerging partners.* www.afdb.org/en/knowledge/publications/african-economic-outlook/african-economic-outlook-2011/

Olamosu, B., & Wynne, A. (2015). Africa rising? The economic history of Sub-Saharan Africa. *International Socialism: A Quarterly Review of Socialist Theory,* 146. http://isj.org.uk/africa-rising/. Accessed 27 July 2017.

Ozga, J. (1990). Policy research and policy theory: A comment on Fitz and Halpin. *Journal of Education Policy, 5*(4), 359–362.

Quist-Adade, C. (2016, March 2). *The coup that set Ghana and Africa 50 years back*. https://www.pambazuka.org/governance/coup-set-ghana-and-africa-50-years-back

Ranson, S. (1995). Theorizing education policy. *Journal of Education Policy, 10*(4), 427–448.

Sachs, J. (2016). Foreword. In *Global education monitoring report. Education for people and planet: creating sustainable futures for all* (pp. ii–iii). Paris: UNESCO Publishing.

Samkange, J. W. T. S. (1980). Samkange's explanation of *ubuntu*. https://en.wikipedia.org/wiki/Ubuntu_(philosophy). Accessed 27 July 2017.

Samoff, J., & Carrol, B. (2004, March 8–12). *Conditions, coalitions, and influence: The World Bank and higher education in Africa*. Prepared for presentation at the annual conference of the Comparative and International Education Society, Salt Lake City.

Sawyerr, A. (2004). Challenges facing African universities: Selected issues. *African Studies Review, 47*(1), 1–59.

Sengupta, M., & Muchhala, B. (2016, April 29). *First FfD review forum fails to deliver meaningful outcomes (TWN)*. New Delhi/New York.

Shivji, I. G. (2009). *Accumulation in an African periphery—A theoretical framework*. Dar es Salaam: Mkuki na Nyota Publishers.

Takyi-Amoako, E. (2009). Development aid: Advancing effectively or withdrawing strategically? *Network for Policy Research Review and Advice on Education and Training (NORRAG) News, 42*, 112–115.

Takyi-Amoako, E. (2010). Examining the current aid effectiveness paradigm through education policy making in an aid dependent country. *The International Journal of Educational and Psychological Assessment, 5*, 4–18.

Takyi-Amoako, E. (2012). Globalisation in comparative and international education: Towards a theory of the confluence. *Journal of International and Comparative Education, 1*(1), 61–70.

Takyi-Amoako, E. (2015). *Education in West Africa*. London: Bloomsbury Publishing.

Takyi-Amoako, E. J. (2017). Education and gender in Africa/Global South. In P. Amakasu Raposo, D. Arase, & S. Cornelissen (Eds.), *Routledge handbook of Africa-Asia relations*. Oxon: Routledge/Taylor and Francis.

Takyi-Amoako, E. J. A., & Assie-Lumumba, N. T. (2018). *Re-visioning education in Africa: Ubuntu-inspired education for humanity*. New York: Palgrave Macmillan.

Taylor, S. (1997). Critical policy analysis: Exploring contexts, texts and consequences. *Discourse, 23*(13), 23–25.

The Education Commission. (n.d.). *The learning generation: investing in education for a changing world by The International Commission on Financing Global*

Education Opportunity. http://report.educationcommission.org/downloads/. Accessed 25 July 2017.

The Global Partnership for Education. (2016). *GPE results report abridged version 2015/2016.* Washington, DC: GPE.

Thompson, J. B. (1991). Editor's introduction. In J. B. Thompson & P. Bourdieu (Eds.), *Language and symbolic power* (pp. 1–31). Oxford: Polity Press.

Thompson, G., & Cook, I. (2014). Education policy-making and time. *Journal of Education Policy, 29*(5), 700–715.

Thompson, G., Savage, G. C., & Lingard, B. (2015). Think tanks, edu-businesses and education policy: Issues of evidence, expertise and influence. *The Australian Educational Researcher, 43*(1), 1–13. https://doi.org/10.1007/s13384-015-0195-y.

Troyna, B. (1994). Reforms, research and being reflexive about being reflective. In D. Halpin & B. Troyna (Eds.), *Researching education policy: Ethical and methodological issues* (pp. 1–14). New York: The Falmer Press.

Tujan, T., & Tomlinson, B. (2008). What should CSOs expect from the Accra high level forum? Real aid reform, measures for aid effectiveness: Global citizens reclaiming democratic mandate for sustainable development.

UNESCO. (2014). *Education for all global monitoring report 2013/14 teaching and learning: Education quality for all.* Paris: UNESCO Publishing.

UNESCO. (2015). *Education for all 2000–2015: Achievements and challenges.* Paris: UNESCO Publishing.

UNESCO. (2016). *Global education monitoring report. Education for people and planet: Creating sustainable futures for all.* Paris: UNESCO Publishing.

Venter, E. (2004). The notion of Ubuntu and communalism in African education discourse. *Philosophy and Education, 23*(2004), 149–160.

Vidovich, L. (2001, December). *A conceptual framework for analysis of education policy and practices.* Paper proposed for presentation at the Australian Association for Research in Education, Fremantle.

World Bank. (1988). *A World Bank policy study: Education in Sub-Saharan Africa policies for adjustment, revitalization, and expansion.* Washington, DC: World Bank.

CHAPTER 13

Conclusion: Towards an Ubuntu-Inspired Continental Partnership on Education for Sustainable Development in Africa— African Union Commission Agenda 2063 Education Strategy

Emefa J. Takyi-Amoako
and N'Dri Thérèse Assié-Lumumba

We conclude this book on the note that the theoretical way has been paved for actual praxis to commence decisively, and argue that for African Union Commission Agenda 2063 in general and its education strategy in particular to succeed, Africa needs a stronger tightly knit continental education partnership for sustainable development under a more robust continental political unity than it currently has, dipping deeply into the major assets of a common cultural root embedded in Ubuntu. This stronger continental entity will then be positioned as the leader at the Confluence to engage effectively with the global partnership not only for Africa's educational progress but also its real socioeconomic development.

E. J. Takyi-Amoako (✉)
Oxford ATP International Education, Oxford, UK

N. T. Assié-Lumumba
Africana Studies and Research Center, Cornell University, Ithaca, NY, USA

© The Author(s) 2018   229
E. J. Takyi-Amoako, N. T. Assié-Lumumba (eds.),
Re-Visioning Education in Africa,
https://doi.org/10.1007/978-3-319-70043-4_13

In this case, the confident view of Aliko Dangote, Africa's top billionaire, holds firm: **"I believe that we will be able to transform Africa by ourselves. Not alone, but we will lead and others will follow"** (*African Business Magazine*, October Issue, 2015, emphasis in the original).

Indeed, the view that ongoing debate on Post-2015 Agenda offers an opportunity is valid (Sachs 2016). This book is an opportunity in the case of Africa to reflect on exactly the educational gains and relevance in the region so far, and what precisely formal/education means for the continent and its progress. For over the past 50 years, Africa's educational, economic, cultural thought systems and partnerships for development, and so on, referred to as Africa's social development, have been hijacked and bedevilled by colonial legacy, colonial proxies, and other imperialist tendencies (Abdi 2010). While neo-colonialism continues unabated in Africa, it has been compounded by capitalist, neo-liberal, and imperialist onslaught of contemporary globalization that favours Western powers and their physical geography. The phenomenon is currently deeply embedded in human existence so much so that revoking its effects is nearly unfeasible (ibid.; Klees 2017). Africa has been at the mercy of the negative aspect of globalization's distributive outcomes for far too long, and the continent now needs to reconsider its positioning in relation to it and to its purveyor, the global strategy for development, and closely determine how to make it work in its favour (Petras 1999). This requires a real sense of urgency and agency.

One would argue that, in the case of Africa, what is mostly required is an active redefining of the continental/regional/national positioning of Africa to external global partners across the education and development landscape. This is because embedded within this landscape is the international/foreign aid structure, comprising the international financial institutions (IFIs) such as the Bretton Woods Institutions (BWIs), bilateral/multilateral donors, and others. These IFIs emerge as the formulators of continental/regional/national/local education policies in Africa. Thus, this concluding chapter reiterates the need to deepen our understanding of how foreign aid donors and international development partners and their actions/initiatives are embedded within Africa's national/regional/continental education policy landscapes and development just like other studies have demonstrated this entrenchment in the politics, economics, and even culture of Africa with significant reverberations for development of the continent (Amoako 2009; Hutchful 2002, 1996; Abugre and Amenga-Etego 2000; Kraus 1991; Toye 1991; Callaghy 1990).

This concluding chapter examines this embedded relation and how it could be viewed as an opportunity for African nations, regional and continental organizations to reposition themselves as leaders at the meeting point/the Confluence of the global (international agents of change) and local (national/regional/continental agents of change) to redefine a more relevant, indigenously reflective, accessible, and quality type of formal education for their people. In the de-culturation and possible reculturation, Africa must aspire for socially inclusive initiatives in which Africa's education, economy and politics, and others must be extensively linked to the continent's needs in terms of history, culture, and genuine concerns with emphasis on its communal mutually dependent values, which is the hallmark of African existence (Abdi 2010). Here the Ubuntu framework increasingly qualifies as the most viable tool to achieve this vision. The continental, regional, and national agendas need to take cognizance of this redefinition or re-visioning. The Agenda 2063 of the African Union Commission (AUC), education strategies of all regional organizations, and others must take cognizance.

Consequently, this concluding chapter recaps Africa's own education strategies such as the AUC Agenda 2063's ten-year Continental Education Strategy for Africa 2016–2025 (CESA 16–25) and the Common Africa Position (CAP) on the Post-2015 Development Agenda (AUC 2014) as well as the Report of Annual Continental Activities (RACA). Although regional economic communities (RECs) of Africa also have education strategies, the main focus here is on the continental education plan for Africa, CESA 16–25, and its positioning in relation to the global education and partnership plan, the education and global partnership SDGs. We therefore restate the question central to this book:

Overall, how can Africa undo the effects of external and internal domination in the global educational policy partnership environment in a manner that would reduce economic, income, and power inequities between Africa and the international community, and within nations/regions/continent for the benefit of its youth, and to what extent can an Ubuntu-inspired global education partnership for humanity harness the potential of its very youthful populations rather than be threatened with the menace that unexploited aptitudes and capabilities of the youth cause?

In answering this key question, we argue that a stronger, tighter continental education partnership for sustainable development at the Confluence embedded with Ubuntu values will enable Africa to navigate and negotiate the durable power inequalities pervading global partnerships for sustainable development to the benefit of its masses while simultaneously promoting the Ubuntu vision to its global partners. We further contend that while this continental partnership building is in process, Africa should re-adopt, re-launch, and pragmatize its original Pan-Africanist vision and strategy, especially proposed and advocated by several leaders on the continent and the diaspora, with the first President of Ghana, Osagyefo Dr. Kwame Nkrumah as the most articulate promoter as stated on the 24th May 1963 that,

> … we must recognise that our economic independence resides in our African union and requires the same concentration upon the political achievement. The unity of our continent, no less than our separate independence, will be delayed, if indeed we do not lose it, by hobnobbing with colonialism. African unity is, above all, a political kingdom which can only be gained by political means. The social and economic development of Africa will come only within the political kingdom, not the other way round. Is it not unity alone that can weld us into an effective force, capable of creating our own progress and making our valuable contribution to world peace? Which independent African state, which of you here, will claim that its financial structure and banking institutions are fully harnessed to its national development?… (President Osagyefo Dr Kwame Nkrumah, 24th May 1963, speech delivered at Addis Ababa at the Founding of the OAU)

Some of President Nkrumah's counterparts, especially the Monrovia Group, rejected his proposal at the time, and out of consensus between the Casablanca Group of which President Nkrumah was part and the Monrovia Group replaced it with one that advocated a loose union. However, it is increasingly becoming obvious that the only way that Africa's incessant colossal resources could be harnessed to boost its economy, to benefit all sectors and people in Africa including the educational development of the massively huge young populations that characterize the continent today, and will continue to define it till the end of the century, is to develop a strong political union with Ubuntu-inspired good governance credentials, promoting the same in national and regional spaces while single-mindedly ensuring the growth of African national economies and productive capacities in a fair manner. Why this urgency and the need for a consciously strategic agency?

Africa's Population Boom: Demanding Urgency and Consciously Strategic Agency

In 2017, children below the age of 15 represent 41 per cent of the population, and the youth between the ages of 15 and 24 years form an extra 19 per cent (United Nations, 2017; see also the Introduction to this book). Over half of the expected increase in population from now till 2050 is anticipated to happen in Africa. Of the 2.2 billion people that may boost the world's population, 1.3 billion will be added in Africa. The continent will be the key contributor to global population increase after 2050. Africa's share of the world's population, which is anticipated to grow from roughly 17 per cent in 2017 to around 26 per cent in 2050, could reach 40 per cent by 2100. Thirty-three of the forty-seven nations classified by the United Nations (UN) as the least developed countries (LDCs) are in Africa with a high chance of their population tripling in size between 2017 and 2100. Some, including Angola, Burundi, Niger, Somalia, Tanzania, and Zambia, will record populations five times their current sizes over the duration (United Nations 2017).

The high population growth rates and increasingly dense populations in these African countries will exacerbate the social problems confronting governments in eliminating poverty, lessening inequality, fighting starvation and malnourishment, extending and revamping health and education structures, enhancing the delivery of essential amenities, and guaranteeing that people are not excluded (ibid.). Currently, the public infrastructure in most of these countries is operating at a deficit. Nigeria, for instance, presently, wrestles to meet the annual education demands of millions of secondary school graduates. Of the ten million candidates that applied to the country's higher education institutions, only 26 per cent were admitted (Kazeem 2017). Yet, the fastest growing population is Nigeria's, considered the seventh largest globally. It is anticipated that its population will exceed that of the United States and will become the third largest country globally just before 2050 (United Nations 2017). What is more, in Africa, the share of the population aged 25–59 is expected to rise from 35 per cent in 2017 to 45 per cent in 2090 (United Nations 2017). Doubtless, the need for bold decisions and initiatives has never been greater, and the time to make those choices and implement them has never been more urgent.

AFRICAN UNION COMMISSION AGENDA 2063: AFRICA'S RESPONSE

The youthful demography in Africa could pay development dividends to the continent, yet it could also be a time bomb depending on the choices made now. To harvest the former, bold vision, investments, and initiatives are crucial. Hence, the timeliness of the launch of the ambitious AUC Agenda 2063 cannot be overstated. The Agenda declares in a united voice and purpose that Africans of diverse backgrounds including those in the diaspora aspire to create a prosperous Africa that ensures inclusive growth and sustainable development within an integrated continent, that is, politically united, steeped in the ideals of Pan-Africanism and the vision of Africa's renaissance with a new generation with Afropolitan consciousness and commitment to the continent (Assié-Lumumba 2016).

The agenda pledges an Africa of good governance, respect for human rights, justice, and the rule of law that engenders peace and security for its people. It articulates with emphasis an Africa with a strong cultural identity, common heritage, values, and ethics whose development is people-driven and depends on the capability of African people, with emphasis on its women and youth, and care and protection for its children. It seeks to create an Africa that is powerful, cohesive, buoyant, and effective global actor and partner.

These message, aspirations, priority, and goals conveyed by the Agenda distil into "The Africa We Want", a single vision of "an integrated, prosperous and peaceful Africa, driven by its own citizens and representing a dynamic force in the international arena". This vision, encapsulated in the Agenda 2063, constitutes the main driver for the future of Africa and was solemnly and publicly declared at the 50th Anniversary Organization of African Unity (OAU), which was renamed the African Union (AU). The eight priority areas of the solemn declaration of Agenda 2063 reflect the goals and seven aspirations of the African people for their continent, regions, countries, and their diasporic communities. The AUC leading the design and implementation of the Agenda 2063 aspires towards a prosperous Africa, based on inclusive growth and sustainable development, with the goal of well-educated citizens and skills revolution supported by science, technology, and innovation. Since education and science, technology, and innovation (STI), as well as a driven skills revolution, form one of the priority areas of the Agenda, it is worth the attention (AUC 2015).

A Strong Ubuntu-Inspired African Continental Partnership on Education: The Way Forward?

The AUC Agenda 2063 has set the course for the profound changes that Africa urgently needs in all its sectors. Accordingly, this section focuses on the manner in which it ought to theoretically and practically re-vision education partnership for sustainable development in Africa. It examines this at the Confluence and within the framework of Ubuntu. The educational sector, like the other sectors of countries in Africa, has been plagued by poor outcomes. Thus, Agenda 2063 represents, in principle, a bold response to the educational lapses and other myriad development challenges that threaten the future of Africa's progress.

Therefore, we reiterate our argument that for an effective implementation of this rightfully ambitious agenda and its educational vision, aspirations, goals, and priority areas in conjunction with the Pan-African and African renaissance perspectives and ideals outlined in the Agenda 2063 document, the AU should establish and lead a stronger continental (education) partnership (e.g. the African Continental Partnership on Education) that can engage effectively on equal terms with entities within the global partnership for development, like the bi-/multilaterals, IFIs, BWIs, and the recently established Global Partnership on Education (GPE) and the International Commission on Financing Global Education Opportunity (Education Commission), at the Confluence entrenched with Ubuntu values for sustainable development in Africa.

This proposed robust African continental partnership, formed from representatives of existing RECs, other regional, continental, and national bodies under a stronger politically united Africa, will enable Africa to effectively navigate and negotiate the power inequalities in order to reposition itself/themselves as leaders at the meeting point/the Confluence of the global (international agents of change) and local (national, regional, continental agents of change) to redefine and actualize a more relevant, Ubuntu-inspired, indigenously reflective, accessible, and quality type of formal education for Africa and humanity. The AUC Agenda 2063, which is a living document and practice, will benefit from this analysis, which aims to help enhance its re-/formulation and implementation.

Ubuntu-Inspired African Continental Education Partnership Strategy

Additionally, the African Union Commission (AUC) Agenda 2063's ten-year Continental Education Strategy for Africa 2016–2025 (CESA 16–25) and the Common Africa Position (CAP) on the Post-2015 Development Agenda (AUC 2014) as well as the Report of Annual Continental Activities (RACA) are relevant. Although regional economic communities (RECs) of Africa also have education strategies, the main focus here is on the global and continental education plans for Africa, education SDG, and CESA 16–25, respectively.

The aim of the education strategy, CESA 16–25, is to establish high standard relevant Africanized system of education and training to produce well-equipped human capital/resources that promote African basic principles needed to realize the dream and objectives of the AU. Those taking charge of its execution will be mandated to re-vision Africa's systems of education and training to align with the know-how, expertise, ingenuity, and inventiveness needed to cultivate African primary values and advance sustainable development nationally, regionally, and continentally. The guiding principles and pillars steer the execution of the Continental Strategy as mirrored in the 12 strategic objectives reinforced by certain spheres of operation.

The six guiding principles emphasized are the generation of skilled human resources that operate knowledge societies, inclusive and equitable education, governance efficiency, harmonized systems of education systems to promote intra-mobility and regional integration, quality and relevant education, and healthy learners. The seven pillars that support these principles include strong political will, to revolutionize education and training, in a harmonious and safe environment, that ensures gender equality, mobilizes resources domestically, consolidates institutional capacity, good governance, a network of actors to initiate democratic and strong partnerships, reorient or re-vision and support at all levels of learning, and favourable conditions for learning. These will ensure the attainment of the 12 strategic objectives captured in Table 13.1.

In fact, the guiding principles, pillars, and strategic objectives all form a fertile ground for a resilient continental education partnership, forged in the Ubuntu fire at the Confluence for sustainable development in Africa.

Table 13.1 The twelve strategic objectives of continental education strategy for Africa 2016–2025

The 12 strategic objectives of CESA 16–25		
SO 1: Revitalize the teaching profession to ensure quality and relevance at all levels of education SO 2: Build, rehabilitate, preserve education infrastructure, and develop policies that ensure a permanent, healthy, and conducive learning environment in all sub-sectors and for all, so as to expand access to quality education SO 3: Harness the capacity of ICT to improve access, quality, and management of education and training systems SO 4: Ensure acquisition of requisite knowledge and skills as well as improved completion rate at all levels and groups through harmonization processes across all levels for national and regional integration	SO 5: Accelerate processes leading to gender parity and equity SO 6: Launch comprehensive and effective literacy programmes across the continent to eradicate the scourge of illiteracy SO 7: Strengthen the science and math curricula in youth training and disseminate scientific knowledge and culture in the society SO 8: Expand TVET opportunities at both secondary and tertiary levels and strengthen linkages between the world of work and education and training systems	SO 9: Revitalize and expand tertiary education, research, and innovation to address continental challenges and promote global competitiveness SO 10: Promote peace education and conflict prevention and resolution at all levels of education and for all age groups SO 11: Improve management of education system as well as build and enhance capacity for data collection, management, analysis, communication, and use SO 12: Set up a coalition of stakeholders to facilitate and support activities resulting from the implementation of CESA 16–25

Source: Created from AUC Agenda 2063's Continental Education Strategy for Africa 2016–2025

AFRICAN CONTINENTAL PARTNERSHIP AS HUMANNESS

Thus, a continental education partnership for sustainable development in Africa will be characterized by Ubuntu, which is simply humanness in symbiotic relation with the broader ecosystem, and will sustain togetherness of African peoples as a single entity and unchanging equals, who share and redistribute (if necessary) resources and complement one another, expressing sympathy and sharing joy, which enables empathy that ensures mutual survival, respect, and tolerance of one another for peaceful and harmonious existence that upholds indigenous wisdom, culture, identity, and knowledge for humanity (Broodryk 2006).

Tutu (1999, p. 2) provides an apt portrayal of one who has Ubuntu:

A person with Ubuntu is open and available to others, affirming of others, does not feel threatened that others are able and good, for he or she has a proper self-assurance that comes from knowing that he or she belongs in a greater whole and is diminished when others are humiliated or diminished, when others are tortured or oppressed, or treated as if they were less who they are.

A strong Ubuntu-inspired African continental education partnership at the Confluence such as the above with its essence of humanness could be employed in deconstructing the existing unequal foundations of global educational partnership for sustainable development in Africa. For instance, a continental education partnership formed under a stronger political unity of Africa, fortified with the Ubuntu principles, could possess a stronger bargaining power at the Confluence of the global and local during education partnership processes with global entities like the multilaterals (e.g. the World Bank, UNICEF, etc.), the bilaterals (e.g. USAID, DFID, etc.), as well as the newly reformed global organizations such as the Global Partnership on Education (GPE) and the International Commission on Financing Global Education Opportunity (aka Education Commission), whose dominant powers, policies, practices, and ideologies, which sometimes undermine Africa's progress, prevail during global education partnership and policy processes with African actors (GPE 2016).

While facilitating the Ubuntu values within the African Continental Partnership on Education, it will, simultaneously, promote these values at the global level so as to deconstruct these structures, which ensure that the global development agreement or strategy is based on a "Faustian Bargain", which pushes African states and global policies to cluster in order to facilitate global integration instead of promoting economic development, through production, employment, and productive capacities in Africa (Gore 2010; ibid.).

Subsequently, the inefficiency of the aid effectiveness principles designed and implemented by the high level forums may no longer be a problem because the African partnership will work with the recipient African countries to devise an exit strategy out of development aid dependency, and aid effectiveness might be achieved. There is evidence that with such an exit plan the power balance between donors and recipients, seen as a crucial catalyst for aid effectiveness, could be realized (Takyi-Amoako 2009).

African Continental Partnership as One Entity, Togetherness, Complementarity, and Mutual Survival

The Ubuntu value of conceiving human beings as parts of one entity **and connected to the social and physical environment** will enable the Continental Partnership to view itself and its members as obverse and reverse sides of one body, which expresses the essence of life as a social and physical interdependence of people irrespective of race, gender, religion, and so on. People are reliant on one another for survival and support. An Ubuntu-inspired African Continental Partnership on Education draws strength from the value of togetherness. A conscious decision by the actors in this partnership to express togetherness and a deep understanding of the fact that one and one's fellow human being originate from the same source, similar life experience, and a shared destiny are what strengthen it. This togetherness leads to a sense of complementarity for mutual survival.

CESA 16–25 resource mobilization plan will benefit from a solid African Continental Partnership on Education. Such a partnership under a robust political continental unity could be characterized as a comprehensive instrument to enable Africa to, for instance, plug the holes that aid capital flight and illicit financial flows from the continent (Ndikumana and Boyce 2011, 2012; Ndikumana et al. 2015; AU/ECA n.d.).

There is strength in collective co-existence and complementarity. There is an African belief that people are reciprocally rewarding counterparts, and sharing represents a vital African value of existence. Humans own different merits, aptitudes, and capital, and they should be distributed in the atmosphere of collaboration for productive survival. Generosity and compassion are key. In support of the "Africa Rising" narrative, the time is ripe for intra-continental resource mobilization for strategic investments. These represent the most underused development prospect in Africa especially during this period of changes in the global trading landscape with reduced flows of foreign direct investment (FDI) from the rest of the world to developing nations, particularly, Africa, whose main export commodity prices have declined drastically since 2014. Despite increase in African trade growth rates (10–16 per cent) from 2000 to 2014, it still lags behind those of other regions (Mataboge 2017). A strong African Continental Partnership on Education built on the above Ubuntu values will enable it to facilitate this Africa-wide initiative that will engender productive capacities, employment, and economic growth for the benefit of Africa's teeming youth and their educational development.

In this case, joint survival is crucial since one's survival is a prerequisite of the other's survival. For a person to endure global tribulations depends on the endurance of others. This mutual dependence of humans guarantees every person's survival, which creates an interpersonal bond of love and warmth.

African Continental Partnership as Sympathy, Empathy, Respect, Tolerance, Equality, Redistribution, Peace and Harmony, Joy

The need for mutual survival demands a redistribution of wealth where necessary. Thus, an Ubuntu-inspired Continental Partnership body in Africa is strong and will engage with a stronger bargaining power within global partnerships for sustainable development to ensure that wealth is redistributed locally, nationally, continentally and globally, while negotiating with hegemonic global institutions for the African people to have their fair share of the global wealth.

In Africa, globalization and sustainable education for development are paradoxically linked. Sustainable educational development facilitates countries or citizens to meet their basic educational needs and experience a good standard of living in a way that will not endanger the important educational needs and good quality life of prospective generations. However, the effect of globalization in African countries has been negative. Globalization represents an intricate phenomenon that has been made even more so by the consequences of imperialism, neo-colonization, and neo-liberalism, all of which have added to the dismantling of sovereignty and cooperative machinery (Abdi 2006; Stromquist 2002; Takyi-Amoako 2008). Thus, the market with other oppressive forces in regard to Africa appropriate nations' authority over education and differentially alters their economic and political right (Stromquist 2002). A strong Continental Partnership grounded on these Ubuntu principles will ensure that the equality of Africa's people is reflected in the education policies in order to subvert existing neo-liberal macro-policies prescribed by the BWIs and IFIs with the support of bilateral donors and Northern non-governmental organizations (NGOs) for a number of countries in Africa. Policy demands for African governments to curb their expenses on higher education while imposing cost sharing have culminated in the commodification and privatization of education and the fact that it is no longer regarded a social advantage but an economic benefit, solely from the perspective of profit that can be gained by investors in education (Puplampu 2006).

The consequence is a restriction of access of the poor to higher education, thus, destabilizing poverty alleviation, and diminishing the role of tertiary institutions as intellect trainers and knowledge producers for Africa's progress. The disinvestment of the state undercut not just educational prospects but also knowledge creation in general, which has an effect on Africans' abilities to cultivate their own models of development and social transformation. Regrettably, the unsuspecting implementation of neo-liberal macroeconomic policies is a prerequisite for donor-recipient interactions in most African nations (Takyi-Amoako 2008).

According to Klees (2017), "[w]hile the World Bank pretends everyone—countries, bilaterals, multilaterals, civil society, and more—is in partnership with it, it is the World Bank which takes the lead on education policy" (p. 5). The Bank's monopoly came after UNESCO, the one-time leader on education globally, was disempowered and compelled to play a lesser role after the United States and United Kingdom withdrew their contributions for years (Klees 2017). A strong African Continental Partnership on Education as an Ubuntu-inspired evidenced-based and data-driven entity will lead the work on Africa's education within the global partnership to tackle the tripartite problem of deprivation, inequity, and employment, futilely fixed on shortage of personal skills and education rather than the capitalist, neo-liberal, and neo-colonial structures whose impact spawns poverty, inequality, and unemployment (Abdi 2010; Klees 2017). Indeed, Africans must be well-equipped with relevant good quality education and skills. However, these must not become redundant but deployed within national, regional, and continental contexts that generate socioeconomic growth devoid of inequalities and unsustainabilities.

African Continental Partnership as Culture and Wisdom

Culture which represents mores and customs is also perceived as law internalized in the community and extended family setting. African law in the various parts of the continent acknowledges the rights of the community and the collective. The interests of the group surpass those of the individual. It is from culture that wisdom stems and one who possesses it is truly human. On this basis, a strong Continental Partnership on Education will formulate and implement policies and initiatives that hold the collective voice and actions of the community in high regard. Hence the Partnership will promote more participatory approaches to sustainable educational development, for example, like participatory budgeting, which originated from Latin America and alternative development systems that emphasize the people's indigeneity and collectivity. It is however important to warn about how a search and adoption of alternative development paradigms can trigger opposition from prevailing dominant powers that prefer to maintain the status quo (Klees 2017). Nevertheless, a strong Partnership on Education firmly grounded in all these Ubuntu values of tolerance, respect, equality, peace, and harmony while promoting them among the African people will enable collective and participatory education policy decisions and processes that will improve their social impact and address the inequalities that pervade Africa's national educational systems.

Also, emphasis on the above values will also facilitate peace and tolerance especially in the conflict zones of Africa, particularly, in the educational spaces, which will become embodiments of these values. A strong Continental Partnership on Education deliberately promoting these values unlocks the African culture in its educational policy processes, and has the potential of endowing cultural and contextual relevance, which is so lacking in Africa's educational systems today.

The Ubuntu values also negate greed, and, therefore, a strong Continental Partnership on Education espousing these principles will check corruptive practices in governance especially in the education sector.

A strong Ubuntu-inspired Continental Partnership on Education in Africa should take the lead in the policy process—formulation, implementation, and financing—since the global agenda has always been prescriptive and unhelpful for African educational systems. Africa must look within, employing history, culture, and the actual lived experiences of its people to view and adopt what works for Africa. More sharing of best practices between African educational institutions could be promoted by this proposed Continental Partnership on Education grounded firmly on Ubuntu principles.

CONCLUDING REMARKS

Rethinking the direction of African education is timely, urgent, and relevant as it touches on the future of the restless youth. Given the rapid changes occurring in Africa in particular and globally in general, credible and sustainable vision of African education thus needs to be rooted in the emerging dynamics of socioeconomic reality and cultural relevance to the aspirations of the youth (Boyd 1992).

Education is one way of humans to define their humanity, to practice humanity, to maintain humanity and to change humanity. Education is a way to connect oneself to the past and to project into the future. (Venter 1998, no page number)

This book, which advances a cogent case for humanity, begins with the contention that Africa needs some deep changes conceptually and pragmatically in respect of its educational systems and poor outcomes. The chapters seek to define fresh paths for education in Africa by theoretically and practically interrogating and re-visioning education within the African cultural and philosophical concept of Ubuntu. Within this context, they attempt to unravel the concept of an Ubuntu-inspired education for Africa and humanity, and explore ways in which and the extent to which the continent can harness the potential of its very youthful populations rather than be confronted with the risk that untapped talents and capabilities of the youth pose. They examine types of policy questions that national/regional/continental governments ought to be asking themselves with regard to educational systems and the global partnership for development processes in Africa, while problematizing the type and level of education quality offered to these growing young populations in the various countries. They endeavour to probe the issue of how educational systems in the different countries in Africa are enabling their graduates or beneficiaries with the above considerations in mind and investigate the choices that governments and decision makers are making to ensure these conditions are fulfilled. They try to critically look into ways and extent to which governments can convert or are converting the fast technological and economic advancement in the international sphere into tangible transformation and enhanced opportunities for Africa's youth, interrogate the gender dimension, and finally, explore the relationship and impact of re-visioned education on socioeconomic and political development of Africa, while providing a critique of the current situation from an Ubuntu perspective, and how the Ubuntu philosophy will inspire a new type of education. For instance, what values and mindset will the concept of Ubuntu bring into content and practice of education? Overall, the book attempts to instigate and rekindle the debate on seeking new paths for education in Africa, and advance fresh thinking and ways of seeing and practising education in Africa in order to increase its relevance to society and national/regional/continental socioeconomic development. Central to all this is the recommendation to the AU to initiate and lead an Ubuntu-Inspired African Continental Partnership on Education to achieve the goals of the AUC Agenda 2063.

Indeed, this book has only re-kindled the debate on the need to re-vision Africa's formal education for improved outcomes by aligning it with Africa's indigenous, progressive philosophies, and in this case, the Ubuntu Philosophy. Consequently, more studies are required to explore how this revisioning, using the framework of Ubuntu, could further be theorized and pragmatized within the context of the continent's formal education systems for sustainable development.

REFERENCES

Abdi, A. A. (2006). Culture of education, social development, and globalization: Historical and current analyses of Africa. In A. A. Abdi, K. P. Puplampu, & G. J. Dei (Eds.), *African education and globalization: Critical perspectives.* Lanham: Lexington Books.

Abdi, A. (2010). Globalization, culture and development: Perspectives on Africa. *Journal of Alternative Perspectives in the Social Sciences, 2*(1), 1–26.

Abugre, C., & Amenga-Etego, R. (2000). International Financial Cooperation for Development. [Online]. Ghana Integrated Social Development Centre (ISODEC). Accessed 6 Oct 2005.

African Business Magazine. (2015, September 28). Read Aliko Dangote's exclusive interview in the October issue of African business – Out now!. http://africanbusinessmagazine.com/press/read-aliko-dangotes-exclusive-interview-in-the-october-issue-of-african-business-out-now/. Accessed 24 July 2017.

African Union Commission. (2014). *Common Africa position (CAP) on the post 2015 development agenda.* Addis Ababa: African Union.

African Union Commission. (2015). *Agenda 2063: The Africa we want (Popular version).* Addis Ababa: Africa Union Commission.

Amoako, E. J. A. (2009). *Shaping policy at the confluence of the global and national: Ghana's Education Strategic Plan.* DPhil thesis, University of Oxford.

Assié-Lumumba, N. T. (2016). Harnessing the empowerment nexus of afropolitanism and higher education: Purposeful fusion for Africa's social progress in the 21st century. *Journal of African Transformation, 1*(2), 51–76.

Boyd, D. (1992). The moral part of pluralism as the plural part of moral education. In F. Clark Power & D. K. Lapsley (Eds.), *The challenges of pluralism education, politics and values.* London: University of Notre Dame Press.

Broodryk, J. (2006, October 12–17) *Ubuntu: African life coping skills- theory and practice-paper delivered at CCEAM conference.* Conference theme: Recreating linkages between Theory and Praxis in Educational Leadership, Lefkosia (Nicosia).

Callaghy, T. (1990). Lost between state and market: The politics of economic adjustment in Ghana, Zambia and Nigeria. In J. Nelson (Ed.), *Economic crisis and policy choice: The politics of adjustment in the third world* (pp. 257–319). Princeton: Princeton University Press.

Gore, C. (2010). The MDG paradigm, productive capacities and the future of poverty reduction. *IDS Bulletin, 41*(1), 70–79.

Hutchful, E. (2002). *Ghana's adjustment experience: The paradox of reform.* Oxford: James Currey.

Kazeem, Y. (2017, June 29). *More than half of the world's population growth will be in Africa by 2050.* Quartz Africa. https://qz.com/1016790/more-than-half-of-the-worlds-population-growth-will-be-in-africa-by-2050/. Accessed 25 July 2017.

Klees, S. J. (2017). Beyond neoliberalism: Reflections on capitalism and education. *Policy Futures in Education.* Prepublished June 29 2017. https://doi.org/10.1177/1478210317715814.

Kraus, J. (1991). The political economy of stabilization and structural adjustment in Ghana. In D. Rothchild (Ed.), *Ghana: The political economy of recovery* (pp. 119–155). London: Lynne Rienner.

Mataboge, L. D. (2017). *Africans need to invest in each other's economies.* http://africanbusinessmagazine.com/sectors/finance/africans-need-invest-others-economies/. Accessed 03 Aug 2017.

Ndikumana, L., & Boyce, J. (2011). *Africa's odious debts—How foreign loans and capital flight bled a continent.* London/New York: Zed Books.

Ndikumana, L, & Boyce, J. (2012). *Capital flight from Sub-Saharan African countries: Updated estimates 1970–2010.* Political Economy Research Institute. www.peri.umass.edu/236/hash/d76a3192e770678316c1ab39712994be/publication/532/

Ndikumana, L., Boyce, J. K., & Ndiaye, A. S. (2015). Capital flight from Africa: Measurement and drivers. In I. Ajayi & L. Ndikumana (Eds.), *Capital flight from Africa: Causes, effects and policy issues* (pp. 15–54). Oxford: Oxford University Press.

Petras, J. (1999). Globalization: A critical analysis. *Journal of Contemporary Asia, 29*(1), 3–37.

Pupulampu, K. P. (2006). Critical perspectives on higher education and globalization in Africa. In A. A. Abdi, K. P. Puplampu, & G. J. Dei (Eds.), *African education and globalization: Critical perspectives.* Lanham: Lexington Books.

Sachs, J. (2016). Foreword. In *Education for people and planet: Creating sustainable futures for all, Global education monitoring report* (pp. ii–iii). Paris: UNESCO Publishing.

Stromquist, N. P. (2002). *Education in a globalized world: The connectivity of economic power, technology, and knowledge.* Lanham: Rowman & Littlefield Publishers.

Takyi-Amoako, E. (2008). Globalisation: An impediment to sustainable educational development in Sub-Saharan African countries. *NORRAG News, 40*, 52–54.

The Global Partnership for Education. (2016) *GPE results report abridged version 2015/2016.* Washington, DC: GPE.

The Joint African Union Commission/United Nations Economic Commission for Africa. (n.d.). *Illicit financial flows: Report of the high level panel on illicit financial flows from Africa.* Commissioned by the Joint African Union Commission/United Nations Economic Commission for Africa (AU/ECA) Conference of Ministers of Finance, Planning and Economic Development. https://www.uneca.org/sites/default/files/PublicationFiles/iff_main_report_26feb_en.pdf. Accessed 25 July 2017.

Toye, J. (1991). Ghana. In P. Mosley, J. Harrigan, & J. Toye (Eds.), *Aid and power: The World Bank and policy-based lending* (pp. 150–200). London: Routledge.

Tutu, D. (1999). *No future without forgiveness.* New York: Doubleday.

United Nations. (2017). *World population prospects: The 2017 revision- key findings and advance tables ESA/P/WP/248.* New York: United Nations, Department of Economic and Social Affairs Population Division.

Venter, E. (1998, August 10–15). *Philosophy of education as a means to educate humanity in a diverse South Africa.* Paper delivered at the Twentieth World Congress of Philosophy, Boston. https://www.bu.edu/wcp/Papers/Educ/EducVent.htm. Accessed 8 July 2017.

Index[1]

A
Academics, 15, 98, 110, 112, 123, 124, 127, 129, 132, 148, 176, 180, 183, 184, 186–189, 196
Account, 27, 40, 42, 56, 58, 61, 79, 80, 146, 155, 183, 190
Accountability, 57, 58, 148, 209
Acculturation, 94, 101, 102
Achievements, 3, 12, 14, 20–22, 25–29, 35, 44, 73, 79, 138, 139, 160, 163, 179, 232
Activist, 45
Actors, 38–40, 46, 99, 209, 210, 213, 214, 218, 220, 222, 234, 236, 238, 239
Adolescence, 88
Adulthood, 31, 88, 131
Advancement, 4, 27, 28, 50, 69, 82, 123, 124, 133, 160, 176, 211, 221, 243
Africa, 1, 19, 20, 22, 24, 25, 27, 31, 35, 63, 64, 65n1, 67, 85–117,

119, 135, 155, 156, 167, 168, 170, 175, 177–179, 185, 186, 190, 201, 202, 205, 229
African-centered, 37
African Continental Partnership on Education, 235, 238, 239, 241, 242
African Economic Community (AEC), 48
Africanness, 35
African Union (AU), 12, 15, 48, 63, 73, 77, 78, 128, 149, 217, 220, 232, 234–236, 239, 243
African Union Commission (AUC), 5, 7, 8, 15, 206, 209, 222, 229, 231, 234, 236
Africa We Want, The, 234
Afropolitan, 234
Agenda 2063, 5, 7–9, 12, 15, 73, 77–82, 149, 151n16, 206, 209, 210, 220, 229, 231, 234, 235

[1]Note: Page numbers followed by 'n' refer to notes.

247

Printed by Printforce, the Netherlands